THE LITTLE CRYSTALLINE SEED

SUNY series, Intersections: Philosophy and Critical Theory
———————
Rodolphe Gasché, editor

THE LITTLE CRYSTALLINE SEED

THE ONTOLOGICAL SIGNIFICANCE OF *MISE EN ABYME* IN POST-HEIDEGGERIAN THOUGHT

IDDO DICKMANN

Cover image: Alexis Arnold, *Untitled (Crystallized Book)*, © 2018 Alexis Arnold

Published by State University of New York Press, Albany

© 2019 State University of New York

All rights reserved

No part of this book may be used or reproduced in any manner whatsoever without written permission. No part of this book may be stored in a retrieval system or transmitted in any form or by any means including electronic, electrostatic, magnetic tape, mechanical, photocopying, recording, or otherwise without the prior permission in writing of the publisher.

For information, contact State University of New York Press, Albany, NY
www.sunypress.edu

Library of Congress Cataloging-in-Publication Data

Names: Dickmann, Iddo, 1972– author.
Title: The little crystalline seed : the ontological significance of *mise en abyme* in post-Heideggerian thought / Iddo Dickmann.
Description: Albany : State University of New York Press, [2019] | Series: SUNY series, intersections : philosophy and critical theory | Includes bibliographical references and index.
Identifiers: LCCN 2018027703 | ISBN 9781438473994 (hardcover : alk. paper) | ISBN 9781438474007 (pbk. : alk. paper) | ISBN 9781438474014 (ebook)
Subjects: LCSH: Poststructuralism. | Mise en abyme (Narration) | Derrida Jacques. | Blanchot, Maurice. | Deleuze, Gilles, 1925–1995.
Classification: LCC B841.4 .D55 2019 | DDC 190.9/04—dc23
LC record available at https://lccn.loc.gov/2018027703

10 9 8 7 6 5 4 3 2 1

To my beloved daughters Hadar Miryam and Talya

CONTENTS

Illustrations	ix
Acknowledgments	xi
Introduction	1

1. The Literary Theory of *Mise en abyme* and its Philosophical Meaning — 11
   - Mise en abyme and mirroring — 11
   - The double-bind of the mise en abyme — 16
   - Strata and undercurrents in the typology of the mise en abyme — 23
   - Mise en abyme in the new New Novel: Reversing mimetologism "in one fell swoop" — 30
   - Mise en abyme in reader-response criticism — 36
   - Mise en abyme in analytic and possible-worlds semantics — 42

2. Jacques Derrida: *Mise en abyme* and the logic of supplementarity — 57
   - Mise en abyme and the infrastructural difference — 57
   - Derrida's denouncement of mise en abyme — 64
   - Iterability and the "lacunal" conception of mise en abyme — 66
   - Misconception of the mise en abyme and its consequences — 70
   - On second thoughts: Intentionality and the "invagination" of text — 72

3. Maurice Blanchot: Heading Toward Death as *Mise en abyme* — 83
   - Death and "ambiguity" — 83
   - Mise en abyme and the "night itself" — 85
   - "Worklessness" and Gide's mechanism of retroaction — 91
   - Worklessness and Iser's "acts of fictionalization" — 95
   - Mise en abyme and the "fatality of the day" — 99

4. Gilles Deleuze: Repetition and Time as *Mise en abyme*	105
Mise en abyme and the ground of difference	105
Mise en abyme and the philosophy of affirmation	114
The prospective mise en abyme and the synthesis of the present	122
The retro-prospective mise en abyme and the synthesis of the past	124
Mise en abyme and "schema" in Kant and Bergson	129
The Klein-bottle and the synthesis of the future	133
5. *Mise en abyme* as a Paradigm Shift I: From Mirror to "Labyrinth of Mirrors"	141
The "mirror of nature" and the principle of *adequatio*	141
Three paradigms of imagination	144
Deleuze on Bergson: Crystallines, convex mirrors and double mirrors	147
Gasché on Derrida: The tain of the mirror	156
Borges and the "monstrosity of mirrors"	160
6. *Mise en abyme* as a Paradigm Shift II: From Play to "Divine Play"	165
The play of the world and the play of Being	165
Gadamer: Play and the hermeneutic circle	168
Eugen Fink: Play as the "symbol of world"	169
Caillois and Levinas: Play and the other-than-Being	172
Deleuze: The divine game and the ethics of becoming	174
7. The Rhizomatic Book and the Centrifugal *Mise en abyme*	187
"Minor literature" and the semiotics of "expression"	187
The rhizomatic book and its reader	190
The rhizomatic book as mise en abyme	194
An empirical example: The Jewish scripture as a rhizomatic book	198
"Diagrammatical" reality and the "sheaf" of transcodation	205
Conclusion	211
Notes	219
Bibliography	245
Index	255

ILLUSTRATIONS

Figure I.1   Gide's escutcheon.   1

Figure 1.1   *Triptyque*.   31

Figure 1.2   Klein bottle.   33

Figure 4.1   Bergson's cone of memory.   128

ACKNOWLEDGMENTS

Warmest thanks to my colleagues and mentors in the recent years (in alphabetical order): Benoît Bourgine (Catholic University of Louvain), Régis Burnet (Catholic University of Louvain), Sylvain Camilleri (Catholic University of Louvain), Paul Cobley (Middlesex University London), Tim Crane (Cambridge University), Kir Kuiken (University at Albany, SUNY), Len Lawlor (Pennsylvania State University), Walter Lesch (Catholic University of Louvain), Didier Luciani (Catholic University of Louvain), Dorothea Olkowski (University of Colorado at Colorado Springs), Susannah Pearce (Cambridge University), Olivier Riaudel (Catholic University of Louvain), Kristupas Sabolius (Vilnius University), Avi Sagi (Bar-Ilan University), Rita Šerpytytė (Vilnius University), Jean-Pierre Sonnet (Pontifical Gregorian University), Ted Toadvine (Pennsylvania State University) and Nathan Widder (Royal Holloway, University of London). It was through intensive dialogue with these inspiring women and men, and thanks to their good advice and support, that this book has come to light.

INTRODUCTION

Mise en abyme is a narratological concept, (but sometimes pictorial or even musical) denoting a segment of the work that resembles, mimics or is even identical to the literary work of art as a whole, "a rebellion against scale . . . a small part carrying 'as much' significance as the whole that contains it."[1] It was christened by André Gide in 1893[2] after a type of a heraldic escutcheon—fictive, argues Bruce Morrissette—comprising a small-scale duplication of its own emblem and contours (Figure I.1). Though sharing much with neighboring terms such as "metalepsis," "metafiction," "surfiction," and many others, "mise en abyme" is reserved for cases where duplication is "immanent" to the text, performed "at the level of the characters" alone, to exclude, for instance, a personal intervention by the author within the narrative. An example of a "simple type" of mise en abyme is Hamlet, where

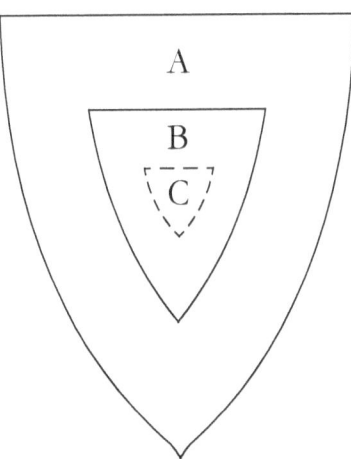

Figure I.1. Gide's escutcheon.

the play within the play repeats the King's crime and the Queen's infidelity. Infinite-aporetic examples, with which mise en abyme is more commonly associated, include night 602 in *1001 Nights*, as understood by J. L. Borges (1962), in which Scheherezade tells of the entire 1001 nights' tales including night 602 itself, the Droste cocoa box depicting a lady carrying the very box upon which she is depicted, and Diderot's *The Nun*, where Suzanne explains the history and reception of a letter within the letter itself.

Though found at the dawn of Western literature (for example, in Book 8 of the *Odyssey*, where Demodocus's songs outline the content and poetic form of the *Odyssey* in its entirety),[3] and despite already being prominent in baroque and romantic texts, it was only with the *nouveau roman* that mise en abyme was "associated from the start and immediately became a distinctive element."[4] Constantine Toloudis provides an illuminating set of examples:

> In Robbe-Grillet's *Le Voyeur*, announcing the rape scene and the nature of Mathias's guilt, a movie poster depicts a scene of violence—a man strangling a young girl, the latter kneeling beside a doll that was ripped. The novel that A began to read in *La Jalousie*, which is about a jealous husband and an unfaithful wife, sketches a situation which parallels that of the story central to Robbe-Grillet's book, involving A herself and alluded to by the book's title. Also in Robbe-Grillet's *Dans le Labyrinthe*, an engraving is described as depicting a place and a situation identical or analogous to those of the scene in the café, the latter becoming the point where all the "threads of Ariadne" lead. In Claude Simon's *La Route des Flandres*, the "fissured" portrait of Captain Reixach's ancestor tells a story that seems to duplicate that of Reixach himself; in his *L'Herbe*, the lid of the cookie tin . . . is decorated by a woman dressed in white who holds an identical box in her hand and is lying in the grass, thus metaphorizing a major aspect of the novel, through a sort of continuous fission of the focal repetition pattern. In Butor's *Passage de Milan*, the canvas being painted by DeVere during the fateful party on the fourth floor is presaging coming events, and as such stands as a metaphor for "passage," the process that the entire book is all about. In his *L'Emploi du temps*, a detective novel being read by Revel (*The Murder of Bleston*), tapestries in the museum and stained-glass windows in the cathedral can all be perceived as vehicles for the device, since they are reflections of one another

and at the same time reflections of the major aspects of the story. Similarly, in Claude Ollier's *La Mise en scène*, the intriguing representations in rupestral engravings become allusions to aggressive gestures and to the murder story which is another major component of this novel.[5]

Flourishing in the *nouveau roman*, mise en abyme boosted a wave of scholarship in literary theory commencing in the 1960s, indeed, "so rich was this scholarly literature that, by the end of the eighties, one might have been forgiven for thinking that something like the last word had been said on the subject of mise en abyme."[6] The key contributions here are Lucien Dällenbach's book of 1977, *Le Récit spéculaire* and Jean Ricardou's *Problèmes du nouveau roman* (1967), *Le nouveau roman* (1973) and others. These works gave the impetus to further research and analysis by Mieke Bal (1978), Linda Hutcheon (1980), Moshe Ron (1987), Brian McHale (1987), Shlomith Rimmon-Kenan (1982) and others.

Not only in literary theory, however, did mise en abyme stimulate a wave of scholarship. Throughout the 1960s and 1970s, I contend, mise en abyme also had an impact on the continental school of philosophy, on contemporary post-Heideggerian, or "post-structuralist," thought. Philosophers, I argue, invoked the concept of mise en abyme to establish an ontology that deviates from that of Martin Heidegger: First, in pursuing the "difference in itself"—un-bound to the ontico-ontological form and unmediated by the laws of contradiction and of the excluded middle—and second, in ascribing ontological significance to heterology, to the Other in its own right, rather than the "Other of the self." The concept thus served in modeling Jacques Derrida's logic of supplementarity, Maurice Blanchot's philosophy of "ambiguity," Gilles Deleuze's philosophy of repetition, Emmanuel Levinas's concept of "proximity," Henri Bergson's philosophy of time, and in a further circuit: the philosophies of Immanuel Kant, G. W. Leibniz, Heidegger himself and more.

The present study is not, however, an enquiry into the history of ideas. It is not my primary aim to unveil the historical impact of the mise en abyme upon these philosophers. My primary aim is to explore its interpretative potential, how mise en abyme can serve in decoding these philosophies, in solving the philosophical and textual problems to which they give rise, and in differentiating them from one another. Mise en abyme could assist us, for instance, in articulating the "almost imperceptible difference"[7] between Deleuze's thought and that of Derrida, or that between Deleuze's synthesis of the past and his synthesis of the future, the nature of which scholars have often found unclear.[8] Or it can assist us in reconciling Blanchot's "fatality of day" with his philosophy of ambiguity; the prerogative he ascribes to the "daylight" (of Being) notwithstanding the uncompromising "ambiguity" he sets—as against Heidegger—between "daylight" and the "night as such."

The "ontological significance" of mise en abyme, I here pursue, both bears the Heideggerian sense and breaks with it. In *Being and Time*, Heidegger launches a new kind of inquiry which concerns Being rather than entities. Philosophers dealing with an ontical inquiry represented Being as a being, or regarded it as a universal, derived by our abstraction from beings, so that Being assumes a substance that remains continuously present throughout all change. By contrast, the assumption underlying an ontological inquiry is that Being is manifested in time; it is a process and it "shines forth" rather than being inferred. However, such concrete, temporalized Being also necessitates in Heidegger's ontology the existence of privileged entities that enjoy ontic-ontological prerogative, that is, that stimulate the question of Being and outline the answer. In *Being and Time*, it is Dasein that performs this role. Ontically distinguished by the fact that it makes issue of its own being, Dasein, as Heidegger would later state (1998b), is the "shepherd of Being." Hans-Georg Gadamer and Eugen Fink, Heidegger's disciples, meanwhile, assign what Gadamer calls "ontological valence" to play—a *Weltsymbol* and a "cosmic metaphor." Gadamer consequently also assigns such valence to art and literature, deriving their mode of being from that of play.

Paul Ricœur defines these privileged entities as symbols, where it is only "by *living* in the first meaning that I am led by it beyond itself."[9] It is only through "engaging" with the symbol, attending to the internal properties of the "picture" that it embodies—and the "play" between them—that I am led to its figurative meaning, the figurative meaning is not given in isolation from the literal one, and the latter is at no stage dispensable. In this "hermeneutics of faith," we are not able to master the similitude intellectually, to judge it formally, but only allow the symbol to master and assimilate us. Is there, however, one or many "pasture lands" to which these "shepherds" can lead their faithful "engagers"? Can a shepherd lead to a concept of Being other than Heideggerian? Gadamer viewed art as bearing "ontological valence," and reflective art, mise en abyme is a form of art. Nonetheless, I wish to argue, the one who engages with the symbol of mise en abyme is "assimilated" into a realm which is not Heideggerian. Mise en abyme indeed embodies a new "shepherd of Being," but not in the sense that play replaced Dasein for scholars belonging to the "hermeneutic turn of phenomenology," or the New Testament did for those of the "theological turn." What "shines forth" in mise en abyme are dyads which are incommensurable and irreconcilable but nonetheless, paradoxically, simultaneous. As such, they epitomize a type of Being which Heidegger's account does not have a grasp of, where the ontic is not "in service" of the ontological and the acute ontological difference does not pass between the ontological and the ontic, but between the ontological and the ontic and their double—the ontological and the ontic understood as secondary powers.

My study will confront writers who failed to "listen" to what the symbol, the mise en abyme itself, "says," or who injected it with meaning extrinsic to the figure in-itself. Hutcheon, for instance, argues that mise en abyme is meant to expose the fact that all fictions are mimetic of "process" (that is of the production of the very mimetic work) rather than "product" (an object or event in real life). However, to assign such instrumental roles to mise en abyme, to view it as a vehicle to pre-established rather than emerging ideas, to judge its meaning from without rather than through "engagement" with the symbol, is to deny literature and art "self-presentation," to render them a function of a "totalizing ideal"—in this case that of "real life"—which fits badly with both Heideggerian and post-Heideggerian inquiry. Moreover, to blur the difference between reflexive and non-reflexive works, to reduce one to the other, is again to subject both to a pre-established ideal—be it aesthetic, political or other—rather than allowing these objects of research to "*make* the difference" between them, a prerequisite for an ontological theory, especially in post-Heideggerian measures.

Failure to engage with the mise en abyme in itself is also manifest in writers like Rodolphe Gasché, who, discussing Derrida, deploys the metaphor of two facing mirrors—itself a symbol of mise en abyme—without fully attending to the actual properties of the device. He associates the device with the totalitarianism of G. W. F. Hegel's "absolute reflection," failing to notice that this "labyrinth of mirrors" was rather invoked by philosophers—Derrida included—to deconstruct Hegel. Derrida, in turn (in one out of my two proposed readings of his work), commits a more complex error of both adopting the mise en abyme and opposing its "logocentric" quality as a demarcated concept, an emblem, and an exclusive category of doubleness. Had he been attentive to the emblem of mise en abyme itself, he would have revealed an entity comprising a "double bind" of plenitude and that which "breaches and broaches" this plenitude *at one and the same time*, thus undermining "logocentrics" in the most radical manner.

In a discussion dedicated to analytic and possible-world semantics of mise en abyme, I shall also put to test my concerns regarding this school committing—to various degrees—to Bertrand Russell's theory of types.

Consisting, as Richard Rorty shows, in "substance ontology," analytic philosophy is superficially incompatible with the "generative" nature of mise en abyme pointed to by continental philosophers and poeticians[10] alike, the fact that the embedding narrative level and the embedded, reflective, one "encounter" upon a ground that did not preexist the encounter. I will argue that whilst analytic semantics has proved invaluable for articulating the paradoxes of the mise en abyme, only continental philosophy, establishing their irreconcilable nature, would be capable of exploiting their ontological value.

The "depth" of the symbol, writes Ricœur, its generation of hermeneutically stimulating nuances, is "inexhaustible."[11] Serving as a paradigm shift and a new ontological symbol, the concept and very emblem of mise en abyme should thus serve as a map, a lab, even a crystal ball to whoever seeks a further exploration of post-Heideggerian philosophy, or whenever a philosophical difficulty may arise. A rich pool of insights and investigations concerning the mise en abyme is nevertheless already at hand in its birthplace—literary theory. Furthermore, only philosophers who attended this pool, I will argue, gained an adequate grasp of the concept of difference, and it goes without saying that only through attending to this pool can I provide an adequate account for the mise en abyme in the philosophy of these writers. It is also true that those philosophers have infused the concept with new meanings, and—more importantly—that the mise en abyme in literary theory was developed against the background of post-structuralist philosophy in the first place. It would be futile—and since Heidegger we also know anti-constructive—to try to eradicate circularities of this sort, but in any case, historically speaking, these disciplines shared an interlaced milieu, materialized for example in the *Tel Quel*, the avant-garde literary magazine, to which both philosophers like Michel Foucault and poeticians like Ricardou contributed on the question of mise en abyme. Correspondingly, the first chapter of this work will explore literary theories of mise en abyme, *but already as a philosophical assessment of those theories*. It will thus anticipate the main body of the study where I explore how mise en abyme functions in post-Heideggerian philosophy.

Chapter 1, surveying the poetics of mise en abyme, is divided into six sections. The first discusses how literary theorists have employed the emblem of the mirror, which has been associated with mise en abyme from the start. It will carry out a differentiation between the static (ordinary) mirror, and the double one (two parallel mirrors), showing how poeticians tended to associate mise en abyme with the latter alone. It shall thus clear the stage for a discussion in chapter 5 of the double mirror as a philosophical paradigm shift. The second section explores poeticians' conception of mise en abyme as an "interruption" to the text, that is as embodying a narratological otherness resulting in paradoxes of time, space, and causality. I will show how these writers viewed this "interruption" to consist in the fact that mise en abyme, far from bearing an "internal essence" embodies what Deleuze would term "pure becoming," a here-and-now juxtaposition between mutually exclusive logical and narratological levels. The third section will show how, aiming at compatibility with an object bearing no "internal essence" and confined to no stable identity conditions, poeticians created a unique, dynamic typology of mise en abyme. It will then explore the phenomenological meaning behind the structure, and choice of types and species, in this typology. The fourth section discusses the transition from the New Novel (*nouveau roman*), which prevailed in the 1950s and '60s, to the new New Novel (*nouveau nouveau roman*), which began around 1970. Aiming to do away with realism and mimetology, the new genre employed "jigsaw contoured" mises en abyme, modeled on "Klein forms" rather than Gide's escutcheon. I shall show, however, how scholars have viewed the very ideological nature of this endeavor as bringing mimetology in through the backdoor. The fifth section shall discuss reader-response theories of mise en abyme, which assigned to the reader an active role in encoding or "inscribing" the work, and to the mise en abyme—a role in creating (and recreating) "gaps of indeterminacy" to be "filled" by the reader. I shall attempt to examine whether the added factor of reader in these theories indeed infuses the poetics of mise en abyme with a new dimension of heterogeneity, qualitatively different than that already existing in formalist poetics. In the final section, I will examine mise en abyme in analytic and possible worlds semantics. By assigning entities intrinsic properties, and by assuming a formal, objectified relation—that of *correspondence*—between entities and their representations, analytic philosophy privileges "static, 'timeless' definitions and conceives of entities standing (a temporally) in Relations."[12] However, can an enquiry that is based upon a static representation, an "internal nature," of entities, account for mise en abyme, an entity that only becomes such by force of here and now juxtapositions?

Chapter 2, opening the philosophical enquiry in this study, shall explore the mise en abyme in the writing of Derrida, using it as a deconstructionist paradigm, "in virtualy synonymous proximity to *supplemanterité* and *différance*."[13] I shall show that *mise en abyme* characterizes Derrida's "quasi-concepts" of "trace," "*différance*," "supplement," and "iterability" and it is the mise en abyme inherent to these concepts, the fact that they are *already différance*-of-*différance*, or supplement-of-supplement—not their innate or even contextual sense—that enables them to serve as an "infrastructural difference" without regressing—like Heidegger's "Being"—to being "transcendental signifiers." The enquiry shall revolve around Derrida's unusual decision to both invoke mise en abyme and to denounce its "presentation," its use as a demarcated concept and emblem. But are Derrida's misgivings toward the mise en abyme justified? Do they agree with the concept's attributes as analyzed by poeticians? And is the discarding of the emblem of mise en abyme favorable to the articulation of Derrida's new, non-"metaphysical" concept of difference? The chapter will examine the implications of this discarding on Derrida's theory of incompleteness of signification as developed in *Limited Inc*. It will offer two competing readings of *Limted Inc*: The one, "transcendent" or "argumentative," follows the face-value meaning of its arguments; the other, "textualistic," focuses on their textual style or what Derrida calls "idiomaticity."

Chapter 3 shall explore the mise en abyme in Blanchot's writing. Drawing explicitly on Gide, Blanchot models his mechanism of "Worklessness" (*désouvrement*) on mise en abyme: heading toward its "absolute exterior," language goes through a series of crossings and re-crossings of the boundary, each both embeds and is being embedded within the others. The chapter shall explore three further writers: Foucault, who in his study "Language to Infinity" brings the mise en abyme in Blanchot's thought to the fore; Wolfgang Iser, whose reader-response theory implicitly draws on (but also illuminates) Blanchot's mechanism of worklessness; and Levinas, whose concept of *il-y-a* and the mise en abyme it implies will serve to solve a textual problem: to reconcile the fact that on the one hand Blanchot's philosophy consists in uncompromising "ambiguity" between two poles—Being and Other-than-Being; "day" and the "night in itself"—but on the other hand argues for the "fatality of day," thus assigning prerogative to the first of these poles alone.

Chapter 4 shall explore the mise en abyme in Deleuze. It will also explore the mise en abyme in Bergson, upon whose work Deleuze's syntheses of time heavily rely, and the writings of Kant, Leibniz and others whose projects Deleuze both contests and completes. Like Derrida, Deleuze invokes the mise en abyme to determine repetition as "vertical," a repetition of repetition, repetition of what is always already "split into two," and difference—as difference-of-difference, a difference given to repetition so as not to depend on the possibility of a pre-established form of difference. As against Derrida, however (if we follow our "transcendent" rather than "textualistic" reading of Derrida), Deleuze would be attentive to the actual poetic emblem of mise en abyme and to what poeticians—such as Ricardou—had to say about it. The principle of coexistence between incommensurable variants which these poeticians formulated, I will argue, underlies Deleuze's concept and practice of "affirmation," his extraordinary choice to be a "thinker of multiplicities" and a "thinker of the univocity of being"[14] at one and the same time. Mise en abyme and its attributes as drawn by Deleuze will further serve for interpreting his syntheses of time. In particular, I shall develop the distinction between Deleuze's synthesis of the past and that of the future, articulating it in terms of the difference between the Gidean escutcheon (as employed in the New Novel), and the "Klein Form" (as employed in the new New Novel).

In chapter 5, I shall argue that post-Heideggerian philosophers—with Goethe, Bergson, and Heidegger himself as precursors—conducted an ontological paradigm shift between the mirror (which Rorty has shown to symbolize "substance" ontologies), and the "labyrinth of mirrors," which those philosophers associated with mise en abyme. I will draw on Richard Kearney's thesis as launched in *The Wake of Imagination,* which argues for a similar paradigm shift with regard to the concept of imagination. Nonetheless, in order to assimilate Kearney's thesis to the question of ontology, I shall modify it in terms of concepts, persons, and especially the lesson to be drawn from this "labyrinth of mirrors." Another prominent thesis that I shall confront is that of Gasché, who, in commenting on Derrida, rather foregrounds the "tain of the mirror" paradigm. I will be required to answer the question as to which type of picture or metaphor qualifies as a "paradigm," and will attempt to respond based on Thomas Kuhn's and Ricœur's criteria.

Chapter 6 shall explore what appears to be an equivalent paradigm shift: From *play* (in the broad sense set by Johan Huizinga) to play-within-play, or mise en abyme. Play has always had an important role in Western literary and philosophical discourse, viewed, since Heraclitus, as a symbol for world and Being. Such discourse culminates in Gadamer and Fink, who redefine Heidegger's relation of Being to beings in terms of a play-player relationship. Viewing its self-seclusion from empirical reality as promoting monocentric logic, Levinas overtly and Deleuze covertly would, however, disqualify the paradigm of play from serving in a philosophy of difference. Drawing upon Friedrich Nietzsche, Deleuze would introduce instead the unique dice game, the "divine" one, where given to chance are not only possibilities within the boundary of the play, but also the variety of factors present in its immediate pragmatic context. The game differs from its "outside" while embedding this differentiation at its very heart: a mise en abyme. Stamped with its Other at its essence, the Divine Game—underlying Deleuze's "ethics of becoming"—is hence a manifestation of what Levinas termed "responsibility," but one aimed toward neither the Other nor the Self, but rather the "middle" between them.

In chapter 7 I shall argue that the book which Deleuze, in *A Thousand Plateaus*, terms "rhizomatic" is distinguished from the object of reader-response poetics, in that the recipient actually inscribes. He inscribes in the sense that the book's text is "hybrid," consisting of a semiotic level of signification—normative inscription—on the one hand, and a pragmatic one—the actual body and actions of its empirical recipient—on the other, without these ceasing to be pragmatic at any moment during the act of reading. In other words, this book fulfills a possibility which poetics all through thought to be impossible: the integration into the narrative of an empirical—rather than an implied—reader. I will provide empirical examples for such a book, and argue that what enables this science-fictional case to be real is a special type of mise en abyme, the "centrifugal," causing the book to "transcode," that is, to signify in a "yet-to-come," radically absent code, in the sense that birds, marking territory, "sing" when it comes to human ears.

CHAPTER 1

THE LITERARY THEORY OF *MISE EN ABYME* AND ITS PHILOSOPHICAL MEANING

MISE EN ABYME AND MIRRORING

Dällenbach, following Magny (1950), views an 1893 paragraph from Gide's Diaries as the first theory and founding "charter" of mise en abyme:

> In a work of art, I rather like to find transposed, on the scale of the characters, the very subject of that work. Nothing throws a clearer light upon it or more surely establishes the proportions of the whole. Thus, in certain paintings of Memling or Quentin Metzys a small convex and dark mirror reflects the interior of the room in which the scene of the painting is taking place. Likewise in Velazquez's painting of the Meninas (but somewhat differently). Finally, in literature, in the play scene in Hamlet, and elsewhere in many other plays. In Wilhelm Meister the scenes of the puppets or the celebration at the castle. In "The Fall of the House of Usher" the story that is read to Roderick, etc. None of these examples is altogether exact. What would be much more so, and would explain much better what I strove for in my Cahiers, in my Narcisse, and in the Tentative, is a comparison with the device of heraldry that consists in setting in the escutcheon a smaller one 'en abyme,' at the heart-point.[1]

A major principle which Dällenbach draws from the charter is that the mise en abyme, as a means by which the work turns back on itself, "appears to be a kind of reflection."[2] Indeed, literary theorists and philosophers alike have associated the mise en abyme with the emblem of the mirror right from the start. The type of mirror which they usually invoke, however, is unique—infinite parallel mirrors ("two mirrors would in fact suffice!"[3])—a device which Deleuze, following Bergson, also terms "dynamic" or "mobile" mirroring. The specular relation prevailing in mise en abyme, writes Ricardou, "is not that of a still mirror, but a dialectical one which elaborates itself, incessantly resettles itself, and which escapes any immobilization."[4] Whilst the static mirror bears a relation of correspondence with the object it reflects, so that one can stably determine any part of the mirror-image to represent a part of the person gazing at the mirror (and that part alone) in the mobile mirror one stands on moving sands. In a mobile mirror where "A reflects B while being reflected by it in continuous mirror effects,"[5] the "selves" (and features) of both the reflecting device and the reflected object incessantly change. Mirror A cannot reflect mirror B without being *always already* a different subject reflecting a different object, it is retroactively transformed into a conjunction such as (mirror A within mirror B), that is, mirror C. The subject and object of the mobile mirror bear not a "coded" identity, to use Deleuze's terminology, but only a "situational" one, deriving from a here and now constellation. This also means that though a difference between the reflected and the reflecting does persist, one cannot stably discern here two respective substances, that is, determine which is the origin and which is the copy. There is no unique, singular, "first time," preceding other instances of repetition temporally or qualitatively: The mise en abyme "does not redouble the unit, as an external reflection might do; in so far as it is an internal mirroring, it can only ever split it in two."[6]

The subject and the object of mirroring, incessantly changing, do not preexist the here-and-now juxtaposition between them. This is to say that the true object of reflection in mobile mirroring is neither the person gazing at the mirror, nor the mirror reflecting this person, but the very "middle" between them, their very juxtaposition. Correspondingly, if *La Tentative amoureuse,* as Gide writes in the charter, "explains much better what he strove for," it is due to bearing what Dällenbach calls a "relational mise en abyme." Mise en abyme, writes Gide, reproduces the "subject of the work itself." Bal notes the ambiguity of the word "sujet," which may designate either the subject-matter or the creative, grammatical, and narrating subject.

Gide, she writes, "was interested primarily in the power of the narrating subject, a power which seems to increase when the subject doubles itself."[7] But, contrary to Bal's interpretation, *La Tentative* in fact shows interest in neither the subject matter, nor the narrating subject. What reproduces itself in *La Tentative* is rather *the relation between the two*: the subject is duplicated "as soon as the work begins."[8] This novel not only attributes to a character in the narrative the activity of the narrator in charge of the narration, but also poses an analogy between the situation of the character and that of the narrator, so that its mise en abyme is "a relationship of relationships, the relation of the narrator N to his/her story S being the same as that of the narrator/character n to his/her story s."[9] If Gide dismissed Poe's story and others' as imperfect examples it is because "the duplication they provide only comprises two of the four terms required (N:S::n:s)";[10] mise en abyme, to stress again, doubles no simple, but what is split into two at its very origin, what is retroactively *already* double. Indeed, in a paragraph adjacent to the "charter"—later to inspire Blanchot—Gide explains the mise en abyme in terms of a mechanism of retroaction:

> I wanted to indicate In *La Tentative* the influence the book has on the author while he is writing it . . . A subject cannot act on an object without retroaction by the object on the subject that is acting . . . An angry man tells a story—this is the subject of the book. A man telling a story is not enough—it must be an angry man and there must always be a continuing relationship between the man's anger and the story he's telling.[11]

In mise en abyme, as in the double mirror, a subject of reflection becomes retroactively its object. In the other adjunct paragraph it is already explicitly a "double mirror" Gide reflects on:

> I am writing on the small piece of furniture of Anna Shackleton's that was in my bedroom in the rue de Commailles. That's where I worked; I liked it because I could see myself writing in the double mirror of the desk above the block I was writing on.[12]

I am not sure how Gide could view himself writing while writing, but it is definitely the case that only in a double mirror can one view oneself gazing at the mirror, that, contrary to the still mirror, one can gaze at the object of reflection and the process, or subject, of reflection, *at one and the same time*. Such principle of simultaneity between incommensurable logical or narrative levels also governs, as we shall see, the mise en abyme. Certainly, in the "charter" itself it is rather convex mirroring which served as Gide's criterion in selecting pictorial examples, but Deleuze would later show convex mirroring to precisely share with double mirroring the principle of simultaneity. Like mobile mirroring, reflecting not only an external object but also the very reflecting device, the convex mirror, capable of condensing within itself almost the entire field of vision that is presented on the canvas, allows the painter to "perform the paradoxical feat of including observer and observed together in the painting."[13]

What Gide terms "retroaction" is the breaking of linearity between cause and effect. The man's telling the story as a cause of the story becomes, through "an act of retroaction," an effect of that story. This system thus comprises two incompatible moments. On the one hand, the cause gains temporal and qualitative priority over the effect. On the other hand—it is the effect which gains such priority; the mechanism of retroaction entails a double articulation, with the two discontinuous "slopes"—to use Blanchot's terminology—separated by an irreducible gap. If metaphysics throughout history invoked the static mirror paradigm—entailing a substance-based distinction between the reflected and the reflecting—to impose binary values upon free-floating variants, poststructuralist philosophy would invoke the double mirror—entailing the irreducible gap of retroaction—to pursue the "difference in itself," unmediated by the binary logic of representation.

It was by taking interest in the poetics of the mise en abyme that philosophers adopted the emblem of infinite mirroring. At the same time, it was through attentiveness to the contemporary philosophical discourse that poeticians like Ricardou were careful to establish a qualitative distinction between static and mobile mirroring, associating mise en abyme with the latter alone. Dällenbach is salient among poeticians who remained blurry as to this distinction. On the one hand, it was he who identified that in Gide's supreme example of mise en abyme, the "relational mise en abyme," "reflexion of reflexion" is a governing principle. Furthermore, in his definition of mise en abyme as "any internal mirror that reflects the whole of the narrative by simple, repeated or 'specious' (or paradoxical) duplication,"[14] he incorporates the term "internal mirror," which Ricardou, as we saw, has already used as an equivalent to mobile mirroring.

On the other hand, he negligently overlooks that it is in fact a *double* mirror which Gide mentions in his paragraph on mirroring, and he recounts "images of mirroring" among writers and theoreticians of mise en abyme, without any discrimination between static and mobile ones.[15] Finally, in articulating the three types of the mise en abyme, he seems to understand this distinction as rather quantitative. The term mise en abyme, he says, applies to three essential figures, corresponding to three "aspects of mirror reflection":

a) simple duplication, represented by the shield within the shield, where a sequence is connected by similarity to the work that encloses it;

b) infinite duplication, represented by infinite parallel mirrors, where a sequence is connected by similarity to the work that encloses it and itself includes such sequence; and

c) aporetic duplication, where a sequence that is supposed to be enclosed within the work also encloses it.[16] This type is represented by the Liar's paradox or other contradictory statements such as "there cannot be anything other than a personal philosophy" (which is itself a personal statement claiming to be a general proposition). At the same time it is represented—like the infinite duplication—by Gide's *The Counterfeiters*, where the main narration "cannot be captured in a single mirror, but is projected, through various filters, in a series of mirrors that open up dizzying perspectives."[17]

These three underlie three types of mise en abyme, respectively: the "simple," the "infinite," and the "paradoxical" (indicted as types I–III in Dällenbach's typology). What is notable here is Dällenbach's implicit association of the "simple type" of mise en abyme—including Gide's important figure of the shield-within-shield—with the still mirror. Alternatively, these "aspects of mirroring" do not correspond to empirical types of mirroring—the simple and the mobile—at all, or else the "infinite" and "aporetic" would not have been differentiated. This indicates Dällenbach's disinterest in the actual mirroring devices and their phenomenology, so that the "mirror reflection" in Dällenbach is an abstract genus whose three "aspects," continuous to each other, differ in quantity rather than quality.

Dällenbach, I will show further on, often employs a conscious and methodical ambiguity in his research on mise en abyme. This is not, however, the case here. His blurriness regarding the significance of mobile mirroring would have been avoided had Dällenbach, like Ricardou, been aware of the ontological paradigm shift—from still to mobile mirroring—which contemporary philosophers, invoking mise en abyme, have conducted.

THE DOUBLE-BIND OF THE MISE EN ABYME

If the first distinctive feature of the mise en abyme—the essential and indivisible feature that distinguishes it from other literary notions—is the idea of reflexivity, the second, writes Dällenbach, is its immanence in the text: Mise en abyme is a "transposition of the subject *at the level of the characters.*" Immanent reflexion is "hypodiegetic" (or "metadiegetic" in Gérard Genette's lexicon[18]). If Achilles and the Tortoise in Hofstadter distract themselves from a tense predicament by reading a story in which two characters called Achilles and the Tortoise read this very story, then "Hofstadter's dialogue projects a primary world, or *diegesis,* to which Achilles and the Tortoise belong. Within that world they read a story which projects a *hypodiegetic* world, one level down from their own. The characters of *that* world, in turn, enter the hypo-hypodiegetic world . . . ; and so on."[19] What Gide was setting out to exclude were reflexive elements that do not concern the "diegesis," or the spatiotemporal universe of the narrative, such as personal intervention by the author within the narrative, or prologues.

However, true "immanence" according to Dällenbach cannot involve the abolition of narratological "transcendence." It rather consists of putting these two vectors—the immanent and the transcendent—in "simple juxtaposition, with no logical constraint necessarily governing the enterprise,"[20] to use Ollier's words. Far from adhering to binary values (entailing as such, as we shall see, a mediating and reconciling unity), this dyad consists in "double meaning"[21]—what Deleuze would term a "double articulation" or "double bind"[22]—two competing hypotheses whose differences cannot ever be reconciled or mediated. Specifically, the reflective utterance (that which conveys the double) operates in two incompatible series at one and the same time. On the one hand, it "continues to signify like any other utterance," succumbing to and reaffirming the totalitarianism of the hegemonic narrative. On the other hand, it "intervenes as an element of metasignification,"[23] an autonomous element, the "other in the text,"[24] that as such diversifies the discourse.

Correspondingly, mise en abyme is "neither opaque nor transparent,"[25] neither an allegory, nor a symbol—as understood by Ricœur. Allegory is signified only by means of *formal* reasoning: A is to B as C is to D. This means that its figurative meaning is external to, and not directly accessible from, its literal one, and its literal meaning could be easily exchanged by another, as long as formal relations between the literal and the figurative are maintained. Allegory is hence "transparent": "once the translation is made, the henceforth useless allegory can be dropped,"[26] as it has no more to contribute to the understanding of the figurative. By contrast,

> In the symbol, I cannot objectify the analogical relation that connects the second meaning with the first. It is by living in the first meaning that I am led by it beyond itself; the symbolic meaning is constituted in and by the literal meaning which effects the analogy in giving the analogue . . . The symbol makes us participate in the latent meaning and thus assimilates us to that which is symbolized without our being able to master the similitude intellectually.[27]

Symbolic signs are opaque "because the first, literal, obvious meaning itself points analogically to a second meaning which is not given otherwise than in it."[28] The symbol—a crucifix, a flag, etc.—constitutes its figurative level as much as it represents it; it represents something, writes Gadamer, "by taking its place."[29] Rather than a formal, fully demonstrable relation of translation between the literal and figurative meanings, the symbol comprises a dissimulation between the two. To use Heideggerian terminology, rather than *adequatio* or correspondence, the truth of the symbol consists in *aletheia* or "self-disclosing"; symbolic analogy is situated in time, so that the analogy "happens," and is always "more" than its (extra-temporal) formalization. Rather than judgment—a comparison of the two sides of the analogy—the symbol consists in giving "faith" in, an "engagement" with one of the two sides, namely the analogue or literal level of the symbol. The symbol provides the analogue which has no existence in disconnection with the symbol. It is by "giving in," by "living in the first meaning" that a reader is led by it beyond himself.[30]

Now the interesting point is that mise en abyme is in fact both an allegory and a symbol. On the one hand, by presenting the content of the whole book in a limited space and by saying the same thing as the story elsewhere, mise en abyme—like a symbol—establishes itself as a self-presenting segment. On the other hand, as in the case of allegory—whose signification depends on a judging, transcendental party—it is the text itself, not only, or initially, the primary meaning of the reflexive sequence that "enacts the analogy by providing the analogue."[31] One can only give a reflexive value to a sequence, says Dällenbach, if the text signals so (for instance, by creating homonymy between the characters of the inserted and enclosing narrative) or if "this is justified by the text as a whole."[32]

Bal (1978) here accuses Dällenbach of being a "closet intentionalist," recovering a "consciousness" which is not immanent in the text, functioning as a substance which regulates and directs its reading, interpretation and criticism. But in truth it is rather in order to avoid substantialism that Dällenbach sets these maxims. In fact, according to Dällenbach, and somewhat to Ron, it is precisely those "who are obsessed with this notion and find it anywhere,"[33] that subordinate the text to substances, by applying pre-established categories of similarity between the reflected and the reflecting, such that are either empty ("any human character is, in some sense, an icon of Man"[34]), or are uncovered only by means of a thorough critical retrospection that can by no means be compatible with a textual immanence. We shall later see how Derrida, being one of those to "find mise en abyme anywhere" (by applying it to textuality in general), also as a result fell—if we are to follow Deleuze's criticism—into the trap of substantialism. What Dällenbach acknowledges is that it is never by negating the transcendental factor that one allows textual immanence, but rather by putting the latter in coexistence with the former. Consisting of a double articulation, mise en abyme comprises the "middle" between these two vectors, an "economy" of totalitarianism (of the dominant text) and defiance (of the autonomous, reflective, segment).

In other words, it is not in itself that the autonomy of the reflexive segment can embody a textual alterity. To the contrary, the reflective utterance bears the potential of substituting one totalitarianism—that of the hegemonic narrative—with another—that of the reflective segment. Self-presenting, the segment, writes Dällenbach, functions as (a Ricœurian) symbol, with which one engages in a "hermeneutics of faith," a concept drawing on the Heideggerian hermeneutic circle: " 'Believe in order to understand, understand in order to believe'—such is its maxim; and its maxim is the 'hermeneutic circle' itself of believing and understanding."[35] However, writers, as we shall see, criticized Heidegger's hermeneutic circle (or the precomprehension of Being latent in the question of Being) for reinstating rather than destroying the truth of Being as a "transcendental signified." Despite comprising a "to-and-fro movement" between the two poles of the primordial difference—the ontological and the ontic—the ontological precedes the latter in both the qualitative and the temporal sense, so that "Being" functions as a totalizing ideal rather than a function of difference. To use entirely different terms and context, the autonomous, metasignifying segment can rather reinforce textual totalitarianism, provided the two become stagnated into a Russellian meta-level/object-level structure. In order to solve the paradox of classes—which we shall discuss further—Russell, in his theory of logical types (1922, 1956), postulates that a class is of a higher type than its members and should not be confused with them. But in such a structure, seemingly incompatible levels are in fact "reconciled," being distributed onto well-distinguished loci upon a hierarchy or a unity. In mise en abyme, to the contrary, such hierarchy "becomes ambiguously reversible."[36] It breaks with such hierarchy, because far from being confined to a single logical or narrative level it is an object that participates *at once* in mutually exclusive levels—both the signifying level and the metasignifying one.

If mise en abyme diversifies the work's discourse; if it forgrounds the "other in the text," it is ironicaly for refusing to blindly succumb to the particularistic and anti-totalitarian banner raised by the reflective utterance. Instead, it puts this anti-totalitarian call *in juxtaposition* with the totalitarian claim of the hegemonic text. There exists in fact a circularity, or even a "mise en abyme" in Dällenbach's very determination of mise en abyme. If mise en abyme is the "other in the text," if it challenges the dominant text's claim for totality and interrupts the consecutive, linear order of time such totality implies, it is not so much because it embodies the small-scale segment that duplicates the whole—thus "challenging" it by means of paradoxes of time, space and causality—but rather because it populates *the seam between that segment and the totalizing whole that embeds it*; it comprises these two incommensurable poles of the bind—the "particularistic" segment on the one hand, the totalizing text on the other—at one and the same time. Far from bearing a coded, "internal" essence, mise en abyme "only becomes such through the duplicative relationship it admits itself into with one or other aspect of the narrative,"[37] a "pure becoming," in Deleuze's terms, to the extent that it is even doubtful "whether a poetics of such a grafted-on function is possible."[38] Difference, for Deleuze, I note in advance, would be likewise a dynamic, complex and always already second-degree entity, such that comprises incommensurable yet "resonating" poles—the Same and the Different at one and the same time. If for Dällenbach the immanence of the mise en abyme means a temporal and logical "interruption to the diegesis,"[39] it is not—as Bal believes—due to the "relay of focalization,"[40] an equivocality caused by the relegation of narration to a character on the hypodiegetic or metadiegetic level, but rather due to the two incommensurable perspectives paradoxically forming a *univocal* diegesis.

Ricardou demonstrates this "economy" of otherness through exploring a mise en abyme in the myth of Oedipus—the sphinx's riddle. "What creature walks on four feet in the morning, two at noon, and three at night?"—"It is man"—replies Oedipus correctly, thus defeating the monster, winning the throne of the dead king, and winning the hand in marriage of the king's widow, his mother, Jocasta. But this is precisely why the solution was also in truth the supreme error. It is by answering correctly that Oedipus *engenders* the true solution to the enigma, which is "Oedipus himself": Who, more than any other, has dragged on four feet during his childhood, stood upright before the sphinx, and finally, blinded, been in need of a walking stick? Oedipus "has indeed made appeal to the saving principle of the mise en abyme, but his timing has remained most imprecise."[41] To perceive an utterance to be reflective also necessitates a knowledge of the text, "a progressive assimilation of all the narrative."[42] The mise en abyme is the "structural revolt of a fragment of narrative against the ensemble which contains it," but the text inevitably "takes revenge": "To what do we turn in truth if not to the revenge of the basic, monovalent narrative . . . against the structural disruptions that the mise en abyme brought to it?"[43] The reflective text is given to "a subtle, tricky game . . . between the hegemonic and the challenging," so that the text "is never enclosed within a single territory,"[44] but rather, the ground upon which mise en abyme encounters the dominant text is diversified *in the first place*. As in mobile mirroring where A cannot reflect B without becoming retroactively the reflected object, an "attack" of A over the hegemonic narrative B is displaced by the very action. It becomes retroactively a counter attack, which in turn, as Blanchot would extensively develop in his mechanism of worklessness, is displaced as well. A transgression of the given toward the exterior entails "the overture of the infinite movement,"[45] an infinite series of crossings and recrossings.

In addition to his main typology, which I will introduce in the next section, Dällenbach recounts three types of dissonance between the time of the narrative and the time of the reflective figure; three manifestations of the attack/counterattack dialectics:

(i) The "prospective" mise en abyme, situated more or less at the beginning of the narrative, reflects the story to come. The "dissonance" which it causes is due to its "overtaking" the fiction, leaving it with "only a past for its future," a room for maneuver limited to reflecting back on this previous reflection. However, as in Ricardou's economy of challenge/revenge, "any 'story within the story' must necessarily challenge the development of the chronology (by being reflexive) while respecting it."[46] The temporal interruption caused by the prospective mise en abyme is effective only if completed by "respecting" the main text, for example if, instead of taking away all the "anecdotal interest" from the fiction by "programming it forcefully," the prospective mise en abyme would provoke tension or gradually enhance the reader's expectations.[47]

(ii) The "retrospective" mise en abyme. If the prospective mise en abyme challenges the text by saying everything before the fiction has really started, the final or terminal mise en abyme has nothing to say save repeating what is already known. Such conforming can only be avoided by "moving on to a higher plane and universalizing the meaning of the narrative."[48] To this end, the mise en abyme might "form a pact" with the themes of the narrative in the shape of a symbol that "seems destined to terminate but never to conclude."[49] However, if a symbol engulfs its figurative meaning, if the latter is not given otherwise than through the symbol, then a mise en abyme embodied by a symbol "transcends transcendence."[50] It entails a peculiar case where mise en abyme, which by definition occupies an inferior narrative level, is found located on a higher level than the primary narrative. It is a paradoxical case where a segment of the text nonetheless precedes and even engenders the whole. Ricardou calls such case *"mise en périphérie"*:

> If the mise en abyme illuminates the fiction, isn't it sometimes so, because it engenders that fiction out if its own image? . . . We should sometimes not hesitate to overturn the entire figure and replace the idea of a micro-narration as a mise en abyme of a macro-story, by the assumption of a macro-story as a *mise en périphérie* of a micro-narration.[51]

An example of such *mise en périphérie*, where the macro-narration becomes a "periphery" of the micro one, is *La Mise en scène* by Claude Ollier. Lassalle, a geologist, arrives at Imlil in the hills of French Morocco. His mission amounts to establishing links: Between a mine and the road below, and between the murder of Jamila, a local girl, and the disappearance of Lessing, his predecessor in this mission, whom Lassalle has every reason to believe also recently met his death in the same region. Toward the middle of the book, while Lassalle is dedicated to his second task, a "proof" breaks out.

Coming fantastically from the past of another memory, an engraving on a prehistoric stone assembles a whole pertinent scene:

> A person straddling a moderately-sized quadruped (a small donkey?) brandishes a mallet with which he threatens a child prostrated with joined hands beside him, to the right. On the opposite side, a body is reclining behind the animal, arms flung wide. In the absence of perspective, the body is shown standing up, but at a lower level than those of the other characters, as if the animal, upon passing, had plowed him straight under the earth: the man has just been struck and lies there, dead or fatally wounded. Still farther to the left, at normal level, a second animal is receding with a raised hoof.[52]

The figures engraved on the stone sum up Lassalle's own story as well as those of Lessing and Jamila: Any foreigner who ascends to those high regions on the left route will fall victim to a deadly assault, while his successor, adopting the right route, will pass through unscathed. "Left" and "right," one must observe, however, are relative directions that can serve in no geographical "outside"; they are designators endemic to the stone, or, more accurately, to the *literal depiction* of that stone in the story. The plot is modeled on *générateurs* which are related referentially to no "outside reality." The interplay between the *words* "right" and "left" *generates* right and left—on the referential level. While mise en abyme usually only *reflects* the work it is embedded in, in the case of *La Mise en scène*, the mise en abyme—despite being a mere segment of the narration, and an object in its spatiotemporal universe, paradoxically *engenders* that universe, which becomes a "periphery" of its mise en abyme. The stone is a "startling otherness," says Ricardou, due to fulfilling the attack/counterattack principle in a unique manner: engendering the narrative it forms a segment of, it breaches its unity and undermines its homogeneity.

(iii) The "retro-prospective" mise en abyme, provides a fulcrum between the "already" and the "not yet," passing from recall to prophecy, from deduction to induction. A prime example is in *Heinrich von Ofterdingen*, where the titular character finds, to his surprise, a book, a miniature version of *Heinrich von Ofterdingen*, which articulates his present and immediate past in uninterrupted succession. Consequently, the protagonist (and the reader, looking over his shoulder) "can easily infer that a book that contains his past and his present so exactly can also be prophetic."[53] By including the "fulfillment' (the second part of the book) at the very heart of the "expectation" (the first part), this mise en abyme causes "irreparable damage to the consecutive order of the narrative," it "allows past, present and future to become interchangeable."[54] But such disruption to the "universe" of the narrative succumbs once again to Ricardou and Dällenbach's principle of revolt and "counterattack." We read in Novalis: "Someone in the midst of this crowd had caught Heinrich's attention—a man he thought he had seen frequently at his side in the book."[55] As in Gide's mechanism of "retroaction," according to which "a subject cannot act on an object without retroaction by the object on the subject that is acting,"[56] the mise en abyme, the reflecting segment, participates *at once* in both discontinuous vectors of the work—the "presumed" and the "resumed." A person presumed to exist is now resumed to exist, and the retro-prospective mise en abyme, in the form of the inserted book, always already "turns back" on the text, thus "implementing" and "dominating" it. It flickers between being the object of interpretation and being the subject and the key to the interpretation of the novel; between subverting the work's chronological order, and functioning as *an ordinary object* in the work's diegesis. The "retro-prospective" mise en abyme produces *a single, yet pluralistic time*, "threads of memory" for which Deleuze would invoke it in articulating his "synthesis of the past," modeled on Bergson's concept of "duration."

STRATA AND UNDERCURRENTS IN THE TYPOLOGY OF THE MISE EN ABYME

What underlies Ricardou's typology of the mise en abyme, or "cross of auto-presentation," is his conception of the narrative as an arena of struggle between two basic vectors, the "ideological" and the "generative," of which the "revolt-counterattack" mechanism is only derivative. Ideological forces attempt to subjugate the text to totalizing ideals—such as the "self" of romanticism or the "real life" of realism—to which the text serves as a mere copy, a cliché. Their objective is "to conceal the text," to deprive it of specificity by "setting a correspondence between what is to be said and the text which says it."[57] Such ideal takes over the surface and infrastructure of thought so fiercely that it becomes "an absolute, pure and simple common sense."[58] It is this "too readily approachable tyranny" that the counter vector of text—that of generation and specificity—defies, aiming to maintain the text's "particularistic" nature. Ideological forces overtake narrations and narratives through reinforcing the referential level of the narrative which points to an extra-linguistic universe—either real or imaginary. The generative vector on the other hand, concerns the literal or material level of the text, the medium through which that universe is communicated or created: The letters, the words, even the ink. The referential and the literal levels of signification are inversely proportionate: "The reader can perceive one only at the expense of the other,"[59] by effacing it at least temporarily, or by subjugating it to the other. A text is then generative when the referential dimension—the diegesis or story-universe—is "in service" of the literal level rather than vice versa. Since the latter is essentially specific and contingent—*no two material levels are identical*—the work modeled on it is a singularity, a leap from totality, and its story—rather than reaffirming a presupposed ideal—comprises a "dramatization of its own working."[60]

Two types of mise en abyme in Ricardou's cross reaffirm the vector of ideology: In type 3, "the horizontal, referential auto-representation," certain aspects of the referential level reflect certain others. As in "The House of Usher," "the story imitates the story."[61]

In type 1, the "vertical, descending auto-representation," aspects of the literal dimension of the work are modeled on certain characteristics of the referential, "the writing is subordinate to the story."[62] In this mise en abyme (which Dällenbach would call "textual mise en abyme"), the predominance of the referential level is affirmed even more strongly, as this mise en abyme lays bare not the concrete, specific, literal dimension of the text, but its general representation, the literal level *as already fictionalized by the narrative*.

In the two other types, by contrast, the mise en abyme manifests the generative forces of the work. In type 2—the "vertical, ascending auto-representation"—certain aspects of the referential dimension are modeled on certain characteristics of the literal dimension, "the story is subordinate to the writing."[63] This category applies mainly to the "generative" novel, a subgenre of the *nouveau roman* descending from Raymond Roussel, and in whose development Ricardou, as both a novelist and a critic, played a key role. In this genre lettristic, syllabic, phonetic, and directly or indirectly anagrammatic factors serve as linguistic generators. In Roussel's "Parmi les Noirs," for example, the plot consists of two sequences. The one recounts events of a certain Balancier, a writer of a novel concerning an old African plunderer (*un vieux pillard*). The other recounts events pertaining to the narrator, a publisher of Balancier, entertaining friends in a country cottage and inscribing a cryptogram on an old billiard board (*un vieux billard*). The two sequences on the level of reference are thus assembled and consequently

THE LITERARY THEORY OF *MISE EN ABYME* 25

generated by a contingent constituent, the purely literal difference between *b* and *p*. Despite the exotic titles, writes Morrissette, "nothing in [Roussel's] works came from outside reality; everything came from inside the text, from the words, their relationships, their interplay."[64] The generative work is generative because the referential dimension (the diegesis or fictional world) is in service of the literal (the letters, the ink, even the book-cover) rather than vice versa, and since the latter is essentially specific and contingent, the work is a singularity. In one of the most striking examples of this genre, Ricardou's novel *La Prise de Constantinople*, the settings, characters, episodes, and descriptions all derive from the letters, syllables, and typographical aspects of the title page itself.

Type 4, the "horizontal, literal auto-representation," is also generative. Certain aspects of the literal dimension of the work serve here as a model for the rest: "writing imitates writing."[65] For example, the syllable OI in Robbe-Grillet's "Three Reflected Visions," common to two major aspects of the functioning of the whole—the trOIs of the triad, and the mirOIr of the reflection the work opens with—also bursts forth in paragraphs that reflect those aspects. Dällenbach would denounce such anagrams—reflecting parts, never the whole of the narrative—as "diffusing" mise en abyme or blurring its distinction from metaphors in general. Ricardou, on the other hand, views type 4 as the ultimate mise en abyme. Like the double mirror, where the subject of mirroring is indistinguishable from its object, the anagram bears "jigsaw" contours, incomplete in essence hence open to its outside.

Dällenbach, we previously saw, distinguished three types of mise en abyme based on three "aspects of mirroring": the simple, the infinite, and the aporetic. If the level of types concerns the "essence" or "form" of mise en abyme, he now moves to introducing four "elementary mises en abyme," "species" in Bal's words, that concern an extrinsic factor—the object of duplication:

1. The "mise en abyme of the utterance" or "fictional mise en abyme," is equivalent to Type 3 in Ricardou's typology. It reflects the referential aspect of the utterance as a "story" or fiction narrated.

2. The "textual mise en abyme," is equivalent to Ricardou's Type 1. It reveals not the actual literary level of a work, but a fictional entity "without being mimetic of the text itself,"[66] a textuality which is already engulfed by the "story."

It is therefore "a sub-category of the mise en abyme of the utterance."⁶⁷ An example of this species is the emblematic metaphor of the text as "fabric," as found in the last pages of Proust's *Remembrance of Things Past*. Text and textiles, interlinked arrangements of elements, are both being interwoven.⁶⁸

3. The "mise en abyme of the enunciation" makes present in the diegesis the anonymous, faceless, producer, production, receiver, or reception of the narrative. Don Quixote, for example, makes a narrative scandal by allowing the characters in the second part to judge the first part (from which they have escaped, as it were). In this mise en abyme, the narrative tries to track down the invisible, immanent author and reader. However, the pre-eminence of the referential vector of the text is again in action. Whilst Ricardou's Types 2 and 4 claim to lay bare the *concrete* production, reception, and literal-material level of a given work, Dällenbach dismisses such possibility, believing them to bring off but an illusion which will "sooner or later be undone."⁶⁹ The text and production which mise en abyme can uncover, he believes, are themselves fictional entities, mere *representations* of text and production.

4. The function of the fourth species, the transcendental mise en abyme, is to reveal something in the text that apparently transcends the text, and to reflect, within the narrative, on what simultaneously "originates, motivates, institutes and unifies it."⁷⁰ In Beckett's *Watt*, for example, we find a picture in Erskine's room comprising a circle and—in the background—a point, or dot, inscribing decentering at the very center of the text, but also guaranteeing ("in an era where the Logos which hangs over the entire history of Western metaphysics no longer subtends words"), the "unfolding of a text deprived of any anchor."⁷¹ However, like the textual and enunciative mises en abyme, this series reflects only a fictionalized "origin" of a work. Since the originating reality is—"by definition," believes Dällenbach—out of reach or already duplicated by the time it comes into play, the transcendental mise en abyme "can only put forward a fiction (or a metaphor) of it."⁷²

In Dällenbach, therefore, we are faced with four species of mises en abyme which eventually merge into one—the fictional mise en abyme. He views the text, the production and the origin revealed by the mise en abyme, as *already* engulfed by the referential level, being part of a fiction rather than the pragmatic circumstances that surround it. This is superficially a harsh monistic stance, and an adherence to a "metaphysical" tradition that has ascribed to these elements of reading, as Derrida taught, the status of *parergon*, "what is only an adjunct, not an intrinsic constituent of meaning,"[73] a fall away from the "essence" rather than a factor defined in its own terms.

In truth, however, such monism is but one out of two incommensurable "slopes" (to use Blanchot's terms) in Dällenbach's typology. Recurring all through *Le Récit* is a methodological ambiguity. Dällenbach establishes a tight formalist model, only to overturn it, to search for "a gap, a contradiction, a point where the project breaks down."[74] He does so drawing on Blanchot's philosophy of ambiguity, Derrida's deconstructionist method, and Roman Jakobson's principle of "dynamic synchronicity,"[75] but above all, this methodologically ambiguous criticism aims at compatibility with the double bind of the mise en abyme, the fact that the latter comprises its other at its very "originary" self.[76]

The "gap," the pluralizing factor which Dällenbach introduces into his typology, is first manifested by an "inevitable implication" of the predominance of the mise en abyme of the utterance, the fact that it governs the formation of the level of types. What determines the simple, infinite and aporetic mises en abyme is the degree of analogy between the mise en abyme of the utterance and the object it reflects:

> It is according to whether the basic reflexion reflects a similar work (resemblance), the same work (mimetism) or the work itself (identity) that it engenders respectively type I, II, or III.[77]

The mise en abyme of the utterance governs the transition between the types through increasing or decreasing the level of this analogy. Type III, for instance, the "infinite," emerges by injecting the title of the book itself into the diegesis or by the inclusion of the book in a reflexive sequence that substitutes it.[78] Whilst his ascribing predominance to the mise en abyme of the utterance is fairly reductionist, Dällenbach, at the same time, exploits the subversive implication of this ascription. Despite concerning an extrinsic factor—the object of duplication—and therefore being subjugated to the level of types, the level of species in fact manipulates the formation of types and the transition between them.

The second "pluralizing gap" Dällenbach infuses into his typology is an ambiguity with regard to the transcendental mise en abyme. This species:

> ... can never be put in the same footing as any other mise en abyme, since it is linked to that which determines all of them. If the transcendental mise en abyme is a metaphor of the primary instance that constitutes the meaning of meaning and enables signs to communicate, does it not follow that it reflects the code of codes, namely that which regulates the possibility of bringing elementary reflexions into play, governs the form of those which are exploited by the narrative and ensures that they form one type rather than another?[79]

While previously viewed as making present in the narrative only a fictionalized origin, here the transcendental mise en abyme is said to reflect a real "code of codes," capable of bringing other reflections into play. What underlies this ambiguity is the Blanchotian meaning and context which Dällenbach ascribes to the category of "transcendence" right from the outset. Indeed, the very category of transcendence breaks with, and is in fact essentially alien to, Jakobson's analysis of verbal communication on whose categories of addresser, addressee, a message passed between them, and a shared code which makes that message intelligible, the other species in Dällenbach's typology are modeled. In Blanchot—explicitly invoking Gide's mechanism of retroaction—a work is created by being in quest of its "origin" or "absolute exterior." Since the point of departure of the quest and that of its destination are discontinuous, that is to say, any common, interdimensional ground to bind them together is absent, any leap towards a pure exterior departing from X, if successful, is transformed by the very action. It takes place *ab initio* in the domain of its *destination*, Y: "[Whoever] purports to follow one slope is *already* on the other."[80] The attempt to leap toward the "outside" of X is always already another attempt—to leap toward the outside of Y, which, due to the discontinuity, hence irreversibility, between X and Y can by no means be X. A leap toward the origin of the work is at the same time an infinite, simultaneous series of recrossings embedding one another, a mise en abyme. In other words, the crucial difference intriguing the mechanism of recrossings is vertical rather than horizontal. It is less that between X and its exterior, Y, than that between the aggregate X-Y and this aggregate put to the nth power, that is its double—X'-Y'. As in a double mirror, where the true object of duplication is neither mirror A nor mirror B, but rather the middle, the very juxtaposition between the two, the true origin of the work which the work is in quest of, the "primary instance that constitutes the meaning of meaning and enables signs to communicate," is the quest itself: X is in quest of (X in quest of Y). The work is in quest of an origin which is nothing but the transcendental mise en abyme it contains, hence, despite reflecting a fictional origin, the transcendental mise en abyme functions *as the origin itself.*

Dällenbach's third "gap" infused into his typology is the pluralization of the level of species. Blanchot's decentering of origin as "simultaneously the cause, of which the text is the effect, and the effect, of which the text is the cause,"[81] leads Dällenbach to assign priority to more than one "dominant," to use Jakobson's term. Jakobson saw the history of literature as forming a system in which at any given point some forms and genres were "dominant" while others were subordinate. However, despite his claim about the monolithic character of a literary history organized in terms of a series of dominants, "Jakobson's concept of the dominant is in fact plural . . . Different dominants emerge depending upon which questions we ask of the text, and the position from which we interrogate it."[82] Dällenbach applies this pluralism in a more radical way. Like doublets in the Pentateuch (the two accounts of the creation in the beginning of the book of Genesis, for instance), he assigns predominance to both the fictional mise en abyme (into which all the others "eventually merge"), and the transcendental mise en abyme (which "can never be put in the same footing as any other mise en abyme, since it is linked to that which determines all of them"[83]), *at one and the same time.* Despite its monocentric appearance, Dällenbach's typology consists of shifts of accent and fluid strata, a "crowned anarchy," where dominance is never stratified and the leader "more like a leader or a star than a man of power . . . is always in danger of being disavowed."[84]

Mise en abyme, an object that "only *becomes* such" through a *hic et nunc* encounter between incommensurable parties, might not be compatible with taxonomical endeavors, which Deleuze, discussing Aristotle's *Categories*, has shown to consist in presupposed, "coded," essences. Dällenbach, well aware of the problem, stops "considering the mise en abyme only from the strictly taxonomic angle . . . but rather from a resolutely 'economic' point of view."[85] He offers a unique, dynamic typology, where species "tend to combine" and none is "uncompromisingly pure and simple"; where a species' "essence" vacillates between a series of claimants, "from one privileged instant to another."[86]

MISE EN ABYME IN THE NEW NEW NOVEL: REVERSING MIMETOLOGISM "IN ONE FELL SWOOP"

Mise en abyme stands out in four epochs: The Baroque, Romanticism, Naturalism-Symbolism and the New Novel prevailing in the 1950s–'60s. It is only with the last, however, that mise en abyme was associated from the start, becoming immediately "one of its distinctive elements,"[87] and indeed this genre has employed self-reflexivity in a more varied and methodical way than any other literary trend in the past. However, the pivotal occurrence in the history of mise en abyme, according to Dällenbach, is the transition that took place around 1970 from the New Novel to the new New Novel, the *nouveau nouveau roman*. At a monumental conference taking place in 1972 at Cerisy la Salle it was already acknowledged that novelists who associated themselves with the militant positions of *Tel Quel* could no longer be thought of as practicing the earlier genre. At the time of this polarization the (old) *nouveau roman*, maintaining relations with the commonsense world, looked almost reactionary.[88] Aiming to break with the prevalence of pre-established ideals (political, aesthetic, noological or any other) in art and thought and to leave mimetologism—the principle which presupposes the "precedence of the reflected over the reflecting work"[89]—behind, these novelists subscribed to a writing that was a radical experiment with language and representation. Like Derrida, using the mise en abyme to liberate the potential of metaphor as free of transcendent, referential frameworks—that is, as bearing an analogue which resonates with yet is not identified in terms of the target—mise en abyme in the *nouveau nouveau roman* serves in generating a diegesis which does not posit the existence of a preordained reality, whether empirical or fictive.[90]

While the *nouveau roman* viewed mise en abyme as Gidean, a "textual equivalent of mirror images,"[91] an encapsulated, "unit-like," and "tidy" contoured image which reflects the "whole of the narrative," the mise en abyme in the *nouveau nouveau roman* comprised "jigsaw"-like segments, reflecting "scraps," never the "whole" of the narrative: "Like the pieces of the jigsaw, their curving edges are designed so that none of them, in isolation, bears the complete image of a character, an animal or even a face."[92] "Unit-like" entities are given to identity conditions. They bear determinable contours, an internal nature and intrinsic properties which remain continuously present throughout all change. Eventually, they presuppose a substance—such as "real life"—that assigns, safeguards and sustains these monolithic identities and properties. "Jigsaw"-like segments, on the other hand, bearing indeterminable boundaries, are meant to break as such with realism, substantialism, mimeticism, or other centrism.

Ricardou's *Les Lieux-dits* for example, conforms to the formula "the whole mise en abyme and nothing but the mise en abyme,"[93] with paragraphs densely populated with repetitions and variants of reflexive elements. For example, the reader of the description of the vast canvas in the museum can recognize the reflexive nature of the *cross* (la croix) in the "centre of the picture," the *crusader* ("le croisé") "in the foreground," and the *banner* ("le bannière") that gives the chapter its title, on which is set the emblem of the crusades ("les croisades"), the *red cross* ("la croix rouge"), on a white background. In accordance with Ricardou's endeavors to disprove idealist suppositions and to assert that "the fiction is mimetic of the narration rather than vice versa,"[94] this excess of mises en abyme—the repetitions and variants which this "cross" ("croix") is subjected to in such a limited textual space—assures that the *literal dimension* of the text is the work's focus and main impulse.

Triptyque by Claude Simon comprises three series A, B, and C, and three reflecting segments a, b, and c. Segments b and c are embedded in A but reflect B and C, respectively; a and c are segments of B which reflect A and C, respectively; and a and b are segments of C which reflect A and B, respectively (Figure 1.1). In such a constellation, each series is enclosed in and unmasked as a text by a mise en abyme belonging to another series,

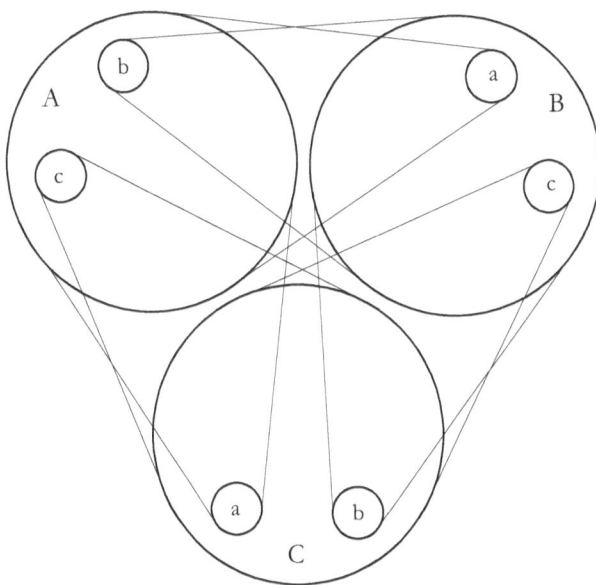

Figure 1.1. *Triptyque*.

and each seemingly closed circle is yet challenged externally by two excluded series, so that the contours of a given "parcel" are never complete. It thus aims to make its individual elements strictly equivalent, without any being privileged in any way, that is, without any relationship of (pre-established) domination between the microcosm and the macrocosm.

Another tactic is what McHale calls "composite mise en abyme." Texts such as Robbe-Grillet's *Projet pour une révolution à New York* are "composites, scrapbooks or patchworks of 'found objects,'"[95] lacking a context to keep them commensurable. A mise en abyme of such texts is therefore an "iconic double," which as such bears a coherence that the original patchwork it doubles, in fact, lacks. It therefore involves us in a conflict with the basic criteria of mise en abyme. Whilst mise en abyme by definition occupies an inferior narrative level, the composite mise en abyme occupies a primary one, such that precedes that work in which it serves as a segment. Here are a couple of intriguing examples artfully put by McHale:

> [W]hat most perfectly duplicates the structure of Robbe-Grillet's *Project for a Revolution* is not any single nested representation, but rather the description of Laura's reading-habits. Laura, we are told, reads several thrillers simultaneously, ignoring the order of the chapters, skipping key episodes, even losing pages or entire signatures from the books. If one were to read as Laura does, the result would be a reading-experience rather close to the experience of reading *Project for a Revolution* straight through in the normal fashion. In other words, Laura's bizarre style of reading captures *en abyme* Robbe-Grillet's abuse of thriller conventions, his disruption of linear development and suspense, and so on. But while the thrillers that Laura reads are nested texts, texts-within-the-text, her own behavior, the means of *relating* these texts and thus of constituting the *mise-en-abyme*, of course occupies the diegetic plane. So is this or is this not a true *mise-en-abyme*? Similarly, in *Les Corps conducteurs* the closest analogue to the bricolage structure of the text itself is to be found in a board fence covered with layers of tattered, superimposed political posters, a fortuitous collage of teasing verbal fragments in which no single word is completely legible. Here the idea of an intertextual space is made literal: these textual fragments only function as a *mise-en-abyme* of *Les Corps conducteurs* when they are brought

together on the physical space of the board fence. But the board fence itself, of course, belongs to the diegesis—so, again, is this truly a *mise-en-abyme*, or not?[96]

This exchangeability of narrative levels is often understood in terms of the Klein bottle, a three-dimensional figure whose inside surface is indistinguishable from its outside, which in many respects replaced Gide's escutcheon as an emblem of mise en abyme (Figure 1.2). As in the composite mise en abyme, this form has neither head nor tail, the narrative line (the exterior or "uncontained" line) penetrates into the duplicated field in such a way that it becomes impossible to distinguish between container and thing contained. In *Projet* for example, Laura deceives a voyeur by holding a lurid book-jacket in front of the keyhole through which he is peeping. When, much later in the text, the voyeur returns with others to break into the house, they interrupt the scene on the book-jacket, which proves not to be a nested representation but a "real" event.[97] The primary representation collapses into a secondary representation to the point where the projected

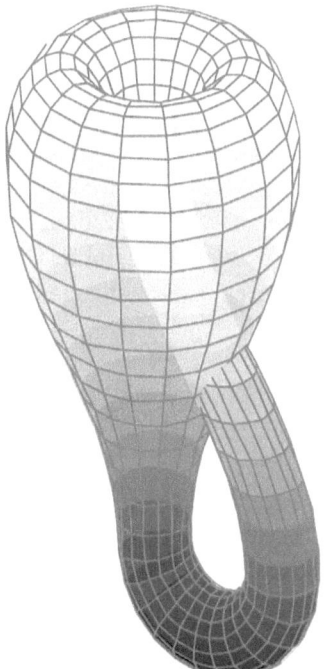

Figure 1.2. Klein bottle.

world is completely destabilized. In a Klein form you have a contained tube and an uncontained tube, a contained hole and an uncontained hole, but, like Deleuze's metaphor of rhizome, as we shall see, "any part of the form can touch, contact, communicate with, flow with any other part, and the parts, the whole, in time flow through each other."[98] Contrary to the classical mises en abyme—the aporetic one included—the Klein form cannot "be stabilized at some point."[99] This form entails "no identifiable center of consciousness through which we may attempt to recuperate the text's paradoxical changes of level and other inconsistencies."[100] It not only *suggests* incompatibility between realms or the lack of logical ground to reconcile them, but also manifests that schism in the *reception* itself, in a process of reading which refuses any "fusion of horizons." Simply put: no ordinary reader can in reasonable time phrase coherently the paradoxical mechanism which governs *Projet*.

While the means and technique of the new genre were undoubtedly innovative, Dällenbach raises doubts as to its principle promise: Does its subversive and uninterrupted duplication really constitute an escape from mimesis?[101] What he seems to really be wondering here is whether not its very *subversive function* renders it "prisoner to Platonic or metaphysical mimesis."[102] Any attempt to reverse mimetologism or to escape from it "in one fell swoop," he cites Derrida, "would only amount to an inevitable and immediate fall back into its system."[103] Ricardou taught, similarly, that any writing conducted by ideology, be it even anti-mimetological, renders the text "in service" of "totalizing," real-world (or in any case extra-textual) ideals. If so, the very *blunt* attempt—ideological as such—of the new genre to have done with mimetology causes the genre to fall back into mimetology.

It is never by negating noological and philosophical totalitarianism, Deleuze would teach, that one is granted a grasp of the "pure difference," unconfined to the binary logic of representation. In Deleuze's "affirmative" philosophy, difference is epitomized less by the Other that breaks with the totalitarianism of the Same, than by the "middle," the very coexistence between these two incommensurable parties. Accordingly, for Deleuze, it is never by presupposing pluralism that a philosophy of pluralism is adequately established. Presupposing pluralism implies presupposing a unity which grounds the multiple instances, thus appealing to differences as "reconcilable" rather than "pure," that is, derived of and defined in terms of pre-established identities. A true grasp of and account of pluralism would only be obtained by a certain restraint, by commencing with what Deleuze has termed "indifference." Dällenbach seems to follow these maxims. Only "instantaneity of representation can provide a compelling and truly vertiginous effect,"[104] he says. Only by restraint and avoidance of overstressing anti-mimetology can a reflective text insert a gap into the structural closure of mimetology.

Deleuze would have further objected to viewing mises en abyme in the "old" *nouveau roman* as "unit-like symbols,"[105] bearing as such internal nature and intrinsic properties. If the infinite-aporetic mise en abyme of this "old" genre is infinite and exponential, then its object of duplication is pluralized as well. If mise en abyme does not redouble the unit, but "can only ever split it in two";[106] if it doubles what is retroactively already double, then a mise en abyme of the type X within X is transformed by this very action of duplication. Its new object of duplication is retroactively no longer X, but X within X, that is Y, or (X within X) within X, that is, Z or is indeed defined in terms of infinite other polynomials. Its pattern is now Y within Y or Z within Z and so on: "The text cannot be the sum and product of continual mises en abyme without the nature of the mises en abyme themselves being compromised."[107] X is therefore a "preindividuated" entity rather than a determinable, "tidy" unit. It is a "molecule," a building block combining with others in innumerable "molar" forms. To use Deleuze's metaphor, X functions like a Go game pellet rather than a chess game-piece. Chess "is a game of State," where identities are shackled to representation. Its game-pieces are "coded," having an "internal nature" "from which their movements, situations, and confrontations derive."[108] Go pieces, by contrast, "are pellets, disks, simple arithmetic units." They have no intrinsic properties, only situational ones, and "only an anonymous, collective, or third-person function: 'It' makes a move, where 'It' could be a man, a woman, a louse, an elephant."[109] The apparently "tidy embedding" mises en abyme of the classical *nouveau roman* in fact function like such "pellets." X, a circuit added to a given mise en abyme, assembles with other circuits upon an "unimaginable space" rather than a pre-established one— "if repetition is possible, it is due to miracle rather than to law."[110] X acts upon a plenitude, but only a situational one, such that does not preexist X. It causes all other circuits to contract into a whole while reconstituting this whole onto which it was added.

Acknowledging that the mise en abyme in the new genre does not fit into the typology established earlier, Dällenbach asserts that mise en abyme is released from the constraining limits that never quite managed to contain it anyway: "The future belongs to a blind Narcissus in search of his own scattered limbs, irredeemably condemned to disintegration."[111] On the other hand, he dismisses the new mise en abyme as a "pseudo mise en abyme"[112] and a "dissolvement" of the concept of mise en abyme altogether. Juliana de Nooy is mistaken in criticizing this ambiguity as hesitation to set loose a "metaphysic" approach to mise en abyme and to embrace the Derridean one—which the *nouveau nouveau roman* supposedly embodies—in its stead. In truth, Dällenbach's ambiguity is again methodological, drawing on Derrida's own ruling against a frontal opposition to mimetism, and aiming at compatibility with the "double bind" nature of the mise en abyme.

Despite this unreconcilable ambiguity, we could perhaps maintain that each of the two genres, the *nouveau roman* and the *nouveau nouveau roman*, embodies a moment or an aspect of the process of differentiation. The new genre emphasizes the moment of break with totalitarianism and the birth of an Other as an "impossible literature"[113] upon an "unimaginable space."[114] This is why it would later be invoked in Deleuze's synthesis of future, marking a break with Bergson's duration of time. The older genre stands for the moment of coexistence, the fact that differing variants nevertheless come as an aggregate. If X and Y are discontinuous, if the ground hosting the encounter can only be heterogenous, then this ground is derivative of or parasitical to the encounter, rather than preexisting it. This is to say that the two parties encounter upon a ground they rather generated, made up of their very encounter, so that an iconic double of this encounter, the coherent (though situational) aggregate X-Y conditions and precedes this encounter.

MISE EN ABYME IN READER-RESPONSE CRITICISM

Dällenbach's later study "Reflexivity and Reading" was part of a large scholarly movement which, drawing on the work of Iser and Roman Ingarden, was moving away from a model of the text as a closed, autonomous entity, toward a new model where the text would be considered in relation to its addresser and addressee. A reception theory assigns to the reader an active role in encoding or "inscribing" the work. By introducing an addressee as the *outside* of the work, and by assuming a communicational deferral between the addressee and the addresser, it attempts to break through the "structuralist closure," and to "pluralize" the text.

According to this school of criticism, the literary work with respect to its reception bears four features:

I. It is undetermined. As opposed to oral, personalized communication, the literary text, where the addresser and addressee are never in the presence of one another, constitutes a deferred communication, "a crossroads of absences and misunderstandings."[115] There is an absence, for the receiver, of the sender and his context, and for the sender, of the receiver and the context of reception.

II. It contains *Leerstellen* which contribute to the overall indeterminacy of the text: holes, blanks, empty spots which have to be filled in by the reader and call for his participation, his imaginative concretization of what is being narrated. If a story begins with the sentence "An old man was sitting at a table," whether the table is made of wood or iron, or is four-legged or three-legged, is left undetermined. No matter how numerous the determinacies are, they will always determine in a partial and schematic manner. But if every real object is absolutely individual, if the general, generic essence appears, as Edmond Husserl would say, only as its individuation, then these "absences" call for the reader's participation, and represent his only creative opportunity.[116]

III. This indeterminacy renders reading an inherently temporal process. The filling in of these gaps presupposes a process of selection from among the possible meanings offered by the text. A single signifier can have several possible signifieds, between which we can decide only by establishing the context, which at each stage we are forced to restructure. The context is "serial," says Umberto Eco (1989), in the sense that rather than being given to a unitary organizing principle, each point along the consecutive line of the narrative "brings along" its own context and even code. Like mise en abyme transformed *ab initio* by any circuit which it produces, the "whole" of the narrative during the process of reading has no existence prior to the here and now act of selection, and in fact comprises—like Bergson's duration, as we shall see—a multiplicity of other, coexisting, "wholes."

IV. The text tends to restrict its indeterminacy. Like the Phenomenon in Husserl, which is generated by being bracketed out from the pre-established state of things but hence—being singled out by essence—dialectically depended on the state of things, a "hole" to be filled comes alongside signals which provide instructions as to its "correct" reading. Gaps are "half-hidden, half-revealed," insinuating the solution at the heart of the "problem." In fact, containing its own paraphrasing system, the literary text "could almost be defined as a statement incorporating a metalanguage."[117]

Mise en abyme, according to Dällenbach, is precisely what can be regarded as one of these guiding signals of "correct reading." Armed with a replica, the reader is able to identify and elucidate obscure elements, notice certain details as relevant, and dismiss others as marginal. However, self-reflection, while removing ambiguity, also creates the gaps and problematizes the text's reading. Far from blocking the gap in a definitive manner, mise en abyme, "by its very varied, insistent, equivocal and always conjectural manner"[118] enables the gap to exist as such; it fills in the holes, but "drills" them as well. Correspondingly, we shall later see how, drawing on Blanchot's mechanism of "worklessness," Iser in his later study *The Fictive and the Imaginary* (1993) would maintain that the "act of fictionalization" committed by the reader, far from ever being complete, comprises a repetition (with difference) of the very undertaking to commit the act. The filling/drilling mechanism often finds expression in an inversion that mise en abyme conducts of the reception programmed into the initial narrative: "every mise en abyme contradicts the overall functioning of the text containing it."[119] If the hegemonic reception calls for a referential reading, mise en abyme clears the way for a self-reflexive reception and a grasp of the work in its textual dimension. If, on the other hand, self-reflection predominates, it reestablishes the rights of a pragmatic reading, which regards the text as referring to something which is not itself. For example, Balzac's instructions as to the correct reading of *La Comédie humaine* is designed to "glue" pieces together and reinforce the credibility of the story. For a contemporary reader, however, it opens the door to a retrospective and deconstructive reading, that is, attention to the fragments from which the text originated, the discontinuous under the continuous, and the chaos under the cosmos.[120]

In *The Narcissistic Narrative*, Hutcheon, like Dällenbach, views mise en abyme as serving both to overcome communicational deferral and to create it. While being made aware of the linguistic and fictive nature of what is being read—and thereby distanced from any unself-conscious identification on the level of character or plot—readers of "narcissistic texts" or "metafictions" are at the same time made mindful of their active role in reading and in making the text mean. They are the distanced, yet involved, co-producers of the novel.[121] The roll of this paradox, argues Hutcheon, is ontological: it stimulates the *production* of fictional worlds that yet comprise actual, empirical resources.

As opposed to poeticians such as Ricardou and Robert Alter (1975), who identified reflexivity with a break from mimetism, Hutcheon views all texts as overtly or covertly both metafictional and mimetic. However, her paradigmatic mimetic case is the "mimesis of process" rather than "mimesis of product," and she views the latter as but a reductive limitation of the former. In a mimesis of product, prevailing in nineteenth-century realism, the reader is required to identify the products being imitated—characters, actions, settings—and recognize their similarity to those in empirical reality, in order to validate their literary worth. In a process-mimesis, on the other hand, the work is meant to reflect the work's own creative processes. It thematizes (but does not imitate in real time) the functions of the reader as responsible in some level for encoding the text. Whereas in "traditional realism" the act of reading is seen in passive terms and the novel only seeks to provide an order and meaning to be recognized by the reader, the reflexive novel demands that he be conscious of the work, that is, the actual construction that he too is undertaking.

Hutcheon considers mise en abyme "one of the major modes of textual narcissism."[122] Mise en abyme stimulates an involved reading by thematizing the role of writer and reader within the narrative, and sometimes by thematizing the metafictional paradox itself, the fact that readers are distanced, yet involved, co-producers. For example, at the end of Borges's "Averroës' Search," the narrator tells the reader: "I sensed, on the last page, that my narrative was a symbol of the man I was while I wrote it, and that to write that story I had to be that man, and that to be that man I had to write that story and so to infinity."[123] However, if mise en abyme is "narcissistically functional" it is above all by making manifest—rather than thematizing—narcissism. Like Dällenbach, Hutcheon views the reflexive utterance as operating on two disparate narrative levels, the signifying and the metasignifying. On the one hand, "it is not different tonally or diegetically from the rest of the narration,"[124] but on the other hand, it belongs to the level of procedures which produce the narration. Consequently, the work itself belongs both to the processes of "art," and to those of "life"; the reader is forced to acknowledge the artifice, the "art" of what he is reading, but at the same time explicit demands are made upon him, as a co-creator, for intellectual and effective responses which are "part of his life experience."[125]

The art/life ambiguity of process-mimesis projects on the "heterocosm," the "universe" of the story, the "coherent autonomous whole of form and content,"[126] to which metafiction refers. Though an absolute otherness, it is not properly speaking "*contra*-factual," but "an effect to be experienced by the reader, to be *created* by him and in him."[127] Rather than comprising a "phantasm," the heterocosm consists of concrete emotional and intellectual resources, which an active reader—intrigued by the work to respond "vitally"[128]—inputs.

The heterocosm is thus neither "real" nor "false" but bears an "ontological status"[129] deriving from precisely this breaking with binary values; a here-and-now existence, responsive to no extra-temporal determination.

Patricia Waugh's version of the metafictional paradox is almost equivalent. Metafictional novels tend to be constructed on the principle of a fundamental and sustained opposition: the construction of a fictional illusion (as in traditional realism) and the laying bare of that illusion. The two processes are held together in a formal tension which breaks down the distinctions between "creation" and "criticism."[130] As in Hutcheon's paradox, the recipient both gives in to an illusion he constructs, and distantiates himself from it in order to construct it. However, whilst Hutcheon views this discontinuity as embodying an "ontological difference" and indicating the "ontological status" of the heterocosm, Waugh assigns to the metafiction an *epistemological* role, namely "explor[ing] the relationship between the world *of* the fiction and the world *outside* the fiction."[131] The pole of defamiliarization serves to make a statement about issues which are external to the immediate process of reading, and even to literature. Metafiction, for example, "helps us to understand how the reality we live day by day is similarly constructed, similarly 'written.'"[132]

The problem with this approach is that it falls into the mimetological trap. It reduces literature to a didactic tool in service of pre-established ideas prevailing in "real life," and thus oppresses true forces of creation. Hutcheon falls into the same pit in agreeing with Waugh that while metafictional texts *expose* the participation/distantiation paradox, "*all* fiction requires 'meta' levels"[133] or is covertly "narcissistic." Such a contention reduces the self-reflexive text to bearing a didactic role, thus denying it self-presentation, essential for bearing the "ontological status" Hutcheon expressly pursued. Waugh, moreover, blurs the phenomenological significance of the mise en abyme by maintaining that descriptions of objects in fiction—any fiction—"are *simultaneously* creations of that object,"[134] and that such simultaneity consequently characterizes the relation between factors in the text. By claiming so, she fails to conceive of the unique, radical simultaneity which prevails between incompatible narrative levels in mise en abyme, and applies a trait—simultaneity—to an entity—fiction in general—which doubtfully belongs to it. "Bipolarists," like Ernst Gombrich, as we shall see, rather describe heteronomy in non-reflexive fiction in terms of "opalescence" or "flickering" between variants, not simultaneity.

Despite its promise, finally, Hutcheon's "heterocosm" fails to embody a singularity of existence, which in post-structuralist measures—as Hutcheon acknowledges herself—is a prerequisite for bearing an "ontological status." Structuralistic thought, writes Hutcheon, "has obvious limitations for the study of narcissistic texts, since it refuses to deal with the subject and with elements outside the closed structure it investigates."[135] A statement, taught J. L. Austin (1975), is to be analyzed not only with regard to its coded meaning, but also with regard to "appropriateness conditions," a variety of factors present in the immediate context of the utterance: the relation of speaker to hearer, tone of voice, paralinguistic gestures, and indexical reference to the immediate surroundings. These, Derrida has taught, are the factors which have been excluded by Western thought as the *parergon* of signification, the "outside" which is merely "adjunct" and supplementary to meaning, and belonging not to its essence. A post-structuralist account breaks with structure by precisely allowing these "inessential" factors ontological significance, and Hutcheon indeed suggested that an act of reading involves not only the semiotic level, the decoding of text, but also the investing of empirical, "live" resources. What her study had promised was to account for them as *here-and-now* resources invested by a *here-and-now*, *empirical* reader.

But at the crucial moment Hutcheon backs off: "The reader is . . . a function implicit in the text, an element of the narrative situation. No specific real person is meant; the reader has only a diegetic identity and an active diegetic role to play."[136] By asserting so, Hutcheon re-succumbs to structuralism, because an implied reader is one whose role, aesthetic understanding, and the code he adheres to have already been formalized and universalized, absorbed into structure. In Hutcheon as in Gadamer, the reader's "horizon" which he infuses with that of the book is not specific and singular, but public—a result of "supraindividual pressures," to use Dällenbach's terminology, himself falling into the same trap as Hutcheon. What interests Dällenbach, he admits,

> . . . is not the response of a given explicit reader, impossible to generalize about, but that of the reader-subject, exposed to the supraindividual pressures of an episteme, ideology, or unconscious desire, and, even more, the response of the implied reader, understood as the reading role inscribed in the text.[137]

Yet an implied reader, far from embodying a gap, a deferral of communication, a point where the structuralist project breaks down, is always already "transformed into structure,"[138] engulfed by a book which "internalize[s] everything."[139]

Both Hutcheon and Dällenbach believe that the integration of the empirical (as against the implied) reader into the narrative is an illusion which "will surely sooner or later be undone,"[140] but is the debarring of the empirical reader from the narrative really self-evident? Could there be a book which addresses a specific, empirical, rather than implied reader and which is, accordingly, mimetic of a specific, empirical—not typified—process of reception/production? Could there be a reception theory where the resources which the recipient invests are fully empirical, corporal rather than intellectual and emotional? Deleuze, in presenting the "rhizomatic book," would answer all these questions in the affirmative.

MISE EN ABYME IN ANALYTIC AND POSSIBLE-WORLDS SEMANTICS

In the analytic tradition of philosophy, the ontological problem of fiction, namely the nature of fictional entities and the logical status of fictional representations, begins with what Lubomir Doležel terms "one-world frame" theories which submit the discourse of fiction to that of the actual universe. According to Russell—endeavoring to eliminate empty terms from logical language—fictional entities, like impossible objects (such as a square circle), lack reference and existence. Fictional sentences are hence false. Frege's treatment of fiction rests on his well-known distinction between two aspects of meaning: reference and sense. He makes no allowance for fictional reference but stipulates that fictional terms are meaningful, that their meaning is constituted and exhausted by sense alone. Fiction for him becomes part and parcel of poetry, where liberation from reference and truth-values allows "aesthetic delight." Another version of one-world frame semantics, the ancient and authoritative doctrine of mimesis, persists into analytic philosophy. Its chief idea is that fictional entities are derived from reality, that they are imitations or representations of actually existing entities. The basic move of mimetic interpretation is to assign an actual prototype to a fictional entity, for example, fifth-century High King of the Britons Riothamus to the legendary King Arthur. Sometimes a particular represents a universal. For example, according to Auerbach, the novel *Madam Bovary* is the representation of an entire human existence which has no issue.[141] The main problem with this semantics, writes Doležel, is that it goes against literature's essence and function. Similar to Ricardou's criticism of "totalizing ideals" in art and criticism, literature, writes Doležel, "is a force of individuation, countering the universalizing pressures of language, customs, social representations."[142] Mimetic interpretation deprives fictional particulars of their individuality and files them under one of its a priori categories; what fictional literature achieves "mimetic criticism undoes."[143] The mimetic and the Russellian semantics of fictionality are not only compatible but also complementary: In both cases, "fictional particulars are sacrificed so that the actual world may preserve its ontological purity."[144]

Thomas Pavel, meanwhile, criticizes what he calls "segregationism" for "marginalizing" the discourse of fiction vis-á-vis the ideal of "real world." Russell allowed importance to fiction only as a cultural institution. Its propositions, he argued, bear emotivistic value but do not concern truth and cannot belong to semantic-philosophical discourse. For Austin, likewise, a literary work is a discourse whose sentences lack the illocutionary forces, and according to John Searle (1979), fictional propositions only pretend to be referring.[145]

Possible-worlds semantics has emerged in Saul Kripke (1974 [1963]), developing modal logic in terms of possible worlds. In the works of a host of logicians who followed Kripke, the universe of discourse is not restricted to the actual world, but spreads over uncountable non-actualized worlds. For both Pavel and Doležel, this discourse marks a true break with Russellian semantics. It avoids segregationism because fictional existence here does not depend on the "truth" of fictional sentences, and fictional sentences do not presuppose the independent existence of the world to which they refer. They rather refer to heterocosms to which they, and they alone, serve as a "semiotic channel."[146]

However, many-possible-worlds semanticists do posit "transworld identity" between worlds, which link fictional entities and their actual prototypes.[147] For example, according to David Lewis (1968), incarnations of a thing in different worlds are linked through a "counterpart relation," a set of determinable essential properties that they all share. Deleuze would object that such posited identity is segregationist. He would argue that predetermination of difference/similarity relations between worlds implies worlds preexisting the sentences that describe them, and consequently a unitary frame that sustains multiplicity, a multiplicity rendered an effect of a unity. The reduction of disparateness between worlds to identity conditions and consequently to contrariety—to a trait one bears and the other not—implies a mediating ground, a judgment allocating the variants to pre-established "rubrics" upon a unitary, virtual, "table of representation" (to use Foucault's words). "There is no dualism without primacy,"[148] taught poststructuralist philosophy, as the law of identity of indiscernibles implies two *presentiated* variants, that is, variants given before a unitary judging faculty. The other-than-given, or "pure difference" poststructuralism has instead pursued, is an unimaginable, rather than predetermined, exterior, an "impossibility" rather than "possibility," to use Blanchot's terminology. The implication is that a true theory of multiplicity, if it is to avoid appealing to differences "only as respectable and reconcilable," should not presuppose multiplicity, but rather launch from univocity; it should allow "*indifference* to subsist,"[149] and difference to be *made* rather than inferred "as in the expression 'make the difference.'"[150]

Both Pavel and Doležel sense this danger of rendering possible worlds effects of pre-established representations or taxonomy. Doležel thus seems to invoke Waugh's paradox of metafiction, arguing that "on the one hand, possibles seem to be brought into fictional existence, since a standard narrative text is written; on the other hand, fictional existence is not achieved, because the text's authentication force is nullified."[151] If "transworld identity" implies a metalevel functioning as an organizing principle that qualitatively precedes and governs the distribution of possibilia onto pre-established "rubrics"; if it adheres to the "meta-language"/"object-language" hierarchy with which Alfred Tarski (1956) and Rudolf Carnap (1937) reaffirmed Russell's theory of types (and the "one-world frame" it entailed), for Doležel the system of possiblia is modeled on mise en abyme, it functions in two excluding logical levels at one and the same time. On the one hand, the possible world, like the reflective utterance in Dällenbach, succumbs to a totalitarian force: the pre-established configuration of possibilia. It reaffirms the "transworld identity" factor that endows the possible world its status of (fictional) existence. On the other hand, comprising a "heterocosm," a universe other than given, the possible world challenges the transworld identity, rendering its "authentication force" "nullified." The possible world is "suspended between fictional existence and nonexistence,"[152] and it is this *very ambiguity*, capable as such of breaking with binary logic and the doctrine of representation, that renders it a heterocosm.

Pavel, likewise, challenges the meta-level/object-level hierarchy by putting it *en abyme*. Exploiting Plantinga's thought experiment, he argues that if each world corresponds with one and only one book, and if there exists a *Magnum Opus* containing the metalanguage, the *Book of Rules*, which explains the ways in which these books relate to these worlds and these worlds relate to the universe, then the indeterminacy of reference, as described by Quine (and generalized to possible worlds by Putnam), would maintain that this metalanguage cannot bridge between a language and the world it refers to without requiring another metalanguage to bridge between itself and the object language it sustains. The paradigm Pavel invokes here is Borges's library of Babel, a classical mise en abyme, where a book aiming to describe all books—itself included—necessitates therefore a second book, then a third, and eventually infinite "shelves" and "libraries."

Pavel seems to allude to Derrida when concluding that "Human books contain but fragments of miscellanea, or amalgamate fragmentary contents of several miscellanies."[153] In Derrida's logic of supplementarity, any "origin," a coherent whole, is "originarily," *always already*, "breached and broached" by a "supplement." Accordingly, each text is always already a "citation" or a "scrap," "open" to other scraps, and thus a component in an intertextual web. Since each scrap belongs, by definition, to an utterly different context, such openness is paradoxical: a scrap "coexists" with others while being disparate from them. In terms of mise en abyme, which Derrida explicitly employs, X cannot differ from Y without that gap between them being nested at the heart of X to begin with. A modern logician, writes Pavel, "would no doubt be horrified by such inconsistency and incompleteness,"[154] but for Pavel as for Doležel, such introduction of mise en abyme—with it non-binary logic—to possible worlds semantics, secures their ontological status, their dependence on no preexisting theorems.

Rimmon-Kenan, setting out to distinguish the poetical concept of "ambiguity" from other types of "plurisignificance," also reflects on Russell's theory of logical types. Her narrow definition of the concept of ambiguity—a "conjunction of exclusive disjuncts"—excludes irony, for example, where the disjunction of multiple meanings enables us to identify the "true" meaning concealed behind the overtly "false" one. With ambiguity no such choice is possible.[155] In narrative, the exclusive variants take the form of two mutually exclusive hypotheses, or fabulas, which the reader has attained by the end of the reading process. Henry James's *The Turn of the Screw*, for example, yields two mutually exclusive finalized hypotheses—"there are real ghosts at Bly" vs. "there are no real ghosts at Bly"—both of which can be equally supported by highly complex clue systems in the text, "so that the gap remains open and no choice between the conflicting hypotheses is possible."[156] "Ghosts vs. no ghosts" becomes ambiguous because of the logical relations created between their components "when applied *to the same object.*"[157] To rephrase: One and the same object participates in two exclusive series *at one and the same time*. In Escher's *White Birds/Black Birds*, by contrast, despite generating two mutually exclusive perceptions, one can only view one of the interlacing "disjuncts" at a time; the two are distributed onto separate points upon time, rather than populating the same temporal spot. This renders the ostensible ambiguity between them rather reconciled. Jastrow's "rabbit-duck" figure is an inadequate example of ambiguity for the same reason.

Escher's famous lithograph *Drawing Hands*, on the other hand, does embody ambiguity. In this lithograph, two pencil-holding hands, identical in form, appear to have just finished drawing the other. In order to make sense of the puzzle, the observer must be able to construe one hand as drawing the other, "but Escher ingeniously subverts the notion of hierarchy, rendering level and metalevel perpetually reversible."[158] Contrary to Jastrow's rabbit-duck, where one can in theory focus on one of the disjuncts perpetually, here the hierarchy between level and metalevel reverses *at the very moment* the observer construes one hand as drawing the other.

Christine Brooke-Rose's *Thru* is a case of ambiguous interchangeability of narrative levels "in its most acute form." Like Escher's *Drawing Hands*, *Thru* is a multi-level structure in which there is no single "highest level," it is impossible to determine who is the author of whom, or which narrative level is hierarchically superior, "if Larissa invents Armel inventing Larissa, Armel also invents Larissa inventing Armel."[159] Being a Klein-bottle narrative, *Thru* "collapses—through reversibility—the very distinction between outside and inside, container and contained,"[160] thus plunging the reader into a situation "not far from Russell's paradox of 'the class of all classes which are not members of themselves.' "[161]

According to this paradox, if R is the set of all sets that are not members of themselves, then if R is a member of itself, then by definition it must not be a member of itself, and if R is not a member of itself, then by definition it must be a member of itself. Russell solved his paradox by the theory of logical types, postulating that a class is of a higher type than its members and should not be confused with them:

> . . . we can avoid commitment to R (the set of all sets that are not members of themselves) by arranging all sentences into a hierarchy. The lowest level of this hierarchy will consist of sentences about individuals. The next lowest level will consist of sentences about sets of individuals. The next lowest level will consist of sentences about sets of sets of individuals, and so on. It is then possible to refer to all objects for which a given condition (or predicate) holds only if they are all at the same level or of the same 'type.'[162]

But it is precisely this hierarchy, writes Rimmon-Kenan, that becomes ambiguously reversible in *Thru*. Rendering logical levels perpetually reversible, *Thru* blocks all possible resolution to the paradox.[163] It also calls into question the notion of mimeticism. To see literature as mimetic is to assume a reality (or a fictional reality) which precedes the act of narration of which it is the object, and thus to confirm Russell's hierarchy between "logical types." Transforming the narrated object into the narrating agency and vice versa, *Thru* renders problematic the very notion of hierarchy—whether between narrative levels, or logical ones. *Thru* does more than thematizing anti-mimetology, it generates a non-mimetological space. If each level in *Thru* is interchangeable not only with the contiguous one but also with the all-inclusive level which is the text we read, then "all hierarchical distinctions within reality or fictionality collapse into true reality, that of the text itself: A text is a text is a text."[164] Rimmon-Kenan (implicitly) draws this notion of "text" from Derrida, according to whom "*il n'y a pas de hors-texte*."[165] In need of a supplement (epitomized by text), any origin (epitomized by "nature"), contains a latent lack, so that the juxtaposition of a supplement with an origin is "originary." It takes place "internally," at the heart of the origin, at the same time as it does "externally," so that "there have never been anything but supplements."[166] This chain of supplementarity does not eradicate the "origin"; if the simulacral world of "text" solves the ambiguity "it does so not by opting for one of the interchangeable alternatives,"[167] but by "reasserting their insolubility," by rendering the actual and the virtual—as in a double mirror—"distinct and yet indiscernible,"[168] distinct—but not according to the law of Identity of Indiscernibles. Like Pavel and Doležel, Rimmon-Kenan acknowledges that neither contrariety nor contradiction-in-itself are relations applicable to the disparity between "disjuncts."[169]

Some theoreticians and critics, writes Rimmon-Kenan, still view the ambiguity of narratives as mimetic, as a vehicle for the reflection, expression and representation of a parallel phenomenon "out there." In its mimetic role, Krook (1967) and Wright (1976) took narrative ambiguity to be "imitating or reenacting the ambiguity of various aspects of life: the moral problem of the coexistence of good and evil in the human soul, the epistemological difficulty of determining whether what we see is fact or delusion . . . and many others."[170] Tadeusz Kowzan, ostensibly, likewise suggested that mise en abyme reflects the political and social reality of human grouping, "founded on different registers, often antinomical and incompatible."[171] As against such a conception of mimetism, *Thru*'s "perverse mimeticism" derives from the logic of the mise en abyme. It imitates a reality while imitating the act of imitation; a reality which did not preexist this act.

Deleuze, as we shall see in chapter 7, would likewise develop a map reflecting the rhizome while being "itself a part of the rhizome," "entirely oriented toward an experimentation in contact with the real."[172] Fredric Jameson's "cognitive map," taking its influence from Deleuze,[173] denotes a guiding device in a fragmented world of "discontinuous spaces." Sharing no monolithic whole, these spaces cannot be reduced to the a-temporal representations which a (statically) mirroring map comprises. Instead, the map is subjective and generative: "The imaginary representation of the subject's relationship to his or her real conditions of existence."[174] It stands for an outside by establishing the very boundary that bestows that outside its status. McHale, drawing on Jameson, views mise en abyme as such a "cognitive map." *Quixote*, for example

> . . . does not just record piecemeal the disparate data of its world; it also models its world globally through its system of structures en abyme. Just as Quixote the novel comprises a single plane punctuated by insets, and unified by partial analogies, so the Mediterranean world of its era comprises a single "universe" broken up into micro-worlds, wherein each micro-world and micro-economy partially mirrors the greater Mediterranean unity-in-diversity.[175]

Mise en abyme in Quixote cannot be said to mirror reality, because that reality is itself "broken up into micro-worlds." Or rather, it is unified only by means of "partial analogies" provided by Quixote itself. If *mise an abyme* reflects the political and social reality of human grouping, "founded on different registers, often antinomical and incompatible,"[176] it does so only by expressing "what is unstated and non-statable,"[177] that is, by the mere juxtaposition between mise en abyme and the reality it expresses.

Robin Le Poidevin and Viveca Füredy are much less inclined to admit the shortcomings of Russell's semantics in appliance to the mise en abyme. We would expect the relationship between an embedded fiction and the fiction within which it is embedded, writes Le Poidevin, to be the same as that between fiction and the real world. But, "notoriously, anything goes in fiction," and Le Poidevin sets out to account for the question of transferability between fictional worlds, appealing to the writings of Ken-

THE LITERARY THEORY OF *MISE EN ABYME* 49

dall Walton (1990) who views fictional representations as continuous with children's games of make-believe. In Walton's account, "in asserting some fictional truth, p, we are not asserting that it is fictional that p, but rather pretending to assert p."[178] In this view, the central metaphysical issue of fictional entities is embodied in the experience of "being caught up" in a story. When immersed in the adventures of Anna Karenina, for example, even if we do not actually believe what Tolstoy's text tells us, we let ourselves be convinced, momentarily and partially at least, of the existence of Anna Karenina. This happens because works of fiction are not mere sequences of sentences but props in a game of make-believe. The reader who accepts that Anna Karenina is unhappy or that she loves Vronsky recognizes that such positions are true in the world of that game. Just as children pretending to feed dolls that in the game are (fictionally) babies become themselves fictional moms, readers of Anna Karenina who cry at the character's tragic end fictionally attend Anna's suicide. Rather than assuming that the readers of Anna Karenina contemplate a fictional world from some privileged vantage point outside it, Walton insists that the readers are located within the fictional world that, for the duration of the game, is taken as real.

In some reflexive novels, the relation between the embedding and the embedded fictions are kept "normal" or realistic. Suppose a novel contains a passage like this:

> Wearily, I pushed away the half-consumed macaroon and started to think about my central character, Fido. I started to write: "Fido remained untouched by the post-structuralist malaise hovering around the bed-sitter. He had his bone. That was enough."[179]

In this type of reflexivity (which due to consisting of a personal intervention of the narrator, Dällenbach would have dismissed as non mise en abyme) the embedded fiction "is just as isolated from the embedding fiction as we are."[180] In Walton's terms, when reading the novel we engage with the first-order game of make-believe in which someone is really eating a macaroon and Fido is only fictionally eating a bone. Alternatively, we can engage in the second-order game in which Fido is really eating a bone, but then the characters of the first-order game disappear, "they have to: since Fido is a real being in this second-order game, there can be no such character as the 'literary creator of Fido.'"[181] As in Jastrow's rabbit-duck, one can either focus on X (in which case Y is marginalized as "fictional" or disappears altogether) or focus on Y (in which case X is marginalized as "fictional" or disappears altogether). In either of the alternatives, mimetism and (hierarchized) dichotomy between the actual and virtual remain.

Le Poidevin proceeds, however, to describe another type, "pathological embedding," where the barrier between embedded and embedding fiction—and correlatedly that between possible worlds—is violated. Flann O'Brien's *At Swim-Two-Birds* presents us with Dermot Trellis, an author who conceives the idea of writing a story about the consequences of wrong-doing. In the course of writing this story, he creates, for the purposes of having her defiled by the base John Furnskey, the ravishingly beautiful Sheila Lamont. So ravishing is Miss Lamont, however, that Trellis ravishes her himself, to the extent of making her pregnant. O'Brien's story breaks the rules of embedded fiction:

> An author (or fictional author) can appear qua character or qua author in her novel, but not both *at the same time*. We can easily imagine a novel in which an author writes a novel in which she ravishes another character. The ravishing takes place in the embedded fiction, not the embedding fiction. The author appears qua author in the embedding fiction, qua character in the embedded fiction. But there can be no such resolution of O'Brien's novel. Here the author qua author ravishes the character.[182]

"Pathological embedding" is not accountable to Walton's schema, according to which in engaging with a fiction, we participate in a game of make-believe in which we imagine that what is stated in the fiction is really happening. If there is an embedded fiction, then our participation in the first-order game requires us to regard the embedded fiction as fictional. But how, then, are we to engage with *At Swim-Two-Birds*? If we imagine Trellis to be real, then Sheila is fictional, and so cannot be ravished by him. If we imagine Sheila to be real, then Trellis does not even exist (since real people are not the creations of fiction-writers, there is no role for Trellis to play), and so cannot do any ravishing. The problem is that we are asked to engage in incompatible games of make-believe.[183]

In order to reconcile the paradox of "pathological" embedding, Le Poidevin proceeds to describe it in terms of Russell's paradox of sets:

> If the fiction embeds another fiction, then there will be a proposition in its set representing all the propositions of some sub-set as fictional. This sub-set constitutes the embedded fiction. It

might appear that a self-embedded fiction appears to generate a set-theoretical paradox akin to Russell's, as follows: "Does the proposition which represents the propositions of a self-embedded fiction as fictional belong to the set of those propositions or not." If not, then the fiction is not self-embedded, but rather embedded within some other fiction. On the other hand, if the proposition does belong to that set, then it falsifies itself, for then the set would contain a proposition which is not fictional, but true.[184]

What Le Poidevin calls "the proposition which represents all the propositions of some sub-set as fictional" is equivalent to what Dällenbach has named "the reflective utterance." According to Dällenbach, it operates on two levels: "that of the narrative, where it continues to signify like any other utterance, and that of the reflection, where it intervenes as an element of metasignification." According to Le Poidevin, the paradox is that, belonging to the embedding level, the proposition is true in presenting the propositions of the embedded fiction as fictional, but false, as this subset hence contains at least one true proposition. His solution to the paradox is that "a proposition is fictional if it corresponds to some fiction, true if it corresponds to the facts. There is no contradiction in supposing that a proposition corresponds to both of these at the same time."[185] What this solution implies is a Russell-like rigid boundary imposed between the meta-level and the object level, so that the reflective utterance is true while functioning as a meta-level, and false while functioning as part of the object-level. The inadequacy of this solution lies in the fact, that the gist of the paradox of "pathological embedding" was precisely that one *cannot* distinguish between the levels in which the reflective utterance is performed; that the utterance is metasignifying *while* signifying. If it is false while pointing to the embedded fiction from within the embedded fiction, but true while pointing to it from without (that is from a metadiegetic level), then it acquires both these values *at one and the same time*.

The other version of the embedding fiction paradox, writes Le Poidevin, is the "ontological":

> The problem still remains of how we are supposed to *engage* with self-embedded fiction. In so far as playing a game of make-believe is pretending that certain fictional propositions are true, are we not required to entertain a self-embedded fiction both as fiction and as truth?[186]

Le Poidevin's solution is that we can pretend to believe—to make-believe—something that we could not, coherently, actually believe:

> It has been suggested that we cannot coherently believe ourselves to be nothing more than brains kept alive in a laboratory and stimulated by an (of course) insane scientist in such a way that it seems to us that we occupy bodies and can interact with the world. But what is to prevent us make-believing that we are brains in a vat?[187]

This solution is again inadequate, being inconsistent with Le Poidevin's own premises. If make-believe games bear "ontological status" in the sense of involving real activities and props, then make-believing something which is utterly incoherent, that is both X and non X, implies being engaged with two incompatible *worlds* at one and the same time, a paradox finding a solution to which Le Poidevin was aiming at to begin with! Unless Le Poidevin has quietly deviated from the initial meaning of "make-believe," employing a new one which entails not an ontological engagement with fiction, but an epistemological state—and a marginalized one in the sense that despite being bedazzling, it involves no implications for real life or even real life epistemology. What he seems to do facing a theoretical framework (Russell's) that fails to apply to embedded fiction is to debar embedded fiction from "serious" discourse altogether, resorting thus to a "one-world framework."

Füredy's concept of "logical levels," set out to account for literary embedding, is also abstracted from Russell's distinction between logical types. Three different forms of boundaries lie between logical levels.

TYPE 1, the "intact and multiplying boundary," comprises infinite recursion: Every metalevel, when discussed, becomes in its turn an object level. John Barth's collection *Lost in the Funhouse* illustrates this effect: "Once upon a time there was a story that began 'Once upon a time there was a story that began 'Once upon a time there was a story that began . . . ,'" and so on. The first "Once upon a time" is on a level which we may call α. The next time it is repeated, it is embedded in the level α, creating a level we may call β. The logical levels in this recursion never "bottom out."[188] Pointing to Gide's escutcheon, Füredy writes:

> We see a shield A, in the middle of which is another shield, B, in the middle of which is an imaginary shield C, the first

of the potential shields expanding the recursion. We have no way of knowing what is "behind" shield B, but we assume it to be the continuation of shield A. This continuation is not, and cannot be, included in shield B, nor does shield B include itself, although it too is part of shield A. In other words, when the point is reached at which the object would have to repeat itself, there is a switch to the next logical level. As in linguistic subordination, the lower logical level fulfills a structural function on the higher level, thus completing it, but, since the lower level itself here is incomplete, this completion is never achieved. At the heart of recursion there is thus a hole, an absence.[189]

The lacuna at the heart of the escutcheon catalyzes the transmission from one discrete level to the other, so that the levels cannot include themselves in themselves. Therefore, believes Füredy, they rather "eliminat[e] paradoxes from Russell's theory of logical types."[190] What Füredy fails to conceive in Gide's emblem, is that for B to represent A it must *always already* include C; A cannot be the object of duplication without that object transforming due to the very act of reflection: from A to (B within A). In other words, the lacuna in Gide's emblem points to a paradoxical coexistence between disparate logical levels rather than to their discreteness.

TYPE 2, according to Füredy, the "intact but reified" type of boundary, is already "malfunctioning." The boundary allows one to cross it on condition that one immediately recrosses it, and one is permitted to recross it only if one immediately re-recrosses it and so on; any crossing entails a "repetition-compulsion." What Füredy describes here is Gide's mechanism of retroaction, later to be exploited by Blanchot in developing his mechanism of "worklessness," and Iser in developing his "fictionalizing acts." According to this mechanism, if Y is incommensurable with X, if the "leap" toward X's "pure exterior"—to use Blanchot's terms—cannot occur upon a mediating space, then the leap, its very undertaking, *always already* occurs in the "jurisdiction" of Y. A leap from X to Y results in Y's becoming retroactively the point from which the leap is taken to begin with:

> Once the boundary between the two levels has been crossed and we are obliged to recross it, what is undecidable is the direction in which we are moving: whether we have returned to the original level of entry or gone on in the same direction as that of the first crossing.[191]

To be precise, the leap is now aimed toward an exterior which, due to the discontinuity and hence irreversibility between X and Y, can by no means be X. Instead, new "departures" engender new grounds—logically disparate to one another—upon which the rupture between the given and the Other occurs. "Crossings" and "recrossings" in fact stand in for the fact that any leap toward the pure exterior has always already taken place upon infinite registers; that any leap implies "a re-petition to be allowed to cross the boundary in the proper one-directional and unconditional way."[192]

TYPE 3 concerns "the interaction of characters across a previously intact boundary."[193] That is, if TYPE 2 consists in infinite "departures" toward the "pure exterior," Type 3 consists in infinite attempts to "land." The example which Füredy provides for this type—a story by Cortazar about a man murdered by a character in the novel he is reading is similar to "From W. S." invoked by Le Poidevin in reflecting on "pathological embedding":

> The plight of L. P. Hartley's author, who is pursued in a series of increasingly threatening messages signed 'W.S.' (in the short story of that name) continues to fill us with horror even when, indeed especially when, W.S. turns up in the flesh to reveal himself as one of the characters created by the author, and who has come to exact revenge for being given an irredeemably nasty personality.[194]

Philosophically speaking, there is no essential difference between TYPES 2 and 3, just as there is no such difference between the paradox of Achilles—where Achilles never reaches his destination—and Zeno's other paradox, the "dichotomy" one, where Achilles never departs. Both illustrate a movement upon discontinuous ground, "lines of flight," in Deleuze's terms, bridging incommensurable "disjuncts." Since the disjuncts—being incommensurable—can by no means share a pre-established ground, they have paradoxically no existence prior to the line stretched between them, hence—as in Hartley's story—their simultaneity, their appearing as an aggregate.

Füredy acknowledges that the undecidability of the direction in TYPE 2, and the transgressibility of boundaries in TYPE 3, cause the distinction between higher and lower logical levels to "lose much of its normal significance."[195] But despite what seems like acknowledgment of the incompatibility of the Russellian framework with the mise en abyme, Füredy, like Le Poidevin, resorts to a sudden "segregationist" stance. The paradox, she says, "can be escaped by jumping out of the system to an inviolate metalevel,"[196] namely real life:

Does the very notion that every boundary is potentially transgressable imply the collapse of Russell's and Tarski's distinction between logical levels on which, as we have in part seen, so much of Western thinking is founded? Or does the fact that there is always a part of the system with distinct logical levels which is not swallowed up by the typeless system indicate that it is, after all, the 'correct' way of perceiving and thinking?[197]

There always exists, she says, "a part of the system with distinct logical levels which is not swallowed up by the typeless system." But does such part indeed exist? If, as Füredy has already admitted, there exists a domain where the distinction between higher and lower logical levels loses its normal significance; where being both embedding and embedded within one another, their logical and spatiotemporal relationship is indeterminable, then one can neither speak of determinable and sustainable boundaries to delimit this domain. If the distance of an entity from a given point upon a boundary is both X and non X, then that point upon the boundary is itself both Y and non Y.

Putting Russell's semantics to action, Le Poidevin and Füredy have revealed not only its shortcomings with regard to "pathological embedding," but also the inadequacy of the *dichotomy* between logical levels found at its foundation. Instead of revising the theory and its postulates, however, these writers put the world of reflective fiction—with its irreconcilable paradoxes—in "quarantine." They assume a domain that is never "swallowed up by the typeless system," one where Russell's "correct way of perceiving and thinking" rests intact.

CHAPTER 2

JACQUES DERRIDA
MISE EN ABYME AND THE LOGIC OF SUPPLEMENTARITY

MISE EN ABYME AND THE INFRASTRUCTURAL DIFFERENCE

Remarkable achievements since Descartes in the philosophy of mind and knowledge came hand in hand, continental philosophy has criticized, with a certain dogmatism underlying these very fields. Philosophy had gone through a process that Nietzsche termed "internalization," where world, acts, entities—in short, the "outside" of mind—have in practice been reduced to concepts, that is, deprived of their specifity and "flesh and blood" existence, transformed instead into representations in the vast—and unitary—"table of representation"[1] of the mind. Philosophy, Husserl and Nietzsche have argued, must cease implying "that it is I who think, that there must necessarily be something that thinks, that thinking is an activity and operation on the part of a being who is thought of as a cause, that there is an 'ego,' and finally, that it is already determined what is to be designated by thinking."[2] It must do away with associating mind with "ego," or any other extra-temporal substance, as such privileging static, timeless definitions and conceiving of entities standing in a-temporal relations.[3]

Heidegger has denounced even Nietzsche and Husserl. With the "will to power" of the first and the reflective phenomenology of the second, neither has done away with the "internalization" of Being. What Heidegger seeks is an ontology where the transcendent subject, while projecting its own world, is at the same time always already "thrown among beings"; where those beings that are surpassed also already "pervade and attune that which projects."[4] Dating back in fact to Plato, the "metaphysical tradition" of Western Philosophy has obliterated the "ontological difference" between Being and beings by representing the Being of an entity as either an entity, a property of an entity, or an empty universal. Philosophers have said much about beings—as biological, economical, or anthropological creatures—but have "forgotten" the fundamental question of Being: What determines a being as being, no matter how it is discussed, biologically, economically, etc.? To "temporalize" Being, to claim it from reduction to an extra-temporal substance or ideal, Heidegger employs the ontico-ontological difference itself. Being is not a being, an object defined by (extra-temporal) identity conditions, thus rigidly distinguished from what it is not. For this very reason, Being is neither some counterpart of beings. It is rather a process in time, the unconcealment of the present in its presence, the very "play" of veiling and unveiling *through a being*. Always already differentiated, or rather being differentiation itself, Being "retreats" in its very unveiling, which is why the forgetting of Being throughout the history of metaphysics is in fact a part of the very essence of Being. The enquiry into Being, correspondingly, "has nothing to do with positing a principle from which a series of propositions is deduced,"[5] it is never through "agreement" of an enquiry into Being with its object that Being is unveiled. The relation between Being and its conceptualization, or indeed between any "thing" and its "representation," is not that of *adequatio* (correspondence), which entails judgment and objectification of the analogical relation and its parties. The "truth of Being" rather consists in *aletheia*, unconcealment through the "body" rather than the coded meaning of a signification. Being unveils through the very question of Being, or indeed the dialectics of the question in general: "Every seeking takes its direction beforehand from what is sought."[6] The question already sets the outlines of its answer, and, by asking the question, the meaning of being is already available to us "in a certain way."[7] Deleuze takes the example of the police in order to demonstrate the imperative character of questions: "I'm asking the questions."[8]

Dasein—the human when not reduced to mind, subject or scientific essence— is "thrown" into a world and finds itself only as a "thrown fact." In "thrownness," it is revealed that Dasein is "always already." Such "alreadiness" is manifest, for example, in the fact that useful things show themselves as such to begin with: We do not just stare at or reason with regard to the thing called "door," but have always already an "average" knowledge as to its purpose, and its proper use, i.e., gripping the knob in order to open it. The "always already" means that Dasein "is its past," that its present is entangled to a primordial "having been." However, thrown back upon its factical There, or gazing at its "having been," Dasein is at the same time "ahead of itself." It is its own "possibility" and it can "choose" itself in its being. Dasein as having-been is "equiprimordially" futural, and the meaning of the being of Dasein is temporality.

It is *always already* due to an opening in Being that Dasein asks the question of Being, which hence grows out of the "average understanding of being in which we are always already involved."[9] Likewise, "any simple prepredicative seeing of what is at hand is in itself already understanding and interpretative,"[10] Dasein interprets discursively what has *always already* been interpreted in a pre-predicative mode, because discursive interpretation is but an effect of a preliminary opening in Being which "uses" that discourse as "home." This preliminary opening belongs to the essential constitution of Dasein, "the 'there,' that is, the clearing of being."[11] It underlines Dasein's making issue of its own being, its being projected into the future, and—as Dasein is never simply a subject relating to objects—its dis-covering or taking into "care" the world into which it is "thrown." Dasein is the site for the disclosure of being, "but have we not thereby demonstrated that a particular being has a priority with respect to being?"[12] Beings bearing an ontico-ontological prerogative are inevitable in an ontology where Being is concrete rather than an empty universal, and shall be sought even in the later Heidegger who turns away from the analytics of Dasein toward an illustrative semantics of disclosure of Being.

Since each particular sense of Being is structurally covered up Being, Being itself is always only in its own deferral, it is difference, it "is nothing in itself, but it is the very 'logical' articulation of its own understanding within which it appears in a multitude of irreducible senses."[13] Heidegger reminds us constantly that the sense of Being is neither the word "Being" nor the concept of Being; that when setting Being before all concepts, he rather attempts to free philosophy from the metaphysical fallacy of an "origin," or of "internalizing" substances. The sense of Being is never simply and rigorously a "signified," and in his study "The Question of Being," he even lets the word "Being" be read only if it is crossed out.

Nonetheless, Derrida asks, in establishing the precomprehension of Being, doesn't Heidegger reinstate rather than destroy the truth of being as "primum signatum"?[14] By determining that anything that is conceived of in its being-present must lead us to the already answered question of Being, Heidegger, he argues, follows the very metaphysical quest of a "transcendental signified" implied by all categories, and precomprehended through each of them. Western metaphysics, says Derrida, has always been structured in dichotomies or polarities, being vs. nothingness, presence vs. absence, light vs. darkness. However, the two terms are not similarly opposed in their meanings, but are arranged in a hierarchical order which gives the first term "the upper hand."[15] "There is no dualism without primacy,"[16] as the first term governs the second axiologically and logically and is assumed a priority in both the temporal and the qualitative sense of the word.[17] What these hierarchical oppositions do is to privilege unity, identity, immediacy, totality, cohesion, and presentness over distance, difference, deferment and separation; they privilege states of reconciliation where the Self internalizes the Other by either identifying him in terms of the Self or putting him as the danger against which the Self is the antidote. Heidegger's Being, even crossed out, is similarly "the first and the last resource of the sign, of the difference between *signans* and *signatum*."[18] While the signifier, Saussure showed, is never contemporary but a "discrepant inverse" of the signified,[19] Heidegger makes of this heterogeneity a unity by declaring that a sign brings forth the *presence* of the signified. He follows metaphysics in reaffirming the precedence of the signified over the signifier, the origin over the copy, the contingent over the essential, and also—putting beings "in service" of the mechanism of unconcealment of Being—the ontological over the ontic. In Heidegger (as I shall expand upon in chapter 6, discussing Gadamer's concept of "play"), the ontic is not equally and symmetrically opposed to the ontological, but is rather defined in terms of it. The ontico-ontological difference, meant to underlie all differences "is tied, if not to a particular word or to a particular system of language at least to the possibility of the word in general,"[20] it becomes dependent on a specific form.

If for Heidegger the ontico-ontological difference underlies all others, Derrida presents four main "quasi-concepts": trace, *différance*, supplement, and iterability that articulate the "infrastructure," the conditions of possibility of the conceptual difference, the minimal structure required for the existence of the ontico-ontological or any other difference.

The "trace" is "the opening of the first exteriority in general,"[21] the "pure outside" within the movement of temporalization, and the intimate relation of the living present with its outside.[22] Let us attempt, explains Gasché, to imagine a concept that has never been held against another in a dichotomous relation. Entirely undetermined, it would be altogether unintelligible, but to say that a concept appears simultaneously with its polar opposite is to admit that that concept can be what it is supposed to be only in distinguishing itself from another term that it adds to itself. The identity of the leading term, therefore, "requires that the possibility of its own duplication and of its reference to another be inscribed within itself. Arche-trace is the name for the universality of this difference."[23] A concept is capable of distinguishing itself from another term only by force of *that very distinction* already inscribed at its very heart—a mise en abyme. Put otherwise, if spacing is both an interval between and an openness upon the outside, there can no longer be any absolute inside, "for the 'outside' has insinuated itself into the movement by which the inside of the nonspatial . . . is constituted."[24] The openness of the inside upon the outside enables the spacing through which the inside and the outside encounter in the first place. The two encounter upon a space primordial to their encounter, but which paradoxically comprises a double of their very encounter—a mise en abyme.

Différance is another name for the primordial gap. In the logic of opposition by which Western metaphysics has always been structured, difference, as Hegel writes, is "already *implicitly* contradiction."[25] Opposing one another *by essence*, each variant "translates itself," becoming a cliché, a manifestation of pre-established theorems of formal logic. Derrida's *différance*, on the other hand, a gap, but also a deferral—an anachronism and dissymmetry between the two poles—is a relation between moments which are not present or presentiated. It cannot mean "to retard a present possibility, to postpone an act, to put off a perception already now possible."[26] but rather (as the *a* at the heart of *différance*, a mutation devoid of, and preceding meaning expresses) it stands for an *originary* retardation, the interval that separates the present from what it is not in order for the present to be itself. By the same token, this interval must "divide the present in and of itself."[27] Movement of time is only possible by an anachronism inherent to time, a gap opened within the present giving rise to a heterogeneous, or multilayered present which as such also heralds the future and clings to the past. *Différance* is hence mise en abyme as well. The non-present that has never been present, the past that is not a modification of a present, insists within the present; the present, distanced from the past, is, in and of itself, *already* hollowed by and keeps within itself the "mark of the past."[28] Deleuze—following Bergson—would argue similarly that time can only move if there exists a multiplicity of times, each—as in mise en abyme—both embeds and is being embedded within the others.

In *Speech and Phenomena*, Derrida points to the *différance* inherent in, or the dialogical nature of, even the sign which Husserl terms "expression," which pertains to the realm of transcendental consciousness that is primordially "my own," and which is ostensibly characterized by immediate, self-presence of meaning. Husserl himself realizes that communication in such solitary mental life involves an abandonment of the privileged sphere, the going-out into a realm of empirical fact. The imagination, for instance, can never be pure, it is always the modification of an antecedent experience, and it testifies to an origin in a realm heterogenous to transcendental consciousness, namely empirical reality. Husserl can consequently preserve the distinction between "expression" and "indication," "inner" and empirical communication, only by recurrent "shift[ing] of the frontier between the primordial and the non-primordial."[29] But these re-settings of boundaries, believes Derrida, are only partially the result of Husserl's futile attempt to homogenize "expression." The other part—as deconstruction always consists in double articulation—is Husserl's succumbing to the fact that every self-presence is "always already split,"[30] rendering the frontier passing not between the pure present and the non-present but rather between "two forms of the re-turn or re-situation of the present."[31] The ideal or form of the present is itself put into repetition within the present, thus becoming multilayered and diversified: a mise en abyme.

Husserl himself accounts for the non-presentiated past in terms of "rememberings in rememberings," or "presentations of a second, third and, essentially of any level whatever."[32] It was moreover Husserl himself who offered the Dresden Gallery fable, a mise en abyme with which Derrida opens and signs *Speech and Phenomena*, to represent these levels:

> We wander through the rooms . . . A painting by Teniers represents a gallery of paintings . . . The paintings of this gallery would represent in their turn paintings, which on their part exhibited readable inscriptions and so forth.[33]

Like Borges's night 602, which includes the entire 1001 nights, the entire gallery is embedded within a single painting. Derrida would nonetheless reproach Husserl for decreeing that "with respect to remembered things at the second level of remembering, there are reflections on perceivings of just these things belonging to . . . the second level."[34] What Husserl, (like Russell, previously) is here doing, is "taming" the mise en abyme by imposing a rigid meta-level/object-level hierarchy on it. He puts levels of self-referential memory into injective correspondence with objects of memory, so that the object of remembered things at the first level is X and X alone, at the second level Y and Y alone, etc. However, as we saw in chapter 1, mise en abyme is a case of ambiguous interchangeability of logical levels. Escher's *Drawing Hands*, or Christine Brooke's *Thru*, are multilevel structures where it is impossible to determine which narrative level is hierarchically superior. To recall, whilst Le Poidevin and Füredy resorted to a segregationist approach to fiction, believing the paradox can be escaped "by jumping out of the system to an inviolate metalevel,"[35] Rimmon-Kenan acknowledged that mise en abyme renders all hierarchical distinctions—that between reality and fiction included—collapsed into a simulacral reality that Derrida called "text." Here Derrida stresses similarly:

> Of the broad daylight of presence, outside the gallery no perception is given us or assuredly promised us. The gallery is the labyrinth which includes in itself its own exits: we have never come upon it as upon a particular case of experience.[36]

Like Derrida's simulacral reality, comprising "nothing but supplements," or "text,"—"*il n'y a pas de hors-texte*"[37]—the gallery does have exits, but the gap between the interior and the exterior is always already double, found simultaneously at the heart of the interior. A simulacral reality or "chain of supplements" is not devoid of "origins." As in a labyrinth of mirrors, the actual and the virtual, the origin and the supplement do differ—but not according to the binary logic of representation. Likewise, the outside of the gallery, while insisting, is indeterminable; we do not pass by continuous transition from one realm to the other.

The "supplement," the third "quasi concept," "is in reality *différance*."[38] but whereas *différance* presents plenitude as an aftereffect of a more "unthought difference," supplementarity emphasizes the instability of such aftereffect, its *manifest* dependence on an (absent) Other.[39] In *Of Grammatology*, Derrida's main target is Rousseau, who believes that origins, nature, animality, primitivism, childhood, and so on are pure and that, compared to these pure and fully present origins, everything else (speech, society, reason) is an exterior addition. What is added is, on the one hand, nothing "because it is added to a full presence to which it is exterior."[40] On the other hand, "the supplement adds itself from the outside as evil and lack to happy and innocent plenitude."[41] Not only must Rousseau assert the danger that follows from the supplement, he must also describe the supposedly pure plenitude of the origins in terms of seduction and threat. These two meanings combined can only be formulated with inherent ambiguity: The "dangerous" supplement breaks into the very thing that would have liked to do without it "yet lets itself *at once* be breached, roughed up, fulfilled, and replaced."[42] It makes up for a deficiency of plenitude, filling "as if one fills a void."[43]

If an origin contains an absence within itself which only a supplement can compensate for, if the "contours" of the lacuna and that which compensates for it fit, then the mark of the supplement has always already existed in the hollowed origin; an origin can invite supplements only if "already inhabited by their negativity."[44] That is why Rousseau is found saying what he does not wish to say, and "describ[ing] what he does not wish to conclude."[45] The supplement in Rousseau's text, apparently exterior and "super-added" to the Origin, is in fact "originarily" interlaced with the (heterogenous) Origin: "What adds itself to something takes the place of a default in the thing, that the default, as the outside of the inside, should be already within the inside, etc."[46] In other words, a supplementation of X by Y is always already embedded within X—a mise en abyme. Any supplement is always already a chain of supplements "in an indefinitely multi-plied structure—*en abyme*—to employ the current phrase."[47]

If "trace," "*différance*" or the "supplement" precede the opening between Being and beings as the possibility of difference as such, it is not due to their coded or even contextual meaning—*différance* is "neither a word nor a concept."[48] What prevents the trace from functioning like "Being" as "master word," and prevents the originary difference it stands for from depending—like the ontico-ontological one—on the possibility of a specific form, is rather *their being mise en abyme*: A trace of trace, a *différance* of *différance*, a supplement of a supplement. Derrida's "infrastructural gap" (to use Gasché's terminology) is less that which underlies difference and which we name "trace," or "différance," but rather the *vertical* difference found *between* the "trace" (or différance) and the structural difference it underlies. The acute difference in mise en abyme is not the static one stretched between variants X and Y, but the dynamic difference stretched between the aggregate XY and the aggregate XY taken to the second degree, that is, a double of XY embedded within the first. Ceaselessly differing from itself and having no "itself to itself,"[49] this vertical gap, a mise en abyme, a difference-of-difference, underlies—and undermines—any static determination of difference.

DERRIDA'S DENOUNCEMENT OF MISE EN ABYME

Yet once establishing that mise en abyme is, to use Dällenbach's words, "in virtually synonymous proximity to *supplemanterité* and *différance*,"[50] Derrida adds a sharp reservation:

> I have never wanted to abuse the abyss, nor, above all, the mise en abyme, I do not believe in it very much, I am wary of the confidence that it inspires fundamentally, I believe it too representative either to go far enough or not to avoid the very thing toward which it allegedly rushes.[51]

Marian Hobson's comment on Derrida's "La double séance" might also apply to this quote from *La carte postale*. With the mise en abyme as a series of reflections or internally contained scale-models of the literary work, she writes, doubles might give consistency and coherence to the literary or pictorial work by encapsulating images which reflect the whole, but Derrida refuses such an analysis. The determination of self-reference and reference to other writing, according to him,

> ... is to be done not just through the textual equivalent of mirror images, that is unit-like symbols, but through textual operations of quotation: by grafts, borrowings, incisions. A work will not then be a mirroring of mirroring through tidy embedding, but a palimpsest of excerpts, an overlapping stratification of quotations.[52]

If a text forms part of a simulacral chain of supplements where an inside cannot be stably demarcated from an outside, if it is devoid of well-defined "contours," then it is practically a "scrap" or a "graft." Its mise en abyme comprises therefore not a reduplication of units as in the Gidean emblem, but *ruptures*, or units with breached boundaries.

Derrida would, however, oppose not only the "unit-like," "tidy" contoured image which "reflects the whole"—the classic, Gidean, mise en abyme—but also the type of mise en abyme prevailing in the *nouveau nouveau roman* and which employed, as we saw in chapter 1, "jigsaw"-like segments that reflected parts, never the "whole," of the narrative. What Derrida objects to is the very "logos" of mise en abyme as an emblem, an exclusive category of doubleness, and a demarcated concept altogether.

Signs, for Derrida, do not owe their signification to an "origin," a "last reason, whether empirical or intelligible, at which its referring function could come to a final halt."[53] As in Saussure's theory of meaning, language is a system of differences before it is a collection of independently meaningful units. A given signifier-signified nexus is a result of simple, "arbitrary" juxtaposition, governed by no logical constraint, so that the parties bear no internal meaning and properties derived from the "compact force of their nuclei,"[54] but only a situational meaning deriving from a here and now encounter. The sign is the place where "the completely other is announced as such."[55] Every sign, marked with the "trace," carries with it, according to Derrida, the possibility of being reproduced, of breaking with its context, not as an accidental predicate but at its very structure. This principle applies not only to individual signs, but to groups of signs and even whole texts; "to write means to graft."[56] All writing involves an incision in language, and texts function only as part of an infinite network of (inter)textuality. Breaking with every given context, engendering new ones in an illimitable manner, does not imply that the mark is valid outside of a context, "but on the contrary that there are only contexts without any center or absolute anchoring."[57] But if there is no "original" context and if, by definition, each text maintains the possibility of further grafting onto other texts, then every text reflects/repeats/grafts/cites itself. In terms of Saussure's framework, if no context preexists the signifier and signified, the only ground upon which they encounter is their very juxtaposition—a mise en abyme. Derrida does not recognize "any structural difference between the mise en abyme and 'grafting' . . . citations all appear to have the same status."[58] To the contrary, mise en abyme as a cohesive and demarcated emblem is a "determined modification of a general citationality."[59] It "arrests the abyss"[60] and it gazes into the gulf "from behind the *garde-fou*."[61]

ITERABILITY AND THE "LACUNAL" CONCEPTION OF MISE EN ABYME

This denouncement of the mise en abyme as a concept would affect Derrida's articulation of his fourth infrastructural articulation—iterability—as developed in *Limited Inc*. Iterability is Derrida's word for the repetition of the same expression in different contexts:

> Iterability alters, contaminating parasitically what it identifies and enables to repeat "itself"; it leaves us no choice but to mean (to say) something that is (already, always, also) other than what we mean (to say), to say something other than what we say and would have wanted to say.[62]

A sign that could not appear in other circumstances at other times would not be a sign but a mere noise, yet if words are by essence public and repeatable, says Derrida, one can never fully designate or be intentional toward a specific object. The word APPLE—to use Gordon Bearn's example—won't do for designating a given apple, for it could refer to any apple at all. We could add more predicates: TART GREEN APPLE, or even infinite predicates, but this gets us no farther. Any designation, if making sense, would always be too universal, repeatable—"whenever I say 'I love you'" to use Bearn's other, colorful, example "I am using a form of words slurred each Saturday into the alcohol mouths of girls without last names."[63] In order to be what they are, things are always less or other than what they "are," so that the sign represents phenomenologically speaking an intentionality without an intentum, and no extra-sign "can ever hope to saturate the text's referring function."[64] Iterability ruins all hope of ever meaning one single serious thing, and each failure to saturate the sign's referential meaning results in further attempts, inherently futile.

Iterability is not intended to be of the same order as an empirical repetition. An empirical or "mechanical" repetition presupposes three interrelated traits: (i) the "uniqueness, singularity, and integrity of a 'first time,'"[65] (ii) an organizing principle governing the spatial and temporal distribution of the instances, and (iii) a unity onto which the instances of repetition are deposited so as to reaffirm pre-established loci. Derrida's heterology set out to undermine such constants and unities in the understanding of meaning. The play of language—the variety formed by the fact that a word can apply in different contexts to different things—is governed by no pre-established ideal. To invoke Borges's example (in "The Analytical Language of John Wilkins"), what enables us to apply the word and concept of "animal" to embalmed ones, tame ones, fabulous ones, sucking pigs, sirens, stray dogs, those belonging to the Emperor, those having just broken the water pitcher, those drawn with a very fine camel hair brush, and those included in the present classification, is not a "coded," "internal" meaning of the word "animal," no type that predetermines its tokens. Though these categories of division in an imagined Chinese encyclopedia on the entry "animal" strike us with wonderment, bearing an "exotic charm of another system of thought,"[66] Derrida believes that the most quotidian usages of a given word are no less heterogeneous; that like these categories, instances of signification draw their meaning and function from no presupposed signified and form together no coherent "cluster."

Pertaining to heterogeneous organizing principles (and series), these instances express in fact a vertical repetition, "repetition of repetition, or repetition in general, repeatability."[67] It is this mise en abyme of Derrida's iterability that Searle has failed to take into account while denouncing the former vehemently. Repetition of signs, argues Searle, is a triviality, "otherwise the rules would have no scope of application."[68] What he fails to acknowledge is that iterability in Derrida precedes rules, that it pertains not to tokens governed by a type, but to instances of repetition of the "type" itself: a sign is iterable even in "the absolute absence of the receiver or of any empirically determinable collectivity of receivers."[69] The sign repeats "nothing that is not itself already double,"[70] it repeats "in extension" (to use Deleuze's terminology), at the empirical level, only in so far as it already repeats "in intension," "within itself and within (an Other of) itself within itself."[71]

According to Deleuze however, as understood by Bearn, Derrida's articulation of iterability implies precisely the master signifiers, the pre-established unities in the comprehension of signification that Derrida attempted to avoid. Deleuze's criticism of Derrida is that like a Kantian antinomy, fulfilment of an intention to mean one single thing embodies in Derrida an epistemological boundary, "the wall that the signifier needs in order to bounce off of."[72] If for Derrida—as for Nietzsche—the plane of existence is like a board game, satisfaction of the intention's desire for completion embodies in Derrida the boundaries of that game, a transcendental condition, not a possibility within the game. The signifier (or the noetic pole of intentionality)—like a squash ball—is confined to possibilities within a domain segregated in advance. Bearn applies here Deleuze's criticism of the "negative" concept of desire in Western philosophy. Plato tells us that when we desire something we must lack it, that this lack is painful, and that what we desire, when we desire, is to stop the desire. This type of desire is construed with reference to an exterior agency, "whether it be a lack that hollows it out or a pleasure that fills it."[73] By contrast, the affirmative one which Deleuze would propose is "defined as a process of production," a desire aimed—as we shall later see—at an object which did not pre-exist the act of desiring. Meaning something in Derrida's articulation of iterability is a painfully empty intention seeking completion. However, were it completely satisfied, the meaning, the wanting to say, would disappear before even commencing. If the act of meaning can only be articulated in terms of lack; if to the latter it owes not only its existence but its very sense, then satisfaction of that lack cannot be a *logical* option, it would annul the gap—essential for communication—which for Derrida is here manifested as that between noema and noesis.

Let us work out this criticism against Derrida based on Derrida's conception of mise en abyme. Because in an acute moment, it seems to be a rather particular conception of mise en abyme which Derrida applies when articulating iterability. "There is nothing more logical than that the mise en abyme is an emblem of Derrida's *différance*,"[74] argues Dällenbach, but Dällenbach argues so in relation to a conception of mise en abyme which I would term the "lacunal," where circles reproduce due to an innate lack, an absence. According to this conception, a setup consisting of shield A, in the middle of which is another shield, B, in the middle of which is an imaginary shield C, is a result of the following dynamics:

> A's acceptance of the ability to be reproduced produces a lacuna within the identity of A because . . . the addition of B to A in fact subtracts from A; from then on the only way B can adequately represent A is itself to include in its center a shield (C).[75]

We have no way of knowing what is "behind" shield B, but we assume it to be the continuation of shield A. This continuation is not, and cannot be, included in shield B, nor does shield B include itself, although it too is part of shield A. In other words—as in Derrida's articulation of iterability, which "leaves us no choice but to mean something that is always already other than what we mean"—according to the lacunal conception of the mise en abyme, this time articulated by Füredy,

> . . . when the point is reached at which the object would have to repeat itself, there is a switch to the next logical level . . . this completion is never achieved. At the heart of recursion there is a hole, an absence.[76]

As in the "lacunal conception," what fuels repetition in Derrida's articulation of iterability is an inherent incompleteness of representation: each failure to intend and to refer results in further attempts, inherently futile. As in the lacunal conception, where the switch to a different logical level takes place just prior to reaching the point where the embedding level is coherently and completely represented by its replica, in iterability a switch to an utterly different intention takes place just prior to the intention being fulfilled.

The "lacunal" picture (though Dällenbach and Füredy fail to note so) is, however, a misconception of mise en abyme. The mise en abyme, says Ricardou, does not redouble the unit, "in so far as it is an internal mirroring, it can only ever split it in two."[77] It doubles no simple unity but only—as in a double mirror—what is itself already double. Embedded within A, it is not A, properly speaking, that B reflects, but rather A as *already* embedding B. B is hence itself *already* a double, if it embeds C it does so *from the outset*, not as a consequence of a lacuna, and not consecutively with preceding or following instances of duplication.

Eradicating logocentrism, being inattentive to the actual emblem of the mise en abyme and objecting—in the name of difference—to any coherence which might hold instances of difference together, Derrida ends up viewing mise en abyme in general, and iterability in particular, as comprising discrete circuits. But extreme discreteness—where each new duplication leaves the others intact—stands incompatible with the fact that added to a mise en abyme, a circuit transforms it *ab initio*. In the two facing mirrors mentioned previously, where A reflects B while being reflected by it, B hence reflects strictly speaking not A, but an object that did not have existence prior to the act of reflection, namely (A as already reflecting B), that is, C. Any new circuit generates the object of reflection. A mise en abyme of the type X within X into which a duplicating circuit X is added is transformed by this very action of duplication. Its new object of duplication is no longer X, but (X within X), that is, Y, and its pattern is now Y within Y. A shield having X as its object of duplication is always already ANOTHER shield, having Y as its object. In true mise en abyme, duplication at the "edge" of the shield affects, reconstitutes, the entire series and series-of-series within the shield. Any instance brings its own ground with it, a ground that comprises all the other instances set into a new constellation, a new whole generated by the instance itself. The relation between instances of mise en abyme, to recall, "is not that of a still mirror, but a dialectical one which elaborates itself, incessantly resettles itself, and which escapes any immobilization."[78]

MISCONCEPTION OF THE MISE EN ABYME AND ITS CONSEQUENCES

Derrida is well aware of the heterogeneity of the circuits in mise en abyme. That which is situated "under" the underneath, he says, "would not only open an abyss, but would brusquely and discontinuously prescribe a change of direction, or rather a completely different topic."[79] He fails, however, to acknowledge that heterogeneous reproductions imply heterogeneity of *plenitudes*. A segment, a circuit added to a series of circuits, retroactively generates the whole, the very mise en abyme to which it was added. Each circuit causes infinite other circuits to *accumulate*, revolving around an organizing principle which that particular circuit becomes. But one finds no such generative quality in an instance of a Derridean iterability.

Confined to a zealous, prejudging ideology of alterity, Derrida refuses to consult the actual emblem of mise en abyme, which he dismisses as bound to a logocentric discourse. Due to that ideology, he also applies to his articulation of iterability a static, degenerated picture of the Gidean shield where each instance of the mise en abyme—as embodying alterity—is maintained discrete from all others. But pure and simple discreteness defeats this very heterological purpose. To imply that an added instance leaves all other instances intact is to imply that instances are deposited onto loci upon an already established whole. Far from each bringing its own organizing principle with it—as was the case in Borges's Chinese encyclopedia—instances of iterability owe their signification and function to a predetermined ideal, a "transcendental signified" that remains constant throughout all change. Far from embodying a difference between the given and the unimaginable, the failure to intend which underlies Derrida's iterability embodies a predicate in the comprehension of that signified. Despite self-association with Nietzsche's philosophy of affirmation, Derrida's philosophy, writes Bearn, is a "saying No" reminiscent of Schopenhauer's pessimism.[80]

We saw in chapter 1 how de Nooy criticizes Dällenbach in that, despite distancing himself from the classical model of mimesis, he was less than enthusiastic about embracing the consequences. Dällenbach's "combination" of elementary mises en abyme, writes de Nooy, can be opposed to Derrida's "dissemination." Whereas Derrida "scatters the seed, cross fertilizes and grafts to produce hybrids," Dällenbach's exclusion "works like selective breeding, of which the prize specimen is the transcendental mise en abyme."[81] What de Nooy fails to notice is that Dällenbach's ambiguity is rather positive and programmatic, and aims at compatibility with the double bind nature of mise en abyme—the fact that mise en abyme "only becomes such through the duplicative relationship it admits to with one or other aspect of the narrative"[82]—and the derived principle of coexistence between variants that governs it, the fact that mise en abyme is less the diminutive segment that reflects the whole, than the very coexistence between that segment and the whole it reflects. The lesson Dällenbach draws from the mise en abyme—and Deleuze would follow him—is that true pluralism is attained not by eradicating unity, identity, immediacy, totality, cohesion, and other "metaphysical" elements from poetics and philosophy—but rather by putting them in coexistence with elements of discontinuity, divergence, and scission. It was indeed only by respecting the exclusiveness and privilege of the transcendental mise en abyme, as we saw in chapter 1, that Dällenbach managed to pluralize the level of elementary mises en abyme, so that both the transcendental mise en abyme and the fictional one became perpetual claimants for being the "prize specimen," and neither could come to dominance without the danger of being disavowed.

It was, ironically enough, Derrida's own warning not to reverse mimetologism in "one fell swoop" which Dällenbach followed in developing this "economic" approach. Derrida insisted that deconstructive interpretation, far from being nihilistic, destructive, or negative, on the contrary "affirms the play of the positive and the negative, and thus it wards off the ethical temptation to liquidate negativity and difference."[83] It was supposed to ward off not only the temptation of metaphysics to negate the "other" but also to negate "negation," namely the metaphysical order. The deconstruction of metaphysics cannot simply combat metaphysics, thus falling in the pitfall of binary logic, "if anything is destroyed in a deconstructive reading it is not meaning but the claim to unequivocal domination of one mode of signifying over another."[84]

However (though our textualistic reading of Derrida will later overturn this conclusion), Derrida's concept of iterability exposes this promise of "affirmation" to be unfulfilled. *Over-emancipating* the mise en abyme, liberating it not only from the Gidean "unit-like" paradigm of reflection, but also from its "logos," the conception of mise en abyme as an exclusive category of doubleness, an emblem, or a concept at all, Derrida ends up *under-emancipating* the mise en abyme. In keeping variants categorically discrete; in banning *any* form or coherence, his mise en abyme (or rather "citationality in general") implies the allocation of those variants onto pre-established loci upon a pre-established unity, a perspective which conflicts with Derrida's anti-metaphysical endeavor. Failure to grasp the difference-in-itself caused Derrida to dismiss the ostensibly logocentric mise en abyme. At the very same time, failure to engage with the mise en abyme as an actual, historical emblem and with what poeticians had to say about it, caused Derrida's failure to implement a Nietzschean affirmation of difference, that is, to recognize the fact that heterogenous, incommensurable variants are nonetheless—and due to their very incommensurability—contracted; that they form a coherence that coexists with difference, an "assemblage" of the Same and the Different, which, being paradoxical and an "unheard of" aggregate, is alone the true and irreducible otherness.

ON SECOND THOUGHTS: INTENTIONALITY AND THE "INVAGINATION" OF TEXT

It is, however, with caution that this criticism against Derrida should be received. Western philosophy, according to Derrida, has granted privilege to reason and the "pure" concept that founds it. Thus founded on the renunciation of the signifier and a corresponding overvaluation of the signified as absolute and unmediated, philosophy "has regarded language as simply a mode of communicating, or perhaps testing, knowledge, but basically as external and accidental to its production."[85] Writing in particular is considered by many of the philosophers Derrida interrogates to be external, physical, and non-transcendental, "an unwieldly intervening medium in need of purification, tightening, and normative rules to ensure clarity."[86] In refusing to see its dependence on writing, philosophy has been able to represent itself as governed only by the Idea, the Concept or Signified, which transcends a more mundane physicality. For Derrida, on the other hand, writing is not originarily subordinate to the logos and to truth, and not "an auxiliary means in the service of science and possibly its object."[87] The signifier does not merely mediate a pre-existent signified, and textual devices are not simply features of the poetic or literary text, but are necessary for all texts to function as such—"deconstruction is after all a mode of reading philosophical texts as texts, as modes of writing, rather than expressions of ideas, a reading that shows up the instability in the relation between what the philosophical text asserts, and how it asserts it."[88] Like the generative novelists, for Derrida, especially in his work on Celan (2005), "a non-transcendent reading remains with the form and language, the signs themselves, perhaps even their materiality as marks on the page."[89]

Consequently, whilst various scholars, especially Gasché, have viewed Derrida as "a technical philosopher in the wake of Husserlian phenomenology,"[90] a substantial school in Derridean scholarlship, J. Hillis Miller for example, has advocated that Derrida's texts themselves should be read according to Derridean measures; that only by toning down "transcendental reading" and logocentric reasoning and employing instead a textualistic reading—a strategy tailor-made to what is idiomatic about the work in question—can we do justice to a Derridean text. Derrida himself often guides his reader toward this type of reading. In *Dissemination*, for example, he warns the reader against drawing out a single thematic nucleus or a single guiding thesis, because that would cancel out the textual displacement that is at work in the text: "we would have to assert right now that one of the theses—there is more than one—inscribed within *Dissemination* is precisely the impossibility of reducing a text as such to its effects of meaning, content, thesis, or theme."[91]

In pursuing a new strategy for reading *Limited Inc*, we must therefore ask what is this book's "signature," or stylistic distinctive feature which might direct us to a new, textualistic rather than "transcendental" understanding of his theory of Iterability? Compared to Derrida's "exuberant, exorbitant, excessive and hyperbolic" works,[92] *Limited Inc* is fairly argumentative in style, and yet a subtle stylistic feature does come to eye, namely, Derrida cites and re-cites *from Limited Inc itself* entire chunks regarding the concept of Iterability. Notably, the following paragraph is cited and re-cited no less than three times:

> The first consequence of this will be the following: given that structure of iteration, the intention animating the utterance will never be through and through present to itself and to its content. The iteration structuring it a priori introduces into it a dehiscence and a cleft which are essential.[93]

Derrida in *Limited Inc* provided some explanation for this deployment of citation:

> I multiply statements, discursive gestures, forms of writing, the structure of which reinforces my demonstration in something like a practical manner: that is, by providing instances of "speech acts" which by themselves render impracticable and theoretically insufficient the conceptual oppositions upon which speech act theory in general, and Searle's version of it in particular, relies (serious/nonserious; literal/metaphoric or ironic; normal forms/parasitical forms; use/mention; intentional/nonintentional; etc.).[94]

If for Austin the poetical or literary speech act is "parasitical" on the everyday one, for Derrida any piece of language, oral or written, is always already parasitic and citational. Even on the first occasion when an expression is used, it is already a repetition or citation; it is literature, "not in the sense that we can make it function any way we like, but in the sense that the possibility of being taken as literature is intrinsic to it just as the serious is built on the non-serious, not the other way around."[95] Reciting his own passages,

Derrida undertakes to reinforce and demonstrate "in a practical manner," that speech acts are always already iterable, and written ones—citations.

However, this explanation leaves much unsaid. I don't see how the status of his statements changing from argumentative to citational, adds value to, or overturns, their argumentative meaning. This change of status functions as an auxiliary demonstration to Derrida's take against intentionalism, more than it promotes a new understanding of it. In "The law of Genre," on the other hand, Derrida does provide a very interesting analysis of the hermeneutical implications of citationality—and citationalization—with which he opens this paper:

> Genres are not to be mixed, I will not mix genres. I repeat: genres are not to be mixed. I will not mix them.[96]

The statement, "I will not mix genres," were it to stand alone, would cause the reader to discern a predicting description, a designation telling in advance what will transpire. Moreover, the word "genre," once sounded, would have drawn a limit, a genre announcing itself, so that one must respect a norm and not cross a line of demarcation. Iterated, on the other hand, the sentence "I will not mix genres," can no longer be taken as a vow of obedience. With two "citations" allowed to resonate all by themselves, the reader is no longer assured of being able to distinguish with rigor between a citation and a non-citation, and his doubt impedes the authentication force of this utterance and of the "genre" (functioning as an organizing principle) it bespeaks. Instead, the utterer is "implicated in a wager, a challenge, an impossible bet—in short, a situation that would exceed the matter of merely engaging a commitment."[97] The citation causes the utterance to transform: from a vow of obedience, into a vow of obedience *uttered within a drama*, possibly a (Greek) tragedy, where the vow rather foreshadows an impossible bet. For Austin, the vow—once transformed into literature or drama—is, while still performative, "infelicitous." For Derrida, on the other hand, this new, tragic type of vow is highly generative. Being equivocal, it erects "the law of the law of genre," which is at once "a principle of contamination, a law of impurity,"[98] *and* imperative to the discourse that follows.

This double characteristic assumed by the iterated utterance is *due to its becoming a prospective mise en abyme:* "Derrida's essays work in a reverse way. They often begin with a concentrated enigmatic statement or speech act that the rest of the essay unfolds through the close reading of some text."[99] Like the oracle's words in Oedipus, the vow not only manipulates the horizon of expectations, but also sets the outlines of the narrative to follow, *whether those expectations are confirmed or not*, whether the oracle, so to say, was right or not. There is no demand for a repleteness of duplication in mise en abyme, writes Ron,

> . . . not only does The Mad Trist (or at least as much of it as went into Poe's story) not include any equivalent of certain events crucial to the plot of Poe's story—e.g., nothing equivalent to Madeline's illness and entombment—but the correspondence as stated by Roderick Usher is based on superficial sensory similarities and is not really an equivalence between two plots or a plot and its summary, complete or partial.[100]

Unveiling the reiterated utterance as a prospective mise en abyme, we now have a better understanding of Derrida's words in *Limited Inc*, according to which citationality reinforces his demonstration "in something like a practical manner." Like the main narrative manipulated by the prospective mise en abyme, what unfolds in the text following the iterated utterance is not an argument interpretative of it, but a *transposition* of that statement. The prospective utterance functions as an analogical rather than a digital message, or to use Peirce's terminology, like an icon rather than a symbol. Whereas symbols for Peirce are mediated by some formal or merely agreed upon link between the sign and its object, such as social convention, or explicit code, icons such as photographs or diagrams are mediated by "resemblance" or "likeness." The unfolding, exposing, text *resembles* the prospective utterance that triggers it.

Mise en abyme shares with the icon the trait of signification through resemblance. Like the icon, mise en abyme consists of signification with the very "physical characteristics" of the sign token; the main narrative assumes the "contours" of the diagram it contains, rather than any "internal," conventional meaning the latter is coded with. Mise en abyme differs, however, in consisting in the "isolability" of the reflecting segment. Pertaining not only to the signifying level, but also to the incompatible meta-signifying one, this segment infuses a logical and diegetic "interruption" to the main narrative.[101] This is to say, that the lack of preexisting incorporating convention causes that without being simply extraneous to the narrative as a whole, the prospective segment is detached from and "indifferent" to this whole. It creates, says Derrida, "a sort of participation without belonging—a taking part in without being part of, without having membership in a set."[102] It forms an "invagination," an "internal pocket" within the whole "that does not, in whole or in part, take part in the corpus whose denomination it nonetheless imparts."[103]

Signifying primarily with its irreducible style or "idiomaticity" rather than with its referential function, the word of literature and poetry, according to Derrida, is "circumcised." Circumcision "must be understood as an event of the body,"[104] it consists in unfolding the layer shielding that body from its outside, and a covenant stamped on the flesh rather than signed in a document. Later in this book, I will show Deleuze's "rhizomatic book" to similarly comprise a hybrid of textual signs and the body of an empirical—rather than implied—reader, so that the work's diegetic level cannot be discerned from empirical reality. I will develop the philosophy and poetics of this hybrid work in terms of the centrifugal mise en abyme. The hybrid work is a case where the meta-level of signification becomes itself an object level, that is, the book itself *embodies* rather than embeds a mise en abyme. However, I will show, this newly created object-level remains an "orphan." Signifying with the "body" rather than the coded meaning of the sign, the pragmatic work breaks through the noematic brackets segregating it from empirical reality; it "invades" empirical reality, enabling its diegetic level to overlap with it. But then, if the mise en abyme which the work embodies overlaps with the present, that which it reflects is the beyond-present. The work comprises an object level which faces a meta-level, but this meta-level it anticipates and bears the trace of, is absent. The absence in question is so extreme that rather than encoding, the radically pragmatic work is transcoding. The work signifies to a yet-to-come recipient and its signs are received in a future, "unthinkable," code, in the way books signify to booklice. Like Deleuze's transcoding book, for Derrida, the word, once circumcised, is "an opened word. Like a wound . . . like a door: opened to the stranger, to the other . . . in the figure of the absolute to-come . . . [whose] coming must be neither assured nor calculable . . . beyond all forms and norms that could be anticipated."[105] It speaks—"as in a prayer"—"even if none of its references is intelligible,"[106] it addresses the other even if the call cannot, by necessity, reach it. It signifies to a radically absent recipient, but that recipient, as in Deleuze's rhizomatic book, receives it in a code that did not preexist the reception, what Derrida calls "migration of languages."[107] Detached from the recipient to come, literature "uses words to 'allow' the other to come, and by no means 'makes' it come."[108] In fact, what justifies Derrida's hyperbolic excess of text, is his obligation "to make his essays speech acts allowing [the] wholly other to come,"[109] and what justifies a textualistic reading of Derrida, is the fact that each of his texts "centers on an attempt to formulate through an obedience to the actual words of the work in question the special, the idiomatic way the other is invoked or allowed to come."[110] Signifying with its "body," "indifferent" to the recipient, the prospective mise en abyme as developed in "The Law of Genre," allows something to happen or makes something happen and "that happening is a coming, though of just what Derrida does not say."[111]

However, in the same "blinking of an eye," this reflecting segment gathers the corpus it anticipates; it "places within and without the work, along its boundary, an inclusion and exclusion with regard to genre in general."[112] Poetization and iteration of Derrida's argumentation in *Limited Inc* "summons" the other not content wise, not in what happens thematically in this text, but in the way this text works, by means of the irreduciblity of the text's "idiomaticity." The prospective mise en abyme, the iterated vow, is detached from, and is incommensurable with, the receiving other, namely the argument it causes to evolve, but due to this very gap, this otherness is "conjoined," and "allied," says Derrida, to the prospective segment. They form a "gathered multiplicity" which Celan calls "by a strong and charged name: concentration."[113] The prospective segment posits "a law of genre," but generates precisely the "outside" of this limit it draws; it cannot come but as an aggregate with that "outside." If semiotic signification is normally made effective by focusing on the coded meaning of the sign and suspending intentionality toward the variety of factors present in its immediate context (such as the type of ink or font the text is written in), signification with the "body"—with "the physical" aspects of the iconic signifier—means that such suspension cannot be done, that the here-and-now, bodily, reception of the message cannot be bracketed out from the messaging. A "surface," writes Nathan Widder with regard to Deleuze's philosophy of sense, the contingent factors of expression, irreducible to the expressed they serve as a channel for, "refers to the plane where divergent realms meet and relate, as the surface of the ocean divides but also connects water and air."[114] The reflecting segment and the main text are always already contracted: "both of them, together—and each time together."[115]

"Summoning" the other-than-presence, the prospective segment breaches the boundary and unity set by the genre, but at the same time forms an aggregate with that other-than-presence or otherness-yet-to-come. The "law of law of genre" it gives rise to, thus establishes a new, ad hoc rather than metaphysical unity, yet a unity no less. The promise "not to mix genres" contracts the genre it demarks and its outside into a single aggregate, where "participation never amounts to belonging," and nonetheless "there is always a genre and genres."[116] The performative giving rise to genre, gives rise by this very action to a "law of law" functioning not as a higher instance in a subjecting (Russell-like) logical hierarchy, but rather as an act of birth, opened to the "yet to come." Derrida studies this law of law through a "double chiasmatic invagination" in Blanchot's *La folie du jour* (*Madness of the Day*). Blanchot's paragraph opens with a demand: "Tell us exactly how things happened." In response, the protagonist performs a semi-promise: "An account? I began. . . ." The subsequent recounting is indeterminate as to whether it embodies that "account" or reflects on the circumstances revolving around the demand and promise to tell it. However, such indeterminacy is sufficient for the reader—and the writing itself—to discredit the authentication force of the genre. The semi-promise to give an account gives rise to a story, but not one "subjugated" to and reaffirming a "boundary" and "genre" set by the promise. Rather, it is a story found at the same narrative level as the promise to tell it, a meta-diegetic one recounting, or rather idly talking of, issues on the periphery of events, similar to the tuning of musical instruments prior to a concert. It is devoid of diegetic intentions and in this sense detached from, and indifferent to, any "law of genre." The indifferent promise and the story do not "belong" together. If the latter evolves from the former, it is due to the promise's analogical rather than digital signification. The promise to tell a story functions in fact as a mise en abyme of the story told.

Blanchot's paragraph then concludes with a second performative: "An account? No, no account, nevermore." This concluding statement resumes the question posed before the "I began," so that the recounting following the latter retroactively bespeaks the commitment made no longer to give an account, despite such account having—perhaps—already taken place. Chiasmatic structure is a literary technique where a series of utterances are followed by a mirror series. A and B—and the relation between them—are followed by variants A' and B', to create a structure A,B,B',A'. The "double chiasmatic invagination" in Derrida is a case where the variant wing of the structure (B', A') itself encapsulates the structure in entire. A' hypermirrors A, with all the latter's predication. It mirrors not only A, but A *as inseparable from a series* including B, B' and A' itself, so that the promise to give an account (A) is followed by a recounting (B), which is retroactively a variant-recounting (B') concluded—but at the same time preceded by—a variant-promise (A'). Like a double mirror, where X cannot mirror Y without Y always already being a different object, "double chiasmatic invagination" is in one aspect a case where mirroring fails. However, similar to the case of the prospective mise en abyme, where failed mirroring subtracts nothing from its being a diminutive model of the work, the second commitment, despite revoking the promise to give an account, or nullifying that already recounted, restores *affirmation* in a unique way. Signifying analogically rather than digitaly, the second commitment—detached from the first—gives rise to a reflection of reflection detached from the one dominated by the first commitment. Consequently, the crucial mirroring occurs not between A,B and B'A', but rather between series A,B,B',A' and its iconic double (A,B,B'A')'. A' cannot revoke A without thus *successfully* mirroring a preceding, primordial act of revoking, but thereby also the existence of A (forming an aggregate with A') which negated by the act of revoking, yet conditions it. Analogical signification means that the "No, no" not only clears the stage for the "Yes, yes," it facilitates its emergence, it gives birth to it. The law of law is a "female" one which the *hors-genre* "neither attempts to escape, nor does he shrink before her,"[117] not due to any reconciliatory principle, but because the escape—like a "second layer of lips," or birth of birth—has already occurred prior to the encounter between the two. With its "double affirmation," the law of law expropriates the integrity of a "first time," but this does not make it foreign to the "genre, genius, or spirit of the law":

> One believes it generally possible to oppose law to affirmation, and particularly to unlimited affirmation, to the immensity of yes, yes. Law—we often figure it as an instance of the interdictory limit, of the binding obligation, as the negativity of a boundary not to be crossed. However, now the mightiest and most divided trait of La folie du jour or of "An Account?" is the one relating birth to law, its genealogy, engenderment, generation, or genre—and here I ask you once more to be especially aware of gender—the one joining the very genre of the law to the process of the double affirmation. The excessiveness of yes, yes is no stranger to the genesis of law (nor to Genesis, as could be easily shown, for it also concerns an account of Genesis "in the light of seven days"). The double affirmation is not foreign to the genre, genius, or spirit of the law.[118]

If we now extrapolate from the "The Law of Genre" to *Limited Inc*, we can maintain that like the iterated vow in the former, the iterated statement regarding the incompleteness of intentionality in the latter functions as mise en abyme, a reflecting segment of the text in entire—not only that of *Limited Inc*, but also of the yet to come critical reception of this statement—such as the present text. In accordance with the previous analysis of "iconic" vs. "symbolic" communication, this mise en abyme reflects, doubles and determines the "plot" which evolves around it whether the latter agrees with the enunciation, that is the coded (rather than stylistic) meaning of the former, or not; whether the "oracle" prediction is correct or not. In this sense, then, and only if we extend the concept of "intentionality" from subjects to statements,[119] we conclude that whilst as an argument the utterance in *Limited Inc* expresses the incompleteness of intentionality, as "icon" it becomes "affirmative," expressing intentionality's inevitable completeness. The interpretation of the utterance, its reception, renders the utterance (retroactively) conjoined with and intentional towards precisely this interpretation. Despite being detached, incommensurable, or rather *due to this detachment*, this act forms an aggregate with its reception to come. Despite, *or rather due to*, iterability and dissemination, the act of signification is, in Deleuze's words, "fated to succeed."

However, is this new, textualistic, reading of *Limited Inc* symmetrically opposed to our previous, "transcendent," reading, where we harshly criticized Derrida's incompleteness of signification? Is it weighty enough? Taking a step backward, we can note two weaknesses in it. First, signification with "idiomaticity," or style rather than content, as developed in Derrida, in as much as it breaks with the referential function, is rendered pale by Deleuze's rhizomatic book and *its* level of analogical or pragmatic signification. When compared to the rhizomatic book's signification with actual, empirical bodies, Derrida's textualistic signification can only metaphorically, or at least relatively, be said to signify "with body." Accordingly, as against the manifest transcoding which the rhizomatic book entails, and the animality, or rather the "becoming animal" type of signification it foregrounds, the recipients of Derrida's text, absent as they are, still receive it in French, or mediated by a translator speaking French, or in any case in a human language.

Second, whereas the rhizomatic book—while transcoding—strongly manifests the principle of simultaneity between the incommensurable parties of the iconic messaging, the fact that "not belonging" together, the reflecting segment and the text revolving around it nonetheless "conjoin," I find it difficult to assess the Derridean case. In the case of the rhizomatic book, it is enough for us to imagine the magnificent universe of carved holes and craters that the rhizomatic book has been turned into transcoding to booklice. The book indeed "has the lice in its head," to rephrase von Uexküll.

Their encounter is radically contigent but therefore paradoxicaly necessary. The reason is that if their encounter cannot imply any preexisting logical and ontological ground, then the only ground the two now share comprises their very encounter, a *primordial aggregate of the two*. Do we see the same type of aggregation between the iterated utterance in *Limited Inc*—while signifying iconically—and the future text that hosts and discusses it; between a statement declaring the impossibility of predicting its reception, and that reception? I think that, unlike the rhizomatic book, such coexistence or simultaneity can only be perceived through laborious intellectual retrospection, not through aesthetic immediacy. However, the reason for this lack of immediacy lies, perhaps, not in the nature of the two disjuncts, but in mere habit, the fact that, as against literature, iconic signification in a philosophical text is not yet a normative reception.

CHAPTER 3

MAURICE BLANCHOT
HEADING TOWARD DEATH AS *MISE EN ABYME*

DEATH AND "AMBIGUITY"

Death bears a crucial role in Heidegger's analytics of Dasein. Giving Dasein nothing to be actualized, it embodies "the possibility of the impossibility of existence,"[1] the very boundary of finitude which assures Dasein's temporality, its distinction from objects at hand, and consequently its ontological prerogative. It is "possibility" due to its remaining within the bounds of phenomenology; a certainty stemming from the observation that the range of possibilities open to one narrows as one's life advances. Moreover, "always essentially my own,"[2] death permits the achievement of authentic selfhood. It brings Dasein face to face with the possibility to be itself, "free of the illusions of the they."[3] Despite the comradeship found in a sharing of finitude, no one else can die for me, "the they never dies because it is *unable* to die."[4] The only ontological significance Heidegger allows to publicly occurring death is negative—the possibility of inauthenticity. Reinterpreting death as public, as occurring every day with others, results for Dasein in an estrangement, its "losing itself in the they."[5] Whenever Dasein says that "one dies," it onticizes death, leveling death down to an event which belongs to no one in particular.

Whilst death bears for Heidegger a mere ontic status, post-Heideggerian thought endeavored precisely to allow philosophical significance to the pure ontic, embodying with its "inessentiality," contingence and specificity the other-than-Being, non-assimilable into structure and reaffirming no totalizing ideal. As against Heidegger, it is precisely the death of the Other, and the death as Other, upon which Blanchot's ontology rests. Death, irreducibly other, asserts itself as continually differing possibility, "the *impossibility* of every possibility,"[6] an experience that transgresses the boundary of the self and is never accessible to it, an enigma, wrote Levinas, rather than a phenomenon.

Yet, the inability to grasp and absorb death, its being otherness, is also what causes death to generate language. Adam's first act, Blanchot cites Hegel, which made him master of the animals, was to give them names, but he thus "annihilated them in their existence,"[7] abolished their particularity as beings. Deprived of their "flesh and blood reality,"[8] things "resuscitate in the universal signification of Being,"[9] they enter language as universals and ideals. What Hegel names "annihilation of existence," Blanchot terms "death" and "murder": "My language does not kill anyone. And yet: when I say 'This woman', real death has been announced and is already present in my language; my language means that this person, who is here right now, can be detached from herself."[10]

Like Derrida's *différance* and "trace" (and like spacing), death in Blanchot is the index of an irreducible exterior. It enables the distances and deferrals of signification—but also its mediation and its openness to the outside. Language as such is *already* constituted by the differences it seeks to overcome: the extra-conceptual singularities annihilated by death do not embody a "real world" to which words refer, no reality prior to the act of idealization, because the latter is what renders them an object of possible address in the first place. Language (like Dasein) heads toward death, gazes at the extra-conceptual singularities it has annihilated, but only at the price of "a movement, a displacement"[11]—its beginning with death. That is, the interval, death, opened between language and the (unreachable) origin it is in quest of, is retroactively the interval opened between point zero, prior to there being language, and the very language which that interval generates: "How can I turn around and look at what exists before, if all my power consists of making it into what exists after?"[12] Death, the "always other possibility,"[13] infuses into philosophy an "ambiguity," "two competing requirements throughout the entirety of Blanchot's work whose differences cannot ever be equalized, reconciled, or mediated by any dialectic whatsoever . . . but only ever affirmed in their fundamental incompatibility, dissymmetry, and discord."[14]

The "ultimate ambiguity" is life, which endures death while "maintain[ing] itself in it."[15] Despite—or rather due to—being an impossibility, death is at the same time what it was for Heidegger: "man's possibility, his chance," through which "the future of a finished world is still there for us."[16] Constituting language, death serves, in some respect, as a foundation of Being and life. Blanchot, writes Deleuze, suggests that death has two aspects:

> One is personal, concerning the I or the ego, something which I can . . . encounter in a present which causes everything to pass. The other is strangely impersonal, with no relation to 'me,' neither present nor past.[17]

The first pertains to Heidegger's concept of death. The second pertains to Blanchot's, but it entails the "state of free differences when they are no longer subject to the form imposed upon them,"[18] namely difference as precisely *stretched between these two "slopes" of a Blanchotian ambiguity*. Blanchot's concept of death, differing from Heidegger's, comprises this differentiation at its very determination—a mise en abyme.

MISE EN ABYME AND THE "NIGHT ITSELF"

To rephrase this "ultimate ambiguity": Death is a foundation for life, but the price of the possibility of any foundation is the impossibility of that foundation. The laying of foundations "is an activity that may take place only within a bottomless abyss."[19] In dialogue with Heidegger's idea of the "foundation" or "origin" of the work of art, Blanchot shows that a true foundation is a "foundation of foundation," a "bottomless abyss" or mise en abyme. In a work of art, says Heidegger, an entity emerges into the unconcealedness of its being. Van Gogh's painting "Pair of Shoes," for example, "is a disclosure of what the equipment, the pair of peasant shoes, *is* in truth."[20] Brought to "light," the artistic image, like entities "ready to hand," function as Dasein's "world" and "worlding." But art also comprises "earth"—the background against which worlding emerges and which is independent from human use and intentionality. If "world" is the image itself—the shoes in Van Gogh's famous picture—then the earth is what comes to the fore when one "erases the image." It is the inner structure organizing the picture, as well as the very material and colors; the "literal" level as against the "referential" one. Art therefore reveals an "essential strife" between "earth" and "world." In its resting upon earth, the world—as the self-opening—strives to surmount it, it will "tolerate nothing closed." Embodying a sheltering and concealing, earth in turn "tends always to draw the world into itself and to keep it there."²¹ Combined, they constitute the mechanism of *aletheia*, the truth of art as unconcealment:

> The earth cannot do without the openness of world if it is to appear in the liberating surge of its self-closedness. World, on the other hand, cannot float away from the earth if, as the prevailing breadth and path of all essential destiny, it is to ground itself on something decisive.²²

The ontological difference, where the ontological is distinguished from the ontic by comprising this distinction at its very determination, is ostensibly a mise en abyme. Likewise, the mechanism of *aletheia*, according to which the "world" of the work, distinguished as such from its "earth," consists nonetheless in the very strife between "world" and "earth," is *prima facie* a mise en abyme too. Heidegger indeed writes: "in the work, the happening of truth is at work, but what is thus at work is at work in the work."²³ The work as disclosure in the world is at the same time also a disclosure within the work itself, a "grounding of grounding," which Heidegger has already pursued in "The Essence of Ground." According to this essay, Dasein at once surpasses and finds itself among the beings it "transcends" or serves a "ground" to. This is because the world it projects is not an a priori category or scheme, but a finite one, comprising the very juxtaposition or seriality of actual—in-time—beings. Consequently, like the reader's act of "concretization" in Ingarden's reception theory, and the subject's "bracketing out" of extra-temporal predicates in Husserl's phenomenological reduction, Dasein's projection of a concrete, fully determined world entails, by necessity, other possibilities that "withdraw":

> Certain other possibilities are thereby already withdrawn from Dasein, and indeed merely through its own facticity. Yet precisely this withdrawal of certain possibilities pertaining to its potentiality for being-in-the-world—a withdrawal entailed in its being absorbed by beings—first brings those possibilities of world-projection that can "actually" be seized upon toward Dasein as its world. Such withdrawal lends precisely the binding character of what remains projected before us the power to prevail within the realm of Dasein's existence.²⁴

This withdrawal implies that Dasein can serve only as a limited ground. It entails as such another, projected, Dasein, which in turn embodies another ground, embracing this time the withdrawing possibilities too, the ones left "abandoned" by the "previous" Dasein. However, as this "new" Dasein itself projects a finite world, its act of grounding entails yet a new "withdrawal," new ungrounded possibilities. Derrida rightly comments, however, that this "underneath of the underneath," this "abyss" (*ab-grund*), does not lead to a conceptualization of the *mise-en-abyme*.[25] Freedom, writes Heidegger, is the ground of ground, yet

> [f]reedom's being a ground does not as we are always tempted to think have the character of one of the ways of grounding, but determines itself as the grounding unity of the transcendental strewal of grounding . . . In its essence as transcendence, freedom places Dasein, as potentiality for being, in possibilities that gape open before its finite choice, i.e., within its destiny.[26]

The ground of ground, the abyss which breaks open upon Dasein's grounding of beings, far from indicating otherness-than-being, reaffirms, for Heidegger, the "grounding unity" that Dasein is. With its self-reduplication, it is precisely this abyss which determines Dasein as "potentiality for being," before which possibilities gape open for it to make "finite choices." If transcendence is understood in the last instance as an abyss of ground, then, according to Heidegger,

> the essence of what was called Dasein's absorption in and by beings also thereby becomes sharper. Dasein—although finding itself in the midst of beings and pervasively attuned by them—is, as free potentiality for being, thrown among beings. The fact that it has the possibility of being a self, and has this factically in keeping with its freedom in each case; the fact that transcendence temporalizes itself as a primordial occurrence, does not stand in the power of this freedom itself. Yet such impotence (thrownness) is not first the result of beings forcing themselves upon Dasein, but rather determines Dasein's being as such. All projection of world is therefore thrown.[27]

The abyss of ground, the ground always already entailing another ground, could have laid bare for Heidegger the mechanism of retroaction latent in his idea according to which "all projection of world is therefore thrown." The idea that the ground, the meta level, is retroactively an object-level—for a yet to come meta-level—could have indicated for him the complete otherness of that meta-level, the radically absent context, surpassing Being, upon which it signifies. Instead, for Heidegger, the exclusivity of Dasein "only becomes sharper" by this. He subjugates this alternation of object-level and meta-level to a pre-established context, namely the presupposed idea of Dasein as an openness for possibilities. Dasein is transcendent to things only to "care" for them, their being immediately compatible with, and a primordial extension of, its existence. Like the oxymoronical "passerby" in Nathan Alterman's poem, yet expected by his surroundings,[28] and like the child in Heraclitus, Dasein is ultimately a narcissistic entity, for whom the sun, wind, hammer, and gun are toys of the gods to play with. The *abgrund* only reaffirms this type of playfulness, the fact that Dasein "has the *possibility* of being a self, and has this factically in keeping with its freedom in each case."[29] The interplay of ground and groundlessness functions at the end of the day in service of the transcendental signifier of "Being." True mise en abyme, writes Derrida, "would not only open an abyss, but would brusquely and discontinuously prescribe a change of direction, or rather a completely different topic."[30] It would comprise an ambiguity which Heidegger's hermeneutical cycle and mechanism of *aletheia* lack. A narrative level in Gide's mechanism of retroaction does not precede another level, without the other preceding it *at the same time*. One finds, however, no such ambiguity in Heidegger, no irreducible double, no unity *always already* hollowed by the other-than-itself.

This point can be demonstrated in terms of Gadamer's ontology of play (upon which we shall expand in chapter 6), transposing the "strife" between "earth" and "world" (and the relation between Dasein and Being), to the player-play relationship. The ontology of play (and hence of art or literature), according to Gadamer, consists in a "to and fro" movement, a recurrent displacement of the player's (or reader's) subjectivity and intentionality from being constitutive of play to being an effect of play, already part of the "script." However, contrary to Gide's mechanism of "retroaction," in Gadamer's thought, the disparate "horizons" do "fuse." The hermeneutical circle is stabilized, so to say, at some point. The ontic (the contingent and specific player or recipient) is "in service" of, and *always already* structured by, the ontological—the "being" of play. It is not in fact an empirical player who is engulfed by play in Gadamer's ontology, but rather an implied one, a player already structured by play.

If Heidegger, Blanchot contends, contrasts earth to world, and correspondingly night—the concealment of being—to day, that night is still "day's night," for it has "day's truth just as it has day's laws."[31] It is the night which serves "in the triumph of enlightenment which simply banishes darkness," and a day that is the whole of the day and the night, the "great promise of the dialectic,"[32] i.e., of the mechanism of *aletheia*. The "underneath" and even the "underneath of the underneath" of the work of art in Heidegger are already "in service" of that work's coming to light, of a pre-comprehended, master word, Being. If the origin of the work of art then repeats, it repeats *mechanically*, with each reduplication populating a pre-established logical level. The ground of ground, writes Heidegger, is not a "formal, endless iteration,"[33] however, by preventing the newly formed meta-level from reconstituting the series of reduplications, by presupposing a static, segregated domain where the reduplication—paradoxical as it is—takes place, Heidegger—like Russell's followers as discussed in chapter 1—implicitly understands the mise en abyme in terms of a static hierarchy between the embedding and the embedded level

Whilst for Heidegger the origin of the work—having "day's truth just as it has day's laws"—is but a channel to the "world" of the work, for Blanchot, that unreachable origin is "the only one which is worth reaching."[34] As against the mechanism of *aletheia* giving rise to the "daylight of being," the mechanism worked out in Thomas the Obscure is "nocturnal":

> The night soon appeared murkier and more terrible to him than any other night, as though it had really come forth from a wound in thought that could no longer be thought, thought treated ironically as an object by something other than thought. It was night itself . . . He could see nothing, and, far from being overwhelmed by this, he made this absence of vision the culminating point of his gaze. Useless for seeing, his eye took on extraordinary proportions, grew beyond measure, and, stretching to the horizon, let the night penetrate to its center in order to create for itself an iris. So it was, by virtue of this emptiness, that his gaze and the object of his gaze mingled together. Not only did the eye which could see nothing apprehend something, it apprehended the cause of its vision. It saw as an object that which prevented it from seeing.[35]

The night "as such" is an absolute rather than relative obscurity, the night that precedes the night, "before the concept and before dialectics." It is impenetrable to the thought of night but at the same time the necessary prior condition of that thought.[36] Its status is ambiguous. Though it enables "worlding," the dialectics of *aletheia*, and even the night—of the *day*—to appear as such, it remains at the same time and *notwithstanding* foreign to all forms of identity, thinkable only as that which is external and foreign to the concept of night; a radical impossibility of night.

Rather than disclosing the being of the work, the encounter between the "world" and the "origin" causes "worldlessness": "Whoever devotes himself to the work is drawn by it toward the point where it undergoes impossibility."[37] Like death found both "before" and "after" life, the origin or "earth" of the work is an "absolute exterior," which cannot serve as the framing of the work without turning, retroactively, into "what exists before," that is, the very "essence" or "world" of the work. Here, however, "we reach the abyss."[38] The first time Thomas perceives this presence it is night, then, a second had replaced the first, "just as inaccessible and just as obscure."[39] Becoming its very "world," the origin, the framing of the work, entails as such another framing, an origin of origin that "deterritorializes" origin. Here we also reach the mise en abyme. If the being of the work of art and the night-as-such that conditions it are incommensurable, the only ground to host the encounter between them is an ad hoc one, made up of the very encounter. In such case, an iconic double of the encounter has preceded and conditioned the encounter, a mise en abyme expressed in the fact that Thomas's gaze and the object he gazes at "mingle together," form an aggregate that paradoxically precedes their incommensurability.

An "enunciative" mise en abyme—making present in the diegesis the receiver of the narrative—furthermore appears at the beginning of the fourth chapter depicting Thomas's reading from a book:

> He entered with his living body into the anonymous shapes of words, giving his substance to them, establishing their relationships, offering his being to the word "be." For hours he remained motionless, with, from time to time, the word "eyes," in place of his eyes: he was inert, captivated and unveiled. And even later when, having abandoned himself and, contemplating his book, he recognized himself with disgust in the form of the text he was reading, he retained the thought that . . . there remained within his person which was already deprived of its senses obscure words, disembodied souls and angels of words, which were exploring him deeply.[40]

Gazing at the night itself, or the origin of his book—Thomas cannot but leap into the realm of the night, and then the night before the night. Since the point of departure of the leap and that of destination are discontinuous, that is to say, any common, interdimensional ground to bind them together is absent, any leap toward pure exterior departing from E, if successful, is transformed by the very action. As in Füredy's recrossing of the "intact but reified" type of boundary, it takes place *ab intio* in the domain of its *destination*, E': "[Whoever] purports to follow one slope is *already* on the other."[41] If Thomas hence "recognizes himself" in the book, it is because he now gazes from the other way round, he "enters with his living body" into the shapes of the words, incarnating as the text gazing at the reader. That is why the text bears eyes, hands, and teeth, and why seeing himself in the "eyes" looking at him,[42] recognizing himself in the form of the text, Thomas becomes himself the word "eyes." Due to the discontinuity between the text and Thomas, the subject and object of the crossing and recrossing incessantly alter. Thomas's gaze at the text is displaced so as to retroactively take place in the realm of the object of that gaze, namely the text, which is therefore stamped with an (enunciative) mise en abyme—a double of the reader's gaze at the text. The person the text gazes back at is not however exactly Thomas. Due to the discontinuity between the point of departure and that of destination, the recrossing does not return to the original point of departure. Thomas and the text bear only a situational identity that did not preexist a here and now gaze. This is why Thomas himself gazes not at a text bearing a coded meaning, but rather at the "*form* of the text," its crude material level, prior to acquiring a code that relates it to meaning or reference; he gazes at the word "eye" as preceding the eye which it is to denote.

"WORKLESSNESS" AND GIDE'S MECHANISM OF RETROACTION

In *The Space of Literature*, Blanchot develops death's double function of exteriority and displacement, drawing explicitly on the mechanism of retroaction in Gide's theory of mise en abyme: "I wanted to indicate in *Tentative Amoureuse*," writes Gide, "the influence the book has on the author while he is writing it . . . A subject cannot act on an object without retroaction by the object on the subject that is acting."[43] Blanchot, citing Gide, writes similarly: "All endeavors transform us, every action we accomplish acts upon us."[44] This principle of retroaction is deployed in Blanchot's mechanism of "worklessness." In the myth of Orpheus and Eurydice, the poet of poets sets out to rescue Eurydice from the Underworld. For him, Eurydice is the obscure origin toward which art and desire seem to tend. Orpheus has been warned not to look upon Eurydice as he rescues her from the Underworld, but faithful to his imprudent force of movement, he gazes back upon his beloved, banishing her again to Hades:

> Orpheus is capable of everything, except of looking this point in the face, except of looking at the center of night in the night. He can descend toward it; he can . . . draw it to him and lead it with him upward, but only by turning away from it. This turning away is the only way it can be approached. This is what concealment means when it reveals itself in the night. But Orpheus, in the movement of his migration, forgets the work he is to achieve, and he forgets it necessarily, for the ultimate demand which his movement makes is not that there be a work, but that someone face this point, grasp its essence, grasp it where it appears, where it is essential and essentially appearance: at the heart of night.[45]

Orpheus does not want Eurydice in her daytime truth, but in her nocturnal obscurity. Grasping the essence of the work can only be done by taking flight from the imperatives of light. By force of the ambiguity of death, Orpheus therefore forgets the task he is to achieve and turns toward Eurydice. The work—betrayed—is immediately undone, but only to give rise to a peculiar dynamic. If Y is incommensurable with X, if Orpheus's gaze, or leap, towards X's "pure exterior" cannot occur upon a mediating space, then the leap, its very undertaking, *always already* occurs in the "jurisdiction" of the point of destination. Any attempt to leap toward the exterior of X is *always already* another attempt—that of leaping towards the exterior of Y—"before having begun, already one begins again; before having finished, one broods."[46] The point of origin at which Orpheus gazes is revealed retroactively to be the starting point from which another exterior is gazed at: "the other night is always other."[47] The leap is indeed aimed at the "origin of the work," but like a Deleuzian "line of flight" it is stretched between subjects and objects which "[do] not seem to have any sort of real prior existence apart from this movement."[48] The attempt to leap—essentially futile—is now aimed toward an exterior which, due to the discontinuity and hence irreversibility between X and Y, can by no means be X: "There is no exact moment at which one would pass from night to the other night, no limit at which to stop and come back in the other direction."[49] Instead, new "departures" engender new grounds—logically disparate to one another—upon which the rupture between the given and the Other occurs. Any leap is *at once* an infinite number of leaps, stretched between no rigid points, engulfing and being engulfed by one another.

Gide, to recall, associates his mechanism of retroaction with writing on a desk while seeing oneself writing in the double mirror of the desk. In "Language to Infinity," Foucault likewise invokes the double mirror paradigm commenting on Blanchot, and setting out to "outline an ontology of literature" beginning with mise en abyme, "the forms of reduplication of language to be found in western literature":[50]

> Before the imminence of death language rushes forth, but it also starts again, tells of itself, discovers the story of the story. Headed toward death, language turns back upon itself; it encounters something like a mirror; and to stop this death . . . it possesses but a single power—that of giving birth to its own image in a play of mirrors that has no limit.[51]

In a double mirror A reflects B while being reflected by it. This means that B reflects not A but rather a conjunction such as (A *as already reflecting* B), that is, C. A reflects in turn not B but rather a conjunction such as (B as already reflecting C), that is, D. Retroactively it is of course also the case that B rather reflects (D as already reflecting C) that is, E, and A reflects F and so on. A is (recurrently) transformed by the very action of reflection, from A to C to E, etc. Another way to illustrate the mechanism of worklessness (and retroaction) is the dialectics of the gift as developed by Jean-Luc Marion, the fact that "to give the gift, the giving must withdraw."[52] Imagine a case where I throw a gift toward someone's property. Once the gift crosses the boundary into her yard, it is already in her possession. When she then grabs it with her own hands, doesn't she receive what has always been hers?

Orpheus's point of betraying the work entails a set of crossings and re-crossings, but this mechanism of "worklessness" is rather the point where the work begins; it is the work's "only chance," because it renders the work devoid of what Ricardou has termed "ideology," that is an "ideal"—political, noological, aesthetical or other—from which the work derives its meaning and which it in turn reaffirms. Orpheus's gaze is the moment where the writer "frees the work from his concern."[53]

Ricardou, as we saw, associates the liberation from ideology with generative qualities, that is, the modeling of the referential level on the literal one rather than vice versa. For Blanchot, similarly, "the tale is not the narration of an event, but that event itself,"[54] and words, rather than being instrumental for some real or fictional universe, endure "only as their space."[55] It is the very literal-material level of the work, its "flesh and blood," as Blanchot says in *Thomas*, that embodies such universe. As in a double mirror, where the true subject and object is neither the mirroring device, nor the images it contains, but the very "middle" between them—the very *process* of mirroring—what repeats in the system of recrossings is neither the object nor the subject of the "gaze," but the very act of gazing, the very endeavor to leap. Orpheus gazes at an exterior which is absolute, and yet neither Orpheus (the writer) nor this exterior have existence prior to the gaze. The gaze, representing the infrastructure of the work of art, the very process of fiction-making and its pragmatic level in general, becomes the work's true "origin." "To write, one has to write already,"[56] it is writing itself—not the heterocosm that writing refers to—which the space of literature consists in. As in Ricardou's generative novels, "words are always there only to designate the extent of their connections":[57] The literal level of the work does not serve as a mere vehicle to the referential level. Rather the signs as signs, the very interplay between words or letters, comprises the only reality "worth reaching." This does not mean that the space of literature is deprived of a "diegesis," a story-universe of actions and events, only that—as in the generative novel—this diegesis is modeled on the literal level. The literal level epitomizes "earth," which being always already an "origin of origin," is retroactively, as we saw, "world."

Blanchot further seems to suggest that if the true object of the movement toward the pure exterior is the movement itself or, rather, the entire series of duplications and reduplications that that movement entails, then mise en abyme not only characterizes the quest for the origin, but also functions as its object—the origin itself: "the mise en abyme which Blanchot discussed so admirably . . . is the song of the Sirens in which is heard, in the innermost depths of the poem, the music of the abyss ('abyme')."[58] The song of the Sirens, the "origin" in search of which Ulysses is dragged to the depths of the poem, is a mise en abyme of that poem. If the mechanism of recrossings means all productions "begi[n] with the end,"[59] if every movement toward the exterior of the work is retroactively a movement initiated at that exterior, then this movement is performed upon a space already opened by a preceding double—"The tale Homer told was simply Ulysses' movement within the space opened up for him by the Song of the Sirens."[60] This means that in every work lies a latent enunciative mise en abyme, or rather—as this double rather precedes and conditions the work—a *mise en périphérie*: The mise en abyme in Blanchot's writing "is simultaneously the cause, of which the text is the effect, and the effect, of which the text is the cause."[61] In a mechanism of recrossings, where the interior and the exterior of the work are interchangeable, the mise en abyme formed by the set of recrossings, while different, is indiscernible from that embedded within the work. Blanchot indeed chooses Borges's "The Aleph" to demonstrate this point. While mise en abyme usually only reflects the embedding work, in "The Aleph" a diminutive encapsulation of the world, lying in a cellar in the world, nonetheless generated the world, so that an effect or segment of the whole paradoxically exists before this whole can exist.[62] Signifying with its literal-material level, the pragmatic rather than semiotic, the book given to the mechanism of worklessness likewise breaks the boundary between the inside and outside of the book, and mise en abyme—up until now a diminutive replica of the work—incarnates as the work itself serving as a diminutive replica of the world. The world and the book "eternally and infinitely send back their reflected images [in an] indefinite power of mirroring."[63] We shall later develop in depth this type of pragmatic signification discussing Deleuze's "rhizomatic book."

WORKLESSNESS AND ISER'S "ACTS OF FICTIONALIZATION"

What Blanchot calls "gaze" Iser calls "acts of fictionalization." In premodern philosophy, all relations to another world were conceived in terms of transcendence, the world that is other than the one we are in is transcendent to it.[64] The way we get from this world to that one is through transcending this one, and the presence, however conceived, of the other world in this one is the presence of something in this world that is transcendent to it. In reading Wolfgang Iser's *The Fictive and the Imaginary*, which draws heavily, though implicitly, on Blanchot, it became clear to Gabriel Motzkin "for the first time," what is wrong with this conception:

> It is not a priori erroneous to suppose that some other world than this one, with other laws, exists. Nor is it a priori erroneous to suppose that we conceive of this other world in terms of laws that do not properly belong to our world. Nor even is it a priori erroneous to suppose that we conceive of one world

in terms of laws that do not properly belong to it, but that have their origin elsewhere. The philosophical tradition's basic error was to presuppose that absolute transcendence, the act of transcending, and transcendence-in immanence, are all the same thing, or indeed that they belong together.[65]

What "premodern philosophy" failed to notice was the discontinuity between the three, the fact that the transcendent world and the act of transcending do not emerge from this world. Like Blanchot's gaze toward the absolute exterior, the act of transcending is transformed by the very act, originating retroactively in a domain disparate to the given. Iser reaches this conclusion by discarding with the old opposition of fiction and reality, and replacing this duality with a triad: The real, the imaginary, and the fictive—which is in fact a fictionalizing act. The three correspond in Motzkin's analogy to the immanent, the absolutely transcendent, and the act of transcending or boundary crossing between the first two. Iser's polemic is directed against those who would derive the fictive from the real, but no less against those who would derive the fictive from the imaginary. Instead, the fictive is a unique hybrid, clearing the stage for "more than just a *contrast* between the two,"[66] namely the non-binary logic of the mise en abyme.

In correspondence with the dialectics of "drilling"/"filling" of gaps developed in Iser's *The Implied Reader*, the fictionalizing act in his *The Fictive and the Imaginary* outstrips the determinacy of the real, but at the same time provides the imaginary with the determinacy that it would not otherwise possess. In each of the two moments—that of selection which disassembles the given order of organizational units by "grafting" them upon the unreal—and that of combination—which turns those units into objects for observation thus transforming the unreal into structure—there is a crossing of boundaries. The reason is that the imaginary is not a guided act, a self-activating potential, but has to be brought into play from outside itself, by intentional acts of fictionalization. Endowing the imaginary with a shape, the fictional act undergoes, in turn, changes itself. As in Husserl's method of phenomenological reduction, where the intentum is inseparable from the intention upon which it casts its own image, the imaginary "appears to be open to all intentions that will always be tied to what they trigger, so that something will 'happen' to the activator."[67]

Motzkin demonstrates this recurrent mutual transformation by invoking the mise en abyme:

> In looking at a picture I enter the world of the picture and then look at myself in and through the picture, since I am now part of the picture.⁶⁸

The "myself" I gaze outward at from within the picture is not the preliminary one which initiated the act of fictionalization. If A—which belongs to the real—is the starting point, and B—which belongs to the imaginary—is the destination point, then B which I retroactively gaze *from* belongs to the real, and A which I retroactively gaze *at* belongs to the imaginary, hence ceases to be "A." It becomes instead a new exterior—C—which belongs to a world just created/discovered by the fictionalizing act. The fictional act, like Orpheus's gaze, is directional, always away from the given:

> A return to the given from the imaginary is simply a boundary transgression from that world. For the movie characters in *The Purple Rose of Cairo* it must be the real viewers who are beyond the line. The real self becomes the dream self of the other. This directionality cannot be changed: there is no towards in the fictionalizing act, it must always be away.⁶⁹

As in Blanchot's mechanism of recrossing, the fictionalizing act in Iser is always already double. Motzkin demonstrates this point employing—like Blanchot, Foucault and many others—the emblem of the double mirror:

> The imaginary me, in seeing itself, looks at an infinite series of mirrors. For an imaginary me to see an imaginary me, it must go through a fictionalizing act of the same kind, and therefore construct an imaginary world of second degree through a fictionalizing act of second degree.⁷⁰

As in a double mirror, the recurrent transgressions toward the imaginary are not performed upon a shared, preestablished ground. Aiming at the imaginary, each act of fictionalization—like Orpheus's gaze—constitutes an "endemic" ground upon which it is (retroactively) performed, "an imaginary world of second degree through a fictionalizing act of second degree." The single space of recrossings comprises paradoxically a multiplicity of (heterogenous) "wholes."

The example Iser provides for the double transformation is the pastoral poetry of antiquity. The pastoral world in this poetry cannot be said to signify the historical, or vice versa. Instead "the artificial world is seen through the eyes of the sociohistorical, and the latter through the eyes of the artificial."[71] Consequently, each of these texts is "a signifier that cannot be fulfilled through what it signifies,"[72] liberated of an extratextual signified or referent governing its sense or referring function. The two texts, mirroring each other without a privileged "first time," establish instead a simulacral space where the referential factor "fades" and each side of the actual/virtual dyad "mak[es] the other unreal."[73] As in Ricardou's and Morrissette's "generative novel," the genre thus draws attention "to the signs as signs."[74]

The mutually exclusive worlds, Iser continues:

> [t]rigger a reciprocal readability in the course of which a *simultaneity* of the present and the absent comes about. The iteration tends to create an illusion of completeness not because it embraces everything but because the reciprocal 'reading' of signifiers is serial in character.[75]

Despite debarring any substance underlying the writing, reading and discoursing of this genre, the series of recrossings put into action by these two worlds forms an ad hoc "completeness," differing as such from plenitudes revolving around (pre-established) totalizing ideals. Governed by the mise en abyme, where an instance of duplication transforms the subject and object of the whole by its very addition, the "completeness" resulting from the "reciprocal readability" is "serial in character," every instance is given to—but also generates—its own organizing principle. In accordance with Gide's mechanism of retroaction, a fictionalizing act is both the cause and the effect of the series of recrossings it generates. It is "a product of activation as well as the condition for the productivity brought about by the interaction it stimulates," and it is this very dual process, writes Iser, "that gives the imaginary its presence."[76]

Heidegger, Husserl, Lask, and Vaihinger all influenced Iser by capturing, to some extent, the heterogeneity and discontinuity between the absolute transcendent, the transcendence-in-immanence, and the transcending act. However, Iser alone, writes Motzkin—and Blanchot before him we here argue—managed to establish a precise, complete, and elaborated phenomenology of boundary transgression. If the two gained a precise account of such transgression, if they captured the ceaseless retroaction entailed with the act of transcending, it is due to adhering to the emblem of the mise en abyme.

MISE EN ABYME AND THE "FATALITY OF THE DAY"

Iser, as we have seen, has acknowledged that series of recrossings toward the "absolute exterior" nevertheless result in a special type of "completeness," a plenitude formed by variants encountering upon no preexisting ground, but one generated by their very juxtaposition. This type of plenitude, I wish to argue, also underlies Blanchot's idea of "day in the form of fatality."[77]

In a sudden turn, notwithstanding the overwhelming ambiguity he stresses between absence and presence, "nocturnity" and "light"—and without reconsidering this ambiguity—Blanchot endows the "day" with the "upper hand":

> if we call the day to account, if we reach a point where we push it away in order to find out what is prior to the day, under it, we discover that the day is already present, and that what is prior to the day is still the day, but in the form of an inability to disappear.[78]

In its quest for its nocturnal origin, literature—like Orpheus—destroys the meaning of words, the capacity to grasp, the answer "understood" in every (Heideggerian) question. Through their song, the sirens guided the sailor toward the region of source and origin where the only thing left was to disappear, "as though the region where music originated was the only place completely without music, a sterile dry place where silence . . . burned all access to the song."[79] However, at this place, "a silence talks even in its dumbness . . . an echo speaking on and on."[80] Though meaning at the point of origin has disappeared, the "meaning of the meaninglessness," the "inescapable degree zero of meaning, to which even the meaningless must bend,"[81] has appeared in its place. Blanchot has never been able to say "Nothing! At last there is nothing," because the void encountered at this place of origin to which the sirens dragged the sailors "doesn't stop speaking."[82] Rather than saying nothing, it seems to be saying something, "a light murmuring,"[83] as if "the unheard-of may be heard."[84] The return to meaninglessness is a futile endeavor, an "ancient accident that has made death impossible."[85]

Attempting to explain Blanchot's bias, Gasché compared the "fatality of day" to Heidegger's question of Being: "Death as the affirmation of an always other possibility begins in that it asks."[86] The question of Being does not entail a linear consecution from question to answer, but rather serves itself as a mode of the answer, a form of the disclosure of Being. Through the mechanism of *aletheia*, Being emerges through the "matter," the body or act of the investigation, and often despite its content, precisely so as to exceed representation by that content. What Blanchot's idea of "fatality of day" means, according to Gasché, is that just as an origin bears "no other existence" than the leap towards that origin, signification is caused by the very attempt to signify, the "body" of the message, regardless of the intention and intentum.

This explanation is correct only to a limited extent. Blanchot's idea of a "fatality of light" does not withdraw from but aligns with the principle of "ambiguity," and the latter, we have already seen, is "not to adhere to the economy of Heideggerian Being."[87] Whereas the mechanism of *aletheia* is governed by the "master word," "Being," which it is preconditioned to "bringing into light," Blanchot's crossing as an act of signification operates within a code not yet present, still in obscurity. It "says nothing, reveals nothing," but instead "announces"—"through its refusal to say anything"— "that it comes from night and will return to night."[88] Like Mallarmé's utopian infinite book, *Le Livre*, which Blanchot's own book title, *Le Livre à venir*—The Book to Come—alludes to, this act of signification belongs to an absent, *yet to come* code. Such absence (as we shall discuss in depth in chapter 7), pertains to the fact that in Blanchot as in Ricardou, the text is a "matter without contour, content without form."[89] It signifies with the pragmatic rather than semiotic level of the sign, generative rather than reduced to a vehicle of pre-established meaning or reference. In such a case, bodies form a message without ceasing to be empirical, here and now existents incompatible with the universalization of their meaning. The code this message is written in cannot therefore preexist its decoding by a here and now recipient. Both the mechanism of *aletheia* and that of recrossings consist in signification with the "body" rather than the "content" of the message, but Blanchot understands "body" differently. He understands it in terms of what Levinas has called *il y a*, the preconceptual and impersonal "flesh and blood," the pure ontic, the ontic as ontic, coexisting with, yet not defined in terms of, the ontological.

Roger Laporte, contrary to Gasché, does observe that Blanchot demands a new "working hypothesis": While Heidegger's Being is "rent apart by the struggle . . . between . . . clearing and non-disclosedness," Blanchot's "come[s] forward to the daylight *whilst* still remaining under cover."[90] The new "working hypothesis" is no longer a "struggle," a bipolarity, what Gadamer would term a "to and fro" movement between variants, but rather a (paradoxical) simultaneity between them. As in Blanchot's fable (alluding to Kafka) of a man that "has forgotten to die,"[91] a zombie, practically, meaning comes forward to daylight *whilst* remaining under cover.

However, have we not already detected this new "working hypothesis"? The paradigm enabling the outside of X to be found *at the same time* at the heart of X is of course the mise en abyme. Let us now see how it governs not only Blanchot's principle of "worklessness," but also his idea of *il y a*, adopted from Levinas, the "strange impersonal light"[92] asserting itself in the "day in the form of fatality."

The day, which has become "fatality," the process where whatever ceases to be continues to be and whatever dies encounters only the impossibility of dying, is like the *il y a*, an "existence without being."[93] The *il y a* is the "universal fact of the there is," the impersonal and pre-personal presence lacking a substantive, but yet is not "nothingness." Indifferent to the movement of concealment and unconcealment that is constitutive of Heideggerian *aletheia*,[94] it "replaces the originary generosity of the Heideggerian gift of Being with the horror and anonymity of being."[95] If we imagine all beings and persons reverting to nothingness, writes Levinas, this nothingness—as in Blanchot's fatality of light—becomes something inextinguishable, the "silence of nothingness" which "murmurs in the depths of nothingness itself."[96]

The *il y a* in Levinas is characterized by a simple juxtaposition between variants, a "proximity" rather than a difference governed by the positive and the negative of formal logic. It was as against the law of excluded middle—the "beyond being posited in doxic theses" and the "an-archical espous[ing] of the forms of formal logic"[97]—that Levinas developed his concept of otherness. Binary logic implies fixed, rigid identities of variants. Stably defined from one another, variants of a given opposition presuppose a mediating ground, and logical loci upon that ground that a judgement allocates them to. By contrast, the ground upon which the variants of proximity encounter did not have an existence prior to the encounter. Therefore, the encounter implies a primordial double, "an allegiance of the same to the other, imposed before any exhibition of the other."[98] Like Derrida's trace—the minimal self-difference within which the sign can repeat itself infinitely "by referring to an Other and to (an Other of) itself within itself"[99]—the *il y a* of Levinas is a mise en abyme, "a series of always anterior repetitive traces whose origin is always lost."[100] The empirical encounter of variants is possible only in so far as the encounter is always *already* split in two, repeating a double found in the "interior" of the variants: "The Same has to do with the Other before the other appears in any way to a consciousness."[101]

Being a mise en abyme, where the embedding circuit is retroactively the embedded one, the *il y a* has "no exits." At the same time, being a mise en abyme, it rather has—as in Deleuze's rhizome as we shall see—"multiple entryways and exits."[102] The place of wandering in the pre-personal space knows no straight line, "one never goes from one point to another in it; one does not leave here to go there; there is no point of departure and no beginning to the walk."[103] A space without an exit, that is without a boundary dividing it (binarily) from its outside, lacks a (stable) point of reference to enable the determinability of two points and the distance between them. Therefore, as in Blanchot's mechanism of worklessness, where the line stretched between the inside and the exterior is always already performed upon another register, the *il y a* is a space where one "never goes from one point to another,"[104] one's movement always already differs from itself. The point to stress here is that each of these lines marks a radical flight from the given: It *reconstitutes* the entire (rhizomatic) *il y a* within which it occurs.

The fatality of light, "the labyrinth of light and nothing else besides"[105] occurs because in the space without exits that makes up the *il y a*, one returns "without ever having left," and begins "by beginning again."[106] One never leaves because the act of "leaving," the leap toward the exterior, is retroactively performed upon a universe "endemic" to the leap, a "completeness" upon which the leap is performed, but which paradoxically did not preexist the leap. In mise en abyme—which the *il y a* embodies—the principle of simultaneity, we have already seen, is responsible for the fact that circuit B added to circuit A transforms the object of reflection *ab initio*—from A to the aggregate (B within A); that added from without to a logically incommensurable whole, B causes this whole to be retroactively stamped with B at its very subject. Despite epitomizing difference, B consists in an ad hoc plenitude made up of all other circuits retroactively constituted and appropriated by B. The principle of simultaneity, established by poeticians such as Dällenbach, Hutcheon, Le Poidevin and many others, is also acknowledged by Blanchot:

> The very bottom, the bottomless abyss belongs to art. And art is that deep which is sometimes the absence of profundity, of the foundation, the pure void bereft of importance, and sometimes that upon which a foundation can be given, but it is also always *at the same time* one and the other, the intertwining of the Yes and of the No, the ebb and flow of the essential ambiguity.[107]

The two incompatible levels underlying art, says Blanchot—the night and the night before the night, or the "foundation" and that "upon which a foundation can be given"—are always given "at the same time." Likewise, in crossing, one is always already recrossing; the two incompatible moments of the retroaction in Blanchot's mechanism of worklessness—the beginning and the beginning again (upon a different register)—despite being "irreducible to one another and absolutely not superimposable on one another,"[108] are nonetheless simultaneous.

Consequently, rather than being discrete, instances of mise en abyme—the series of recrossings—necessarily accumulate to form ad hoc *plenitudes*. Day is a "fatality" because the inevitable signification which lies—instead of nothingness—at the origin of language is no other than the accumulated attempts of language to reach its origin:

> From the day that men began to speak toward death and against it, in order to grasp and imprison it, something was born, a murmuring that repeats, recounts, and redoubles itself endlessly.[109]

The murmuring which language encounters at its origin was born once man "began to speak towards death," it embodies man's *very set of accumulated recrossings* toward the absolute exterior. The principle of simultaneity governing mise en abyme compels us to define death beyond the negative and positive valorizations "as affirmation—of the *possibility* of nothingness."[110] It "intertwines the 'Yes' and the 'No,'" the two slopes of ambiguity, and this coexistence of the "Yes" with the "No" renders the "No" by necessity part of an inevitable continuum: a "Yes."[111]

The coexistence between the two slopes of ambiguity projects on that between the book—its diegesis—and its empirical outside. Ahab and Melville are brought together "in one space." Despite each being "an absolute world, which would make it impossible for [it] to coexist with the other absolute world," the "greatest desire" of each, is for "this coexistence and this encounter."[112] Foucault describes this "heterogenous space" as bearing an "ontologically density." The murmuring embodied by the set of recrossings "has undergone an uncanny process of amplification and thickening, in which language is lodged and hidden"[113]—language, encountering the murmuring at the origin of this language, is at the same time lodged within that murmuring. Deleuze would term such "density" "indivisibility." If mise en abyme is always already "coupé en deux," if one cannot identify a subject of duplication (X within X) without already being compelled to identify another subject (Y within Y), then mise en abyme "may be divided, but not without changing its nature."[114] What might be divided is only a determination "carved" from, a suspension or interval of, the true, indivisible mise en abyme.

CHAPTER 4

GILLES DELEUZE
REPETITION AND TIME AS *MISE EN ABYME*

MISE EN ABYME AND THE GROUND OF DIFFERENCE

We have encountered in previous chapters Derrida's criticism of the metaphysical "dreams of plenitude," where concepts of unity, totality, and cohesion precede difference and separation; where defined in terms of opposition—that is, the laws of contradiction and the excluded middle—difference is reduced to states of reconciliation. There is no dualism without unity taught Derrida, as dichotomies or polarities are arranged as such in a hierarchical order which allows one of the terms a qualitative and temporal priority. To challenge the "logic of negation"—where binary oppositions and mono-centrism interdepend—is the undertaking of Deleuze as well. Deleuze, however, who—far from embracing Heidegger's and Derrida's notion of the "end of metaphysics"—declares himself to be a "pure metaphysician,"[1] and who often uses for his models "philosophers whose own work has been considered tightly unitary or monistic"[2] would accordingly refuse to negate negation, to debar "logocentric" discourse from the articulation of the "difference in itself." He would establish that the other logic, that of "affirmation," is to be obtained not as an opposite pole, but in the "middle" between the pole of "negation" and that of "affirmation"; that affirmation, in other words follows the logic of mise en abyme.

For Deleuze, the acute difference lies not between Being and beings—or any other pair of variants—but between instances of that which *grounds this gap*. A central problem in *Difference and Repetition* is to uncover a concept of difference which ran throughout the history of philosophy parallel—though in disguise—to the hegemonic one defined in terms of identity or representation. This recovered difference would be stretched between and reduced to no pre-established constants, a "pure difference" or "difference in itself" "that is not contained in the 'from' of the 'x is different from y'—in which case, difference would be relative to identity."[3] Constants, or (rigidly determined) identities, succumbing as such to the Law of Identity of the Indiscernibles, differ from one another as X from non-X, that is, by means of a contrariety which is nothing but opposition. This correlation between "identity" and binary logic has already been expressed—and to a large extent established—by Hegel, who viewed opposing variants as bearing as such an "internal"—rather than situational—essence: "One of the variants in a pair is the positive and the other the negative but the former as a positive *which is such within*, and the latter as a negative *which is such within*."[4] Such pre-established constants also imply a substance, a pre-established shared unity into which they have been allocated in advance so as to "populate" predetermined loci. Stably defined from one another, opposing variants presuppose a mediating ground, a "reconciling" judgement to keep the two from transgressing one another's "rubric." They imply a single set of coordinates, a unitary taxonomy cast upon the two, singling each out according to an "internal nature" that it bears, or—more accurately—an "internal nature" which any taxonomy or categorialism inevitably transforms its objects into the bearers of. It was as against such Aristotelian taxonomy that Dällenbach, in his typology of mise en abyme, exploited the logic of the mise en abyme to allow species to "slide" into and "amalgamate" with one another.

Establishing his categorialism in his studies *Categories* and *Metaphysics*, Aristotle faces three options from which to select the paradigm of difference. Would he choose that prevailing between genera, species, or individuals? He opts for the middle, the "specific difference," the "greatest and most perfect," since it is the only one to comprise contrariety in the *essence*. Two terms differ only when they are other "not in themselves, but in something else, thus when they also agree in something else."[5] Species differ by a given property—such as having or not having wings—only with respect to a common denominator—the form or genus. While the difference which Deleuze pursues is generative, that is, it lies between variants that have no reality prior to that difference's self-making, variants in Aristotle's categorialism presuppose a form which is continuous throughout change and which governs the differentiation.

Above and below the level of species, difference according to Aristotle tends to become simple otherness and to escape the identity of the concept. Generic difference is too large, being established between uncombinable objects which do not enter into relations of contrariety. Individual difference is too small: prima facie contrarieties such as white/black for humans or male/female for animals pertain only to matter, they are mere "accidents" and hence have no contrariety either. Aristotle thus embodies "the Greek eye which sees the mean and which has lost the sense of Dionysian transports and metamorphoses."[6] Rather than forming an irreducible interval, his difference ensures coherence and continuity in the comprehension of the concept. Difference is already "in service" of classification, and presupposes, or carries with itself, the genus. Only mediated—reduced to the "shackles" of identity and opposition—and only represented—related to the requirements of the concept—could difference for the post-Dionysian Greek cease being monster.

Since a genus only comprises species between which there *are* differences, and since between genera lies not difference but mere otherness, Being cannot serve a genus. Such emancipation of genera would have served as a new chance for the philosophy of difference, leading toward a concept of what is free of mediation and subordination to representation. Nothing of the kind, however, occurs with Aristotle. With genera, an identical or common concept still subsists. Maintaining that Being is "equivocal," and decreeing an analogy between the many ways Being is "said of," Aristotle *distributes* Being in proportion to the different terms of which it is predicated. He distributes those variants, those "many ways," onto an (implied) unity, to fulfill pre-established representations. The instance capable of proportioning the concept to the subjects of which it is affirmed is judgment, but judgment means that all modes of Being are given *at once* to whoever judges, and that the measurements which that judge applies are unitary. This can only occur if all modes, all objects of judgment, have already gone through a process of standardization, transformation into representation, so as to become compatible with the judging measurements. Judgment occurs when the two sides of difference are always already homogenized, reconcilable, and continuous with one another. Deleuze's difference, on the other hand, consists of dissymmetrical sides: "instead of something distinguished from something else, imagine something which distinguishes itself—and yet that from which it distinguishes itself does not distinguish itself from it."[7] Aristotle's "Difference in the concept" determines the "other side" in advance; Deleuze's "difference-in-itself" implies *pure* transition from one mode of Being to the other, without one being able to tell where difference would lead.

Hegel, like Deleuze, discovers in serene representation "the intoxication and restlessness of the infinitely large."[8] At its limits, believes Hegel, any supposed identity is, in fact, ill-defined. Each time we think we have arrived at the final identity of all things, it is open to a contradiction. But Hegel, like Aristotle, errs in determining difference in terms of contraries or opposition of extremes. Each of the opposing variants is "self-subsisting," "a unity existing for itself and excluding the other from itself."[9] It is this bearing of the opposition to the Other in the Self's very identity that renders Hegel's triads incessant, but also causes contradiction to "resolve itself in one unity." It posits the Other as the Other *of the Self*, and renders the dyad in entirety—since each variant is "the whole opposition"[10]—a cliché of a pre-established form: the theorems of binary logic. For Deleuze it is not difference which "as such is already *implicitly* contradiction,"[11] but opposition which presupposes difference. Forcing difference into a previously established identity rather betrays and distorts difference, and beneath opposition would always bustle "a pluralism of free, wild or untamed differences."[12] If Hegel takes the principle of identity "particularly seriously,"[13] it is mainly due to *presupposing* multiplicity, hence its form. Despite apparent "restlessness," Hegel's triads are "closed in the logic that governs the endless spiral of contradictions and syntheses,"[14] and variants become parasitic to loci upon this pre-established "tree."

Differently put, despite each "disjunct" in a Hegelian opposition being itself "the whole opposition,"[15] the tree of triads does not form a mise en abyme. To recall, Derrida's iterability (in our "argumentative" rather than "textualistic" reading), despite comprising an act of signification that repeats "externally"—at the pragmatic, empirical level—only due to being doubled "internally"—in its "essence"—cannot be regarded as mise en abyme either. In both cases this is due to the dispersion of variants "in extension," allocation of instances (in practice) onto a pre-established unity. Hegel terms the enormous system of dialectics "absolute reflection," but the "absolute reflection" of the mise en abyme—represented by the labyrinth of mirrors where A cannot reflect B without turning retroactively into the very object of reflection—consists of a recurring transgression of boundaries between levels, which Hegel's system lacks. The "nth" level in the double mirroring is "distinct and yet indiscernible"[16] from the (n-1)th one, distinct but not according to the Law of Identity of Indiscernibles. Those levels logically exclude one another but ontologically coexist. Reflection in double mirroring consists of transgression of logical boundaries into the "other side" of representation, which Gasché (as we shall see in chapter 5) would term "the tain of the mirror." Hegel, on the other hand, allocates the "nth" power and the (n-1)th one in advance onto a unity which Gasché terms the "specular play," to populate loci *well differentiated* from one another. In true mise en abyme, a circuit cannot be added to a whole without transforming its very subject. Such transformation caused by a contingent, diachronical addition is impossible, however, in Hegel's logic, where the quantitative unit is "the dialectical synthesis of limit and alternation implied by qualitative or determinate being"; where quantity is derived from quality and is "an external modification of being that must be reintegrated dialectically."[17] Transformation is impossible in Hegel's triads, where multiplicity is *postulated* in advance, and variants function as mere clichés of branches upon a pre-established "tree." It was precisely so as to dismiss mechanism and atomism as abstract understandings, writes Widder, that Hegel externalizes quantity, and this confrontation of mechanistic quantification he rather shares with Nietzsche and Deleuze; "one might even see Deleuze as both rivaling and completing Hegel's project of immanence."[18] However, the quality he introduces instead, rather than marking heterogeneity, is quality in the form of equality, imposed externally upon quantity—and the difference germane to it—thus reinvoking problematic abstraction. The circuit of mise en abyme is incompatible with the Hegelian scheme, being both quantitative, a here-and-now creation, a "grafted-on function," as we saw in chapter 1, and qualitative, being generative of the entire series it is grafted to.

As against Hegel's pre-established, homogenous ground, Deleuze maintains that a variant *brings its own "ground" with it*. Difference lying between disjuncts of "entirely different nature"[19] means that no *presupposed* ground can host it. If E' is incommensurable with E, then the breaking (or encounter of) E' with E—the given and the unimaginable—is eternally "that which has just happened and that which is about to happen, but never that which is happening."[20] The very undertaking of differentiation, the breaking from E and the "leaping" towards E' is transposed rather than given to a final halt. If the two are discontinuous, then the crossing, if successful, retroactively occurs in the "jurisdiction" of the point of destination—E'—which, unimaginable, did not exist prior to the act of crossing and can only be *endemic to that act*. What Heidegger failed to acknowledge was that the acute difference lies not between Being and beings, *but between instances of that which grounds this gap.* Deleuze's repetition is a "correlation of the grounded and the ground."[21]

This idea of a plenitude paradoxically generated by rather than preexisting the entity acting upon it is predominantly expressed by Duns Scotus. If Scotus's is the ultimate ontology, it is because, as against Aristotle, Hegel and Heidegger, it rather starts from "indifference," the theological upshot of which, is that "one can say 'God is wise' and 'Socrates is wise' without invoking an identity between God and Socrates, but also without wisdom itself being said equivocally even though God's infinite wisdom eludes human comprehension."[22] Like God, who according to Scotus manifests his properties in humans in an unmediated fashion, "Being is univocal." However, while Scotus limits the univocity of being at this point; while "univocity establishes a relation between finite and infinite substances that otherwise share nothing in common," Deleuze would apply this form of heterogeneity to the individual difference, extending univocity to the relation between the essential and nonessential senses of being.[23] An ontology would employ the wrong concept of "ontological difference" and a philosophy of multiplicity (possible worlds semantics, for instance) would go astray, should they *presuppose* a multiplicity of variants, hence a unity onto which these variants have always already been allocated. True philosophy of multiplicity rather allows difference to be "made," or make itself, "as in the expression 'make the difference.' "[24] Being multiplies *due to* univocity. The fact that no other "voices" are presupposed implies that the single voice occupies no predetermined time and space, bears no fixed, determinable identity, and is confined to no presupposed form, meaning and context. Resultantly, "when we speak the univocal, is it not still the equivocal which speaks within us?"[25] If univocity is by essence "deterritorialized," there are *at once* infinite subjects who utter it, and infinite constellations, grounds—generated rather than presupposed—upon which the voice is announced.

Scotus allows difference to be "made" because while Being is said in a single and same sense, that of which it is said differs: Being repeats *as univocal* in "unheard-of-world[s],"[26] upon an unimaginable rather than pre-established ground: Repetition is possible "due to miracle rather than to law."[27] Being repeats with difference, but that difference pertains to no taxonomical property that distinguishes one instance of repetition from the other (at least not primarily). It derives from the ground, the (unimaginable) constellation onto which the (one and single) voice is transposed. While Aristotle's distribution of Being according to "common sense" and "good sense" is "agrarian" or "sedentary," Scotus's is "nomadic." The agrarian division pertains to a *given* space, and to elements that are distributed upon it so as to populate it. The nomadic division, on the other hand, *constitutes* space as a function of dispersion, nomads "distribute *themselves* in an open space—a space which is unlimited, or at least without precise limits."[28]

Univocity of Being means that each instance of Being is Being in its entirety, but multiple plenitudes, cannot, by definition, align with one another, or else they would presuppose a fundamental plenitude which they all shared. Instead, they form a mise en abyme where repetition—unlike in the case of the empirical version—cannot take place "in extension." Reproduction does not add a second and a third time to the first whose integrity and uniqueness is presupposed, but is rather an "intensive" repetition, a split at the heart of the reproduced: "Every intensity is E-E', where E itself refers to an e-e', and e to ε-$\acute{\varepsilon}$ etc."[29] The attempt to leap toward the exterior of E is *always already* another attempt—that of leaping towards the exterior of e or ε. Every difference is already a difference-of-difference, and every repetition—a repetition of repetition—a repetition that doubles only what is already double—"It is repetition itself that is repeated."[30] Repetition can indeed be comprehended properly only when bearing the emblem of mise en abyme before one's eyes: what Deleuze means when he states that "each series . . . is not implied by the others without being in turn fully restored as that which implies them,"[31] is that repeating instances bear the trait which Dällenbach terms "aporetics"; that despite heterogeneity and exclusiveness they embed while being embedded within one another.

Being, we have established, repeats upon "unheard of" grounds. Leibniz, for whom "the ground plays a greater role"[32] than Hegel, is thus also a philosopher of multiplicity, of a "bacchanalian delirium." Leibniz discovers "the restlessness of the infinitely small."[33] If Aristotle dismissed the differences "in matter"—contingent by necessity—as mere accidents, for Leibniz the acute difference—ascribed with unprecedented ontological significance—is the "inessential." If contingent predicates such as Adam's "eating the apple" and Caesar's "crossing the Rubicon" are not as absolute as the lemmas of mathematics, they nonetheless suppose the sequence of things that God has freely chosen, "a sequence based on God's first free decree."[34] Infinitely small differences can generate utterly divergent worlds and the "small to infinity" in Leibniz's calculus nonetheless determines acute properties of the curve. But the contingent difference, the difference "in matter," embodies this "inessentiality" only in so far as it stands for singularity and specifity, not when reduced to *contrariety* (Adam ate/did not eat the apple). Worlds "vice-dict" rather than contradict each other, they oppose not within a preexisting universe but upon a ground "endemic" to the act of differentiation: "God did not create Adam as a sinner, but rather the world in which Adam sinned."[35] Like the infinitesimal, the "inessential" difference is indeterminable, it pertains less to the gap between distinctive features, than to the displacement of the ground upon which they differ. Worlds X and Y differ upon a ground generated by their very encounter, a ground comprising the very "aggregate" X and Y, a mise en abyme.

It is due to this mise en abyme that Leibniz's Law of Identity of the Indiscernibles cannot be received in isolation from his Law of Continuity. If each instance in a mise en abyme retroactively constitutes the whole upon onto which it is added, if it is composed of varying organizing principles, then mise en abyme is "indivisible" as no unitary measurement of division can apply: "Intensity is primarily implicated in itself: implicating and implicated . . . For this reason, intensity is neither divisible, like extensive quantity, nor indivisible like quality."[36] Divisibility is only possible when parts are "determined by the unit," not when they both embed and are being embedded within it.

Furthermore, it is due to mise en abyme that, despite indefinite posibilia, a world in Leibniz might assume the status of "actual" and even an ethical prerogative as the "best of all possible worlds," the *measure* of good. In mise en abyme—where an added circuit transforms the very object of duplication (from X to (X within X)) and consequently its very pattern and subject (from (X within X) to (Z within Z)), the ground upon which a variant emerges comprises a *series* of all other variants set in a new constellation, a new "compossibility" which the new, dominant or actual variant has cast by its very addition to that series. In Leibniz's words: "every substance involves in its present state all its past and future states and even expresses the whole universe *according to its point of view*."[37]

Finally, it is due to mise en abyme that monads, far from being distinctive points, are "pre-individual singularities."[38] As explained in chapter 1, in a mise en abyme of the type X within X, the indeterminate X turns from being a diegesis, a (literary) "universe," into a molecule or building block of universes whose form and identity incessantly change. It participates at once not only in units embodied by X, but also in units representable by polynomials such as (X within X), that is, Y, or ((X within X) within X), that is Z, etc. Like Deleuze's Go game pellet and unlike the chess piece, as we have seen, it bears only "situational properties" and a collective subject, an "It," that transforms upon a nomadic—rather than "sedentary"—space. It bears an identity which has no reality prior to the gestalt that contains it, but that gestalt in turn has no reality prior to the particular variant added to it. A gestalt comprising a conjunction of a, b, c, and d is discontinuous with one comprising a, b, and c, and has no reality prior to the addition of d.

Deleuze's proclaimed task is "to overturn Platonism,"[39] to deny the primacy of original over copy and to establish that "things are simulacra themselves."[40] But such overturning conserves many Platonic characteristics. Platonism indeed represents the subordination of difference to the powers of the One, the Analogous, the Similar, but like "an animal in the *process* of being tamed," the Heraclitan world "still growls in Platonism," and our mistake lies in trying to understand Platonic division on the basis of Aristotelian requirements. Platonic division is not a question of dividing a determinate genus into definite species. The method of division between the genus and its species, or between an origin and its copy, is rather selection among rivals, "the testing of claimants."[41] Plato allows such rivalry by introducing myths. The "simple play of myth" establishes circulation, both because it involves a further task to be performed, "an enigma to be resolved,"[42] and because (pre-Homeric) myths are recounted orally, so that each copy of an oral book—as we shall expand upon in chapter 7—differs from all others by mutations input by a specific reciter. Copies differ, for example, according to "rivalry between several cities for the birth of a hero."[43] If in all recounting of myths—by different agents and in different settings—any of the claimants is found salient, if it is found to be an "origin" before which others are copies, it is due to passing the test of repetition rather than judgment.

The other claimants, however, are not eradicated, but persist in the myth in their simulacral fashion. Derrida has already taught that the supplement supplements "originarily," at the very heart and outset of the origin; that it emerges equivalently rather than posteriorly to the latter. Deleuze argues similarly that "the essential contains the inessential in essence."[44] If the variant that outdoes the other claimants repeats as that which outdoes them, then so do those claimants—they align with the repeating dominant. But division is hence "capricious," "jump[ing] from one singularity to another."[45] Neither of the claimants can function as an anchor, a (sustainable) pivot in a hierarchy between the actual and the virtual; all claimants bear a potential "after," that of overthrowing or being overthrown. Repetition enables unpredictable changes of settings where a claimant ceases to assume the role of the dominant. It is this seriality, this inseparability of the actual from the non-actual, which Dällenbach, I argued in chapter 1, applies to the level of "elementary mises en abyme" in his typological model, assigning predominance to *both* the "mise en abyme of the utterance" *and* that of the "origin," thus turning the level of species into a "crowned anarchy."

But despite or rather due to this "capriciousness," the important lesson in Plato is again the ground difference brings along, its comprehensiveness. Once a claimant has been selected, the series of other claimants that come along with it, are "recruited" to form an ex-post "ground" that revolves around that claimant as a focal point. Plato's claimant—if victorious—transforms the enormous series of duplications and reduplications into the necessary basis of its "crowning." The dominant generates its own ground of justification: "Justice alone is just, says Plato."[46]

MISE EN ABYME AND THE PHILOSOPHY OF AFFIRMATION

The Heideggerian *Not* refers not to the negative in Being but to Being as difference. But does Heidegger conceive of difference radically enough?—"It would seem not," answers Deleuze, "given his critique of the Nietzschean Eternal Return."[47] For Heidegger, the basis of Nietzsche's Eternal Return lies in its *determination* of Being as becoming, its substantialization of becoming, so that "becoming" turns into a metaphysical principle, a "will to power in its most profound essence."[48] However, far from being an ideal that precedes and defines the instances of Being, Eternal Return, writes Deleuze, the "supreme repetition," is the "becoming *in itself*," it comprises *the very ideal* of becoming given to repetition. Eternal Return, writes Kir Kuiken, passes not between the identical and the same "but rather between the identical, the same or the similar . . . and the identical, the same and the similar understood as secondary powers,"[49] a vertical repetition, a repetition of that which has already doubled. Contrary to Derrida, Deleuze does follow Heidegger (as well as Hegel and Hyppolite) in maintaining that "philosophy can only be an ontology,"[50] but at at the same time, for Deleuze "there is no ontology of essence, there is only an ontology of sense,"[51] where the expression, like Spinoza's "mode," brings along the expressed, the substance or essence, that did not preexist it. Any difference between events upon a substance entails *at once* a more primordial difference: between those events and their double as sustained by a double of that substance; any difference between essences or rigid identities entails *at once* a difference between instances of that which grounds the two. Heidegger's failure to grasp the verticality of difference, the fact that the *crucial* ontological difference *prevails less between instances of repetition than between instances of that repetition given to repetition*—a mise en abyme—results in practice in subordinating the ontological difference to representation, in rendering it dependent on the possibility of a specific form.

Kuiken, who articulates the difference between Deleuze and Derrida in terms of their understanding of Nietzsche's Eternal Return, does so implicitly in terms of their acknowledgment of the mechanism of reconstitution which governs the mise en abyme. For him—as for Bearn—the "almost imperceptible difference" between the two passes between affirmation and negation. Whereas Derrida "is the one to insist on the reinscription of the simulacrizing effect, of its return in the necessary and irreducible undecidability of a dissimulation of dissimulation," Deleuze insists "on the *decidability* of the simulacrum."[52] If repetition repeats no first term, only what is already double; if there is no substance—in the form of a genetic or structural or other principle—to ground that repetition (unless given itself to repetition), then any actual which the Eternal Return selects out of other "claimants," would still be a simulacrum. If, as in a double mirror—where the mirroring object is itself reflected—the actual and the virtual return *aside one another*; if "the essential contains the inessential in essence"[53] at the very "outset" and "heart" of the essential, then one cannot discern the actual from the virtual. Yet, from this fact, Deleuze and Derrida infer completely different conclusions.

For Derrida, the Eternal Return "gives rise to the problematic of the limit and of the decision that would draw the line between the text of metaphysics and its other"[54]—or indeed between any two simulacral claimants. Since there is no "as such" of difference, only dissimulation or sheer dislocation, Derrida—who refrains in the name of difference from all logocentric discourse that as such ascribes entities with demarcation and individuality—bans any decision. He allows no salience to a particular variant; no claim of a variant for the status of "actual" or other prerogativeness. However, by keeping any potential dominant from transgressing its boundaries, from invading other claimants' "rubrics," Derrida "flattens" the difference between them. He keeps them discrete from one another, but thus—as we saw in chapter 2—confined to pre-established loci, and ultimately presupposing an allocating judgement, a totality.

It is indeed mise en abyme, what Kuiken here calls the "dissimulation of dissimulation," that gives rise in Derrida to "the problematic of the limit," but Deleuze's philosophy—Kuiken fails to stress—is also underlain by mise en abyme and the ambiguity it infuses into philosophy. Only that Deleuze would acknowledge the true nature of this ambiguity, the "double meaning" of the mise en abyme as previously introduced, the fact that radical and uncompromising as this ambiguity is, it coexists with—in fact, implies—a coherent whole made up of the very juxtaposition between its "disjuncts." If Derrida bans a "claimant" from assuming the status of an "actual," for Deleuze the Eternal Return is "the site, place, or territory where the discord between a 'being-in-the-world' and a 'virtual universe' . . . *is* decided."[55] The keyword here is "territory," ground. For Deleuze, each instance of the Eternal Return is a center of involution. Each instance assimilates, or retroactively transforms, all previous ones into a series conducted by or revolving around that particular instance; each return brings its own infrastructure with it, a substance set into action by the mode rather than vice versa: The Eternal Return "does not bring back 'the same,' but returning constitutes the only Same of that which becomes."[56] It is a special type of substance, here and now plenitude, generated rather than presupposed.

In Derrida's mechanism of iterability, an endeavor or an event is aborted *right* when the point is reached at which it is to become complete and coherent, but this implies instances of repetition confined to logical and epistemological boundaries set in advance, and a totalizing, "internalizing" mind setting them. Derrida's error, as we saw in chapter 2, was adopting the lacunal conception of mise en abyme that in practice treats the space of mise en abyme as homogenous, a pre-established substance. Derrida was well aware of the heterogeneity of the circuits in mise en abyme, but did not acknowledge—unless in our counter, textualistic, reading of *Limited Inc*—that heterogeneous reproductions imply the heterogeneity of *plenitudes*. For Deleuze, the dominant is indeed "formed from one mask to another . . . from one privileged instant to another,"[57] but the amalgamation that "crowns" it—despite being one among many—is a coherent whole. Like a new circuit added to a mise en abyme and thus transforming it, rendering its object of reproduction retroactively other, the dominant, added to a previous series, *displaces* that series. A "claimant"—if victorious—renders the entire series of duplications and reduplications as the setting which necessitates its emergence.

Deleuze's and Nietzsche's parable of this repetition of becoming is a unique game of dice to which we shall return in chapter 6. Whereas regular play is "distinct from ordinary life both as to locality and duration,"[58] that is, it consists in the bracketing out of the empirical world, in Deleuze's game it is not only the possibilities within the board that are played, gambled on, given to chance, but also the framing of that board—play's contingent, pragmatic circumstances:

A *throw* you made had failed. But what of that, you dice-throwers! You have not learned to play and mock as a man ought to play and mock!⁵⁹

The gambler's actual interaction with the game, his attitude toward the results of the dice rolls, are all further circuits of rolls and results: "Nothing is exempt from the game."⁶⁰ In this "Divine Game"—a mise en abyme due to having the game itself as its object—difference prevails not between segments of a dissected Being, but between instances of a "univocal Being." To say that the framing itself of this game is given to chance is to say—above all—that the rules of the game are given to chance. Difference prevails not between instances governed by a set of game rules, but rather between instances of that which grounds the game, two instances of the very set of rules given to repetition. Each roll is paradoxically rolled within a set of rules, a framework that did not exist prior to that roll. If the boundary between an affirmative and a negative philosophy passes "between a Derridean game you can never win and a Deleuzian game you can never lose,"⁶¹ it is not because the latter lacks rules, but because each roll brings its rules along with it; "tailor made" ones that would render it "necessarily winning."

Correspondingly, if Derrida's act of signification was—despite Derrida's antimetaphysical endeavors—trapped in a pre-established unity, if, like a squash ball, it "bounces off" the wall set up by a generality, "and fall[s] back onto the strata," Deleuze's linguistic instances "cross the barrier [to] reach the unformed, destratified element of the plane of consistency."⁶² In Derrida's iterability, the signifier is confined to possibilities within a domain segregated in advance. These possibilities are well distinguished from the boundaries, that is the conditions of the "game." They are confined to a meaning and place derived from those boundaries, and cannot transgress the threshold into the other level—where matter and concepts are made rather than given. In Deleuze, on the other hand, acts of signification "break on through to the other side of representation,"⁶³ writes Bearn, and the other side they leap to, the "plane of consistency"—Bearn fails to develop—is not a void. It is an unimaginable rather than pre-established ground, such that did not exist prior to that act, yet a plenitude all the same, "chance is not liberated by the breaking of regular verse: on the contrary, it is subject to the exact law of the form that responds to it and to which it must respond."⁶⁴

To untie linguistics from postulates of "deep structure," whether syntactical, morphological, or phonological—Deleuze would introduce a special speech-act-theory, a radical pragmatics where "the meaning and syntax of language can no longer be defined independently of the speech acts they presuppose."[65] Each proposition—in accordance with the *singularity* of the act that conveys it—would bring its own, "endemic" code and syntax with it. Sense, writes Deleuze, "is strictly copresent to . . . its own cause and determines the cause as an imminent cause."[66] Not only does sense not exist outside of the proposition which expresses it, but it is also the "attribute of the state of affairs,"[67] namely it reconstitutes empirical "things" while denoting them. In *Cinema 1* the expression "state of affairs" or "state of things" similarly designates reality or rather its hegemonic mode—"individual characters and social roles, objects with uses, real connections between these objects and these people,"[68] all confined to (coded) identities and representations within a pre-established unity. There is also, however, the molecular aspect of reality, sustained by "affects" or "qualia" which cannot be reduced to the state of things. A police report of a murder scene would record the victim, the lamp, the bread-knife, the assassin. But there are also, writes Deleuze, referring to Pabst's 1929 film *Pandora's Box*, "the brightness of the light on the knife, the blade of the knife under the light, Jack's terror and resignation, Lulu's compassionate look."[69] Now the interesting point is that these singular, here-and-now qualities which the report would not include constitute, nevertheless—as cinema well exploits—the "expressed" of the state of things—the face of reality. The affect—like a face with regard to a body—"does not exist independently of something which expresses it, although it is completely distinct from it."[70] It "*gathers* and expresses the affect as a complex entity, and secures the virtual conjunctions between singular points of this entity (the brightness, the blade, the terror, the compassionate look)."[71] The paradox is that the state of things, despite logical precedence to their qualia, cannot be concretized—and hence be real—prior to the qualia. The qualia reconstitute the state of things which they merely express, and are therefore mises en abyme: "it is only in the Mobius strip, unfolding and untwisting, that the dimension of sense appears for itself."[72]

Like a circuit upon a mise en abyme, a given, here-and-now act of signification reconstitutes the constellation upon which all other acts of signification were performed. Rather than being discrete, as in Derrida's iterability, the entire web of language is "recruited" and assimilated by the single instance of signification, rendering the compatibility of intention and its object self-evident. We saw previously how iterability, where the sign represents an intentionality without an intentum, ruins all hope of ever meaning one single serious thing. However, in opposition to Derrida's incompleteness of signification (as in our first, "transcendent," reading of *Limited Inc*), where an act is stillborn, vanishing before fulfilment, in our textualistic reading of Derrida, as well as in Deleuze, the act of signification is fated to succeed. Saussure is the thinker "who puts the arbitrary character of the sign and the differential character of the sign at the very foundation of general semiology,"[73] writes Derrida, but Deleuze acknowledges that arbitrariness and fatedness come hand in hand. To say that the signifier and signified did not exist as such prior to their arbitrary encounter is to say that the dyad emerged upon a constellation it itself has generated; that the dyad emerged upon a ground revolving around and necessitating that very encounter. "Derrida is unable to say Yes, because he thinks Yes must always have a point,"[74] writes Bearn, but to be precise Derrida (in our "transcendent" rather than "textualistc" reading) is unable to say Yes because he thinks Yes must have a *predetermined* point. It is not the case, inversely, that Deleuze's Yes is "as pointless as a work of art,"[75] as Bearn believes. An intention does bear an intentum and an act of signification does aim at a "true meaning," but just as each instance of duplication in mise en abyme paradoxically reconstitutes (in fact generates) the infinite set of duplications to which it was added, this "true meaning" does not come to existence prior to the specific act of signification that aims toward it.

Establishing such (ad hoc) plenitudes in the midst of pursuing difference (that rather breaks with structural closures), Deleuze, like Dällenbach and Blanchot, exercises an "economical" approach, a systematic ambiguity derived from the double bind nature of the mise en abyme as presented in chapter 1. Such an approach is preeminent in Deleuze's concept of repetition. There are two types of repetition, he writes:

> The first repetition is repetition of the Same, explained by the identity of the concept or presentation; the second includes difference . . . One is static, the other dynamic. One is repetition in the effect, the other in the cause. One is extensive, the other intensive. One is horizontal, the other vertical. One is developed and explicated, the other enveloped and in need of interpretation. One is revolving, the other evolving. One involves equality, commensurability and symmetry; the other is grounded in inequality, incommensurability and dissymmetry . . . One is a "bare" repetition, the other a covered repetition, which forms itself in covering itself, in masking and disguising itself.[76]

The first type of repetition is governed by generality and its instances are already taken over by their representations. The second is the Deleuzian type of repetition, the "repetition for itself," which functions as the "infrastructure" of the first type, its "interiority" and "heart," "the condition for repetition prior to any consideration of a repeated thing."[77] However, what Deleuze here stresses is that *the reverse is also true*: The repetition-for-itself "forms itself in covering itself, in masking and disguising itself," it can prevail *only* if disguised by a represented form of repetition. In other words, though opposing elements, the repetition-for-itself and the mechanical repetition co-depend, or rather, the repetition-for-itself comprises two coexisting orders, not only itself, but also its Other. It comprises less the repetition which breaks from representation, than the *middle* between these two orders. This *coexistence* between the equal and the unequal at the heart of repetition; this "play of the *unity* of stems and their difference,"[78] renders the concept of difference in Deleuze's thought "an object of affirmation."[79] Pure difference entails or rather consists not only of that which differs, but also the plenitude from which the former has broken. Only this double bind can be compatible with the dissymmetry of difference, the fact that "the distinguished opposes something which cannot distinguish itself from it."[80]

Deleuze, unlike Derrida, does not eradicate "logocentrism" from language and philosophy. To the contrary, he asserts, "intensity is individuating." True, a selected actual cannot serve as a sustainable pivot in a hierarchy between the actual and the virtual, and is always in danger of being disavowed, but this potential does not prevent it from bearing a coherent and demarcated identity, in as much as the latter consists of a contraction of all antecedent (and even anticipated) "claimants" established by the very addition of the claimant at stake and directed by it: "The act of individuation consists . . . in integrating the elements . . . of the disparateness into a state of . . . internal resonance."[81] Deleuze was willing first and foremost to adhere to an individuated and privileged concept of doubleness: the actual Gidean emblem of mise en abyme. It is true at the same time that this emblem granted Deleuze the idea of a "resonance" of the Different and the Same in the first place.

To conclude: Attentive to the actual emblem of the mise en abyme and to what poeticians (such as Jean Ricardou) had to say about it, Deleuze was alert to three interrelated features of the mise en abyme:

First, mise en abyme consists in a "double meaning" or "double bind." It comprises less the small-scale segment that reflects the whole—the "other in the text" that "disrupts" the structural closure which the main narrative has cast—than the very "assemblage" between these two incommensurable narrative levels.

Second, and by force of the double bind nature of the mise en abyme, is the principle of simultaneity. Incommensurable narrative levels of the mise en abyme, and incommensurable variants in general, nonetheless coexist: "the essential point is the simultaneity and contemporaneity of all the divergent series, the fact that all coexist,"[82]

Third, and by force of the principle of simultaneity, is the principle of reconstitution. Every instance of mise en abyme reconstitutes the (accumulative) chain of circuits to which it was added. A mise en abyme of the type X within X into which a duplicating circuit X is added is transformed by this very action of duplication. Its new object of duplication is no longer X, but (X within X), that is, Y. The instance of repetition contracts all antecedent and even anticipated ones into a constellation, a "compossibility"—in Leibniz's words—thus establishing a decisiveness in its favor and generating its own ground of justification.

Dismissing the logocentricity of mise en abyme—the actual concept and emblem as developed by poeticians—Derrida at a fatal moment adopts instead the "lacunal conception" of the mise en abyme where there is a switch to the next logical level whenever the point is reached at which the circuit would have to get completed. As in this lacunal conception, what fuels repetition in Derrida's articulation of iterability is an inherent incompleteness of representation. Careful attention to the traits of mise en abyme as stemming from the Gidean emblem, however, reveals a severe flaw in both the lacunal conception and Derrida's iterability. Both comprise radically discrete variants which imply as such pre-established loci within a pre-established unity onto which these variants have been distributed in advance by a presupposed organizing principle, a totalitarianism that fits badly with Derrida's heterological endeavors.

For Deleuze, on the other hand, mise en abyme bestows the acknowledgment that incommensurable variants coexist, and that the "difference-in-itself" is ironically to be articulated in terms of this (ad hoc) plenitude. Mise en abyme, taught poeticians, is less the "revolt" of the autonomous, reflective segment against the "hegemonic" text—to use Ricardou's terminology—than a dialectics of "revolt" and "counterattack." Therefore, difference demands an affirmation not only of that which differs, but also the plenitude from which the former has broken. It is one of the ironies of Gilles Deleuze, writes Todd May, that "the thinker of multiplicities, of haecceities, disjunctions, and irreducible intersecting series, is also the thinker of the univocity of being."[83] Difference for Deleuze is vertical, a mise en abyme. It is less the Other that challenges totality than the very "middle" between the Other-than-totality and the totality it challenges, the very assemblage between incommensurable variants, that as such is compatible with no taxonomical order.

THE PROSPECTIVE MISE EN ABYME AND THE SYNTHESIS OF THE PRESENT

Deleuze's three syntheses of time are associated, respectively, with Hume, Bergson, and Nietzsche. In the first synthesis, the Humean, which Deleuze calls the "passive synthesis of habit," habit and imagination establish, by means of contraction of repeating instants, a line of time. This synthesis contracts the successive independent instants into one another, thereby constituting the lived, or living, present. The contemplating self is where this synthesis takes place, but Deleuze's ontology is far from being anthropocentric. A soul must in fact be attributed even "to the rat in the labyrinth and to each muscle of the rat,"[84] though a contemplative soul whose entire function is to contract instances—or rather serve as *the very seam between them*. Deleuze coins here in fact a new usage of the term "subject," "no longer the subject of an action, nor therefore the human subject, but rather a passive subject."[85] Habit "*draws* something new from repetition—namely, difference,"[86] meaning that the contemplating self is the *agent* of difference, rather than a subject of generalization, it is the *site in which variants come into a relationship*. This site is mise en abyme, because the instants to be contracted, like Blanchot's "il y a," encounter by definition prior to there being the line of time, therefore upon no ground other than the ad hoc one formed by their very encounter, and which the self embodies.

Being a mise en abyme, the contemplative subject is passive due to always already repeating a double: "we speak of our 'self' only in virtue of those thousands of little witnesses which contemplate within us."[87] This is to say that to this living present belong both the past and the future constituted in time as dimensions of this present. The passive subject transforms from the particulars which it envelops by contraction to the general which it develops in the field of its expectation. An instance, adjoined to previous ones, forms together with them—contracted—the living present, but it was "selected" to adjoin them by force of a primordial juxtaposition in the first place, a "virtual" encounter, embodied by the mind and which conditions both the given (contracted) variants, and the anticipation of the non-given one. The human subject is not a self-sufficient principle for this activity of retention and anticipation. Like "an actor play[ing] . . . [while] beholding himself playing"[88]—Bergson's metaphor for the paradoxes of time—absorption and transformation of particulars entail a subject *acting while contemplating himself acting*. It involves our "thousands of little witnesses" too. A contemplation is a repetition (with difference) not only of the contemplated, synthesized instants, but also of *the synthesis itself*. The synthesis of the present, a mise en abyme, involves "innumerable micro-constructions, which literally go all the way down, there are no instants in themselves that are subsequently synthesized; rather the instants are themselves differentials."[89] There are no fundamental instants, no first time, but each instance is always already split in two, embedding while being embedded within others: The many selves "are all different syntheses *of one another*."[90]

Deleuze chooses however not to ascribe an aporetic quality to this particular mise en abyme, no potential to cause "irreparable damage to the consecutive order of time," to paraphrase Dällenbach.[91] He reserves that for the second and third syntheses of time. The order of time established by the first synthesis is rather characterized by continuity, and the mise en abyme that might well represent the first synthesis of time is the simple type, especially the "prospective mise en abyme," which despite *hinting* at severe paradoxes, generally "respects our prevalent beliefs about empirical reality."[92] Oedipus's recognition for example, "can only come about once the information suggested by the oracles is confirmed by the results of Oedipus's rational-empirical investigation." The Oracle's utterances may be termed "prophetic" "but that is not directly relevant to temporal anachrony in narrative,"[93] as indeed the story might have been developed so as to prove them misleading.

The prospective mise en abyme, taking place at the start of a narrative, provides a "double" for the fiction in order to "overtake" it. The reader, like the novel itself, "is also 'oriented.' "[94] As in Deleuze's first synthesis of time, the transformation between retention and expectation which the contemplating subject or reader embodies is passive, "oriented" by an undercurrent of micro-contractions rather than judgment. The prospective mise en abyme restricts the fiction's room for maneuver "because the remainder of the narrative is fated: tolerating its own revelation by a precursor, it must follow the latter's directives."[95] It is "fated" in the sense that the mise en abyme provides the directives for its reading, it affects the reader's interpretation of the work and his recognition of important parts. But as in Deleuze's first synthesis, where the actual future might well differ from the possibilities which the contemplating-self awaits, the plot which embeds the prospective mise en abyme, as we have already discussed in our second reading of Derrida, might yet twist from the "fate" ordered of it by the latter. Ricardou has shown with his "challenge-revenge" mechanism how such twists "swarm" beneath every prospective mise en abyme, and inevitably come to actuality in some.

THE RETRO-PROSPECTIVE MISE EN ABYME AND THE SYNTHESIS OF THE PAST

The claim of the present is precisely that it passes. But the static line of time which the first synthesis creates cannot account for such passage. While the first synthesis is the "foundation" of time, the "empirical" or apparent time, the second is the "ground" of time. We have seen in chapter 3 how for Blanchot every grounding "earth" always already transforms into a grounded "world," entailing as such another ground or "night"—the "night before the night"—a mise en abyme. Similarly, the ground of time according to Deleuze is *another* time upon which time, constituted by the first synthesis, passes. The second synthesis is hence formulated as mise en abyme right from the outset: "This is the paradox of the present: to constitute time while passing in the time constituted. We cannot avoid the necessary conclusion—that there must be another time in which the first synthesis of time can occur." [96]

The second synthesis is Bergsonian. The "other time" upon which the present passes is the "pure past" which has never been present. Bergson holds duration to be

> . . . the reflux of the past into the present, arguing that because the mark of the past remains in the present, no mechanistic understanding of causality and no linear conception of time can adequately capture the vitality of life. The past remains present as a virtual temporality in addition to the past, present, and future of linear chronological time.[97]

The dominance of the past in Bergson's concept of duration, the fact that the present includes the past in principle and not merely in fact, and that "[p]ractically, we perceive only the past,"[98] implies the heterogeneity of the duration. Time in Bergson's duration "has to split itself in two at each moment as present and past, which differ from each other in nature, or, what amounts to the same thing, it has to split the present in two heterogeneous directions, one of which is launched towards the future while the other falls into the past."[99] Like mise en abyme and the "difference in itself" consisting in a state of "double bind," every moment in Bergson's duration is already split into two dissymmetrical jets, one of which makes all the present pass on, while the other preserves all the past. The continuity of the duration hence holds within itself "the seeds of its own discontinuity and differentiation":[100] What Bergson means by stating that "every perception is already memory,"[101] is that every perception is found to be memory by a mechanism of retroaction, hence belonging at once to heterogeneous dimensions. The duration consists not of a single, but of multiple, heterogeneous threads of memory. Every perception, transformed into memory, reconstitutes the series that precedes it while coexisting with the original series. The threads that weave time are not horizontal lines of succession, but "vertical transmissions within a duration";[102] antecedent series "insist" within the reconstituted past, *even following that reconstitution.*

Bergson illustrates such reconfiguration of a series accounting for how a skillful chess player may be able to play several games at once without looking at the chessboards. Such play indeed involves a "visual memory," yet "the image of the chess-board with its pieces is not presented to the memory, clean cut and ready-made, as in a mirror," instead "at every move in the games the player has to make an effort of reconstruction."[103] The player mentally recounts the *history* of the game from the beginning, but not as a series of consecutive moves, but as a coherent whole, a gestalt, an idea of the whole which enables him to visualize the elements. Like Deleuze's Divine Game (as we shall see in chapter 6), this play depends upon the reconstituting of the successive events which have brought about the present situation in light of a new axis which the fresh move (still anticipated) embodies; every fresh move is a point zero fitting all previous ones into a new history, a constellation through which they are to be retroactively comprehended. In this sense it generates a different game "with a character entirely of its own."[104]

The dominance of the "edge" move, constitutive of the game in entire and bestowing it its form and *raison d'être*, subtracts nothing from the pluralism inherent to the game. A *single game* is a multiplicity of heterogeneous, discontinuous, yet coexisting games, each of which is a coherent whole: the set a-b-c "insists," as a coherent whole, within the new one, a-b-c-d—a mise en abyme. A multiplicity of plenitudes can populate the same duration, because time "is not the interior in us,"[105] a monolithic object, "internalized" by mind, but to the contrary "the only subjectivity"—

a univocal, hence pluralized, whole. Like Derrida's "text," this subjectivity, while retaining the divide between inside and outside, the virtual and the actual, the text and the "hors-texte," renders them interchangeable. In the multiple chess-game example, whilst every new move in this game reconfigures all that precede it, it cannot take place unless the player recalls the game, but hence already reconfigures it. The player reconfigures the game, so to say, prior to reconfiguring it. In order to play he must identify the game, but in order to identify it, there is need for the new move to orient the course of events and provide the game its "character." When performing the move in actuality, the player only doubles *what has already been performed in virtuality*, that which "without being or resembling an actual x, has nonetheless the capacity to bring about x"[106]—a mise en abyme. That the "virtual" in Deleuze is a mise en abyme of the actual is apparent in the example he gives from developmental psychology:

> On the one hand, the child goes beyond the bound excitations towards the supposition or the intentionality of an object, such as the mother, as the goal of an effort, the end to be actively reached "in reality" . . . But *on the other hand and at the same time*, the child constructs for itself another object, a quite different kind of object which is a *virtual* object . . . or centre and which then governs and compensates for the progresses and failures of its real activity: it puts several fingers in its mouth, wraps the other arm around this virtual centre, and appraises the whole situation from the point of view of this virtual mother.[107]

A child's active endeavor to walk toward an actual mother is conditioned by a diminutive icon of the act, a virtual walking toward a virtual mother.

Deleuze subsequently presents four further paradoxes of the past aimed to establish that Bergson's duration—a mise en abyme—"is defined less by succession than by coexistence."[108] Let us demonstrate how the four parallel four aspects of the mise en abyme.

The first paradox is "the contemporaneity of the past with the present that it *was*": "no present would ever pass were it not past 'at the same time' as it is present; no past would ever be constituted unless it were first constituted 'at the same time' as it was present."[109] If a present had to await the arrival of a new present in order to be constituted as past, then it would continue to wait—and us with it—in a perpetual and frozen presence, "the only way for the present to pass is if it passes while it is present—if the past is given along with itself as present and is internally implicated in it."[110] This paradox parallels, I believe, the Gidean principle of retroaction, according to which the reflecting segment cannot reflect the whole without being transformed due to that very action, turning retroactively into the very object of reflection. In Blanchot's version of the paradox, the point of destination of a leap toward the exterior becomes retroactively that of departure, so that the leap itself repeats upon multiple logical levels. Correspondingly, in Deleuze's first paradox the past, the other-than-presence toward which a passing present is headed, is constituted in contemporaneity with the leap. It becomes retroactively the point of departure, the "other time in which the first synthesis of time can occur."[111] The mechanism of retroaction is mainly manifested in the retro-prospective mise en abyme, a type which consists, as we saw, in "including the 'fulfillment' at the very heart of the 'expectation.'" Since Heinrich, to take Novalis's example, possesses a book which recounts his entire past, every present, opened for future possibilities, is at the same time—as in Deleuze's first paradox of time—a fulfilled past, it is retroactively discovered to be *already* recounted in that book.

The second paradox is that of coexistence. If each past is contemporaneous with the present that it was, then "*all* of the past coexists with the new present in relation to which it is now past."[112] In terms of mise en abyme, if circuit X represents time and circuit X' represents the "other" time upon which the first passes, then due to the exponential and aporetic nature of the mise en abyme the entire, infinite set of duplications of the gap between these two is at once duplicated at any "infinitely small" level, specifically: In the very interval X-X'. Therefore, the entire past is confined between X and X'. In terms of Heinrich's paradox, the book, recounting each instance of Heinrich's present passing into the past, is, at the same time, an object in that past, so that Heinrich's *entire* past—folded in that book which recounts all passing presents—is contemporaneous with a specific past.

The third paradox, that of "pre-existence," derives from the first. If the past is contemporaneous with the present that it *was*, "we necessarily speak of a past which never *was* present,"[113] "a pure, general, *a priori* element of all time,"[114] which conditions the present. If circuits of mise en abyme can symbolize instances of the past, and if those instances—due to mise en abyme's exponentiality—persist in duplicating and reduplicating centripetally, even when no new, centrifugal circuit—representing the present—is added, then that past is a past which never was present.

The fourth paradox derives from the second as well as from the third: "Not only does the past coexist with the present that has been, but, as it preserves itself in itself (while the present passes), it is the whole integral past."[115] If the past pre-exists the present in general, then the past is not dependent on the present for its existence. Rather, the past "preserves itself in itself." This paradox, writes Deleuze, is the meaning of the famous Bergsonian metaphor of the cone where the whole past "coexists with *itself*, in varying degrees of relaxation and of contraction at an infinity of levels."[116] Bergson's inverted cone, SAB (Figure 4.1), represents the totality of the recollections accumulated in memory. Whenever a recollection appears in consciousness, it descends from the heights of the motionless base, AB, situated in the past and comprising pure, unconscious memory, down through different regions of the past to the precise point where the action is taking place. The summit, S, indicates at all times my present, and unceasingly touches "the moving plane p of my actual representation of the universe."[117] It is inserted into the plane, and this participation in the plane "implies that my body is more than a mathematical point, . . . with the cone image, we are dealing with factual perception."[118] "Factual perception" does not imply a

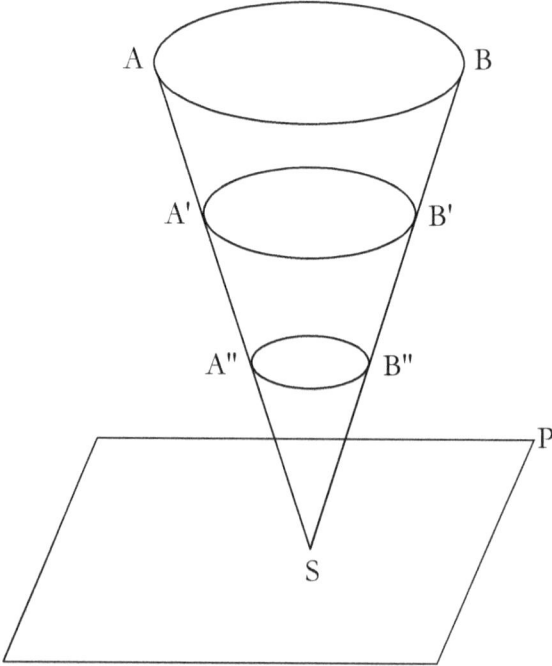

Figure 4.1. Bergson's cone of memory.

purely sensory-motor state, it is complex and concrete because it is mixed with, or "impregnated" by memories. The sensory-motor state S

> . . . only marks out the present direction of memory, being nothing else, in fact, than its actual and acting extremity . . . this memory itself, with the totality of our past, is continually pressing forward, so as to insert the largest possible part of itself into the present action.[119]

The extreme of actuality only marks the direction of memory, it is a function of difference and repetition, or the outermost event that reconstitutes memory only to retroactively occur within boundaries, *always already within memory*. From this double effort result, at every moment, an infinite number of possible states of memory, figured by the sections A'B' and A"B" (sharing the same apex S) in Bergson's diagram. Each section of the cone "is larger or smaller according to its nearness to the base or to the summit," and yet these sections are "repetitions of the whole of our past life,"[120] each includes "not particular elements of the past, but always the totality of the past."[121] The cone is a mise en abyme because, as in Gide's escutcheon, any level of the past, any embedded cone, nonetheless reflects the embedding cone in entirety—the "whole past." In terms of the retro-prospective mise en abyme, if the plot in *Heinrich*, the series of actions, is both the subject of the story—thus constituting "actual time"—and its object—thus serving as a virtual time in a story *already recounted*—the work comprises the whole past as a parallel "thread of memory," autonomous to the present.

If the memories are descending toward the summit, writes Leonard Lawlor, and images are ascending up from the bottom, if the difference between matter and memory consists in these two opposite directions,

> then we have to say that the cone image as Bergson presents it is incomplete; there is a second cone, a cone of matter, below the cone of memory. Being a double, like a mirror image, this second cone would have to be the inverse of the first.[122]

However, given that the concept of "mirror" Bergson uses, and Lawlor here alludes to, is—as I show in chapter 5—a double mirror, internal to that which it mirrors, I believe that the "second cone" Lawlor describes is in fact embodied by the centripetal movement of doubles *within* the single cone of memory. The mirror cone Lawlor speculates on, the cone of matter, does not comprise a stream of pure sensory-data. Being a *Bergsonian cone*, as defined above, each datum is always already appropriated by a series. It is saturated with meaning and telos as generated by that series, and is a function of historical strata and pragmatic needs rather than a priori principles. Such future series is therefore itself a thread of memory; the (speculative) cone of matter comprises less a series of future presents, than a series of *future pasts*. Its stream of images does descend from its base towards its summit (which it shares with the cone of memory), but it retroactively does so while embedded within the cone of memory, doubling rather than countering the stream descending from the pure past toward the actual present—a mise en abyme. By arguing for the cone of matter as inhabiting the cone of memory, I by no means seek to override dualist conceptions of Bergson. The dyad Matter-Memory is indeed crucial in Bergson. Rather, I suggest that, like the actual and virtual in post-structuralist philosophy of simulacra, the difference between the two exceeds contradiction, which is "less than difference and not more."[123]

MISE EN ABYME AND "SCHEMA" IN KANT AND BERGSON

The transition from Deleuze's second to his third synthesis of time passes through a discussion of Kant in relation to Descartes. Descartes's Cogito is operated with two logical values: determination and undetermined existence. The determination ("I think") implies an undetermined existence ("I am"), and determines it precisely as the existence of a thinking subject.[124] The Kantian critique, on the other hand, amounts to objecting, against Descartes, that it is impossible for determination to bear *directly* upon the undetermined. We have previously found in Iser (drawing implicitly on Blanchot) that the fictionalizing act mediates between the imaginary and the real; that the real cannot be grafted onto the imaginary by means of a Jakobsonian function of selection without that selection retroactively taking part in a *third domain*, i.e., the fictive. Iser's third domain is not therefore a synthesized middle, or a being at all, but a function of difference, deterritorialization of the very gaze toward the imaginary. Kant, according to Deleuze, follows this (Blanchotian) logic of discontinuity. Kant's third logical value, the "determinable," is more than its embodiment by schemata, or "forms of experience," through which the categories are applicable to intuitions and sense-impressions. It rather amounts to a "discovery of Difference"—"no longer in the form of an external difference which separates, but in the form of an internal difference which establishes an a priori relation between thought and being."[125] The crucial transcendental difference is not stretched between features of a (logical) category, or even between categories. It no longer assumes the form of an empirical difference, stretched between two determinations. It is rather a *vertical* difference, stretched between the determination as such and what it determines, between the very conditioning difference and the difference which it conditions.

Critics were highly concerned about Kant's "schema" intervening between our concept and our experience: "What could that be, and isn't there a danger that once we have found that we might need yet another intermediary to apply *it* to our experience, and thus be off on an infinite regress?"[126] However, if we follow Deleuze, the transcendental difference does not affect the empirical one by force of mechanical repetition, like an ideal to a cliché, and the schema does not stand for the linear succession that such mechanicalness implies. The schema, vertical, mediates to intuition not the category, but rather its very "crossing" into the sense data; the very difference between the aggregate which the two form, and that aggregate taken to the nth power. The schema, like the Deleuzian "map" we shall later discuss, mediates between the a priori and the appearances *by being a mise en abyme of this very relation*. Kant proposes

> that the schemata must be various "transcendental time-determinations," features of the structure of time or of relations in time, that can be associated with the categories. Such transcendental time-determinations will be "homogeneous" with the categories because they are universal and *a priori*, but will also be homogeneous with "appearance insofar as time is contained in every empirical representation."[127]

But it is mise en abyme alone, "intervening as an element of metasignification," yet "continuing to signify like any other utterance," as Dällenbach showed, that can be "homogenous" with both transcendental determinations and apearances. An immanent transcendental determination, performed "at the level of the characters," mise en abeme alone can function as Kant's schema.

Kant's discovery is that despite the fact that sensory data or empirical concepts are structured by a priori forms, these forms depend on things as well: "Thoughts without content are empty, intuitions without concepts are blind."[128] However, the synthesis between a priori forms and sensory matter, determination and the undetermined, is an "assemblage" between disparate parties rather than a coherent dialectics caused by a qualitative precedence of the forms over the matter. What Deleuze calls the "*a priori* relation between thought and being" is therefore the mise en abyme that such assemblage—a deterritorialized encounter—implies, the fact that this synthesis can only occur upon a preceding reproduction—with difference—of itself. It is the mechanism of retroaction entailed in such double that underlies the Copernican Revolution[129] and it is this gap—not the a priori forms per se—which serves as the transcendental condition for knowledge. Furthermore, it is due to this mise en abyme that time is the form under which undetermined existence is determinable, and that together with space it is the intuition that "underlies all intuitions."[130] According to Kant, the representation of space cannot be obtained through experience from the relations of outer appearance since "this outer experience is itself possible at all only through that representation."[131] To rephrase, the *very differenc*e between the subject—with its a priori forms of space and time—and the world of appearances is conditioned by that intuition of space. Similarly, time is not an empirical concept that has been derived from any experience:

> Neither coexistence nor succession would ever come within our perception, if the representation of time were not presupposed as underlying them a priori. Only on the presupposition of time can we represent to ourselves a number of things as existing at one and the same time (simultaneously) or at different times (successively).[132]

If the encounter between the subject and the world is actual, if it takes place in the world of appearance, it is due to the subject and its intuition of time *being already in time*. Only *in time* "is actuality of appearances possible at all."[133] Any synthesis between forms and data entails a mise en abyme. It entails *another dyad* of actively casted a priori forms and passively received sensory matter; it entails another transcendental ego against which the first one becomes a passive and indeed mere phenomenal one:

> The spontaneity of which I am conscious in the "I think" cannot be understood as the attribute of a substantial and spontaneous being, but only as the affection of a passive self which experiences its own thought—its own intelligence, that by virtue of which it can say I—being exercised in it and upon it but not by it.[134]

Bergson's criticism against Kant amounts to maintaining that a priori conditions must be rather conceived as temporally determined and experiencible.

But the mise en abyme, the principle of retroaction rather than final halt, governing both the interaction between Kant's a priori (the categories) and sense-data, and the interaction between Bergson's a priori (the past that has never been present) and sense-data (or rather memory images), renders Kant's critical philosophy contributive to Bergson, more than the latter perhaps realized.

In particular, in developing the concept of "dynamic schema"—and it would be surprising if Bergson does not allude by it to Kant—Bergson perhaps inherits from Kant the idea of schema as mise en abyme of the encounter between the a priori and the sense-data. What the chess player from Bergson's previous example remembers is "a representation of the whole which enables him at any moment to visualize the elements."[135] The representation of the whole, which Bergson qualifies as abstract, writes Lawlor, is like a physiognomy, "the 'physiognomy' of each game is singular and unified, although the elements of the game are reciprocally implicated in this single representation. The single physiognomy of each game gives him an impression of each game *sui generis*."[136] Rather than symbolically, the schema outlines its object physiognomicaly, or iconically. It stands for its object in a relation of resemblance rather than (universalizable) correspondence. However, Lawlor's characterizing of the schema in terms of "physiognomy" cannot in itself resolve the paradox we have previously extracted from this example, namely how can the player perform a correct move within a game, a reconstituted whole, a *physiognomy*, which did not exist prior to the completion of the movement?

The solution for this difficulty lies, perhaps, in the fact that the iconic signification characterizing the schema is rather a mise en abyme. The crucial physiognomy is perhaps less the one involved in relation R_0, between a game and its "internal organization"—a representation whose elements are reciprocally implicated—but rather the *second degree physiognomy*, pertaining to a relation of relations, between R_0 and the relation to come R_1, once the moving of the chess piece reconfigures these elements. Indeed, the image Bergson provides to help us understand the dynamic schema and its movement is the pyramid, but the pyramid, writes Lawlor, is a variation on Bergson's famous cone image of memory in *Matter and Memory*.[137] With the dynamic schema being the summit, and perceptual images being the base, in the pyramid as in the cone, the hypothetical solution the player has "in mind," is the movement "down from the plane of ideal, incorporeal or spiritual representations to the sensible, corporeal or material images."[138] Far from being a static, mediating synthesis, the pyramid, like Kant's schema, comprises a representation of a dynamic dyad:

> The descending movement encounters obstacles. The encounter with obstacles is very important for understanding the schema's dynamism, that is, for understanding its ability to be transformed. These obstacles are matter, either the memory images of things actually perceived or the perceptual images of things.[139]

The schema, mediating between the a priori past and the present matter, is nothing but a diminutive double of the relation between the two, a mise en abyme.

THE KLEIN-BOTTLE AND THE SYNTHESIS OF THE FUTURE

With Kant's division between the active (synthesizing, transcendental) ego and the passive (empirical) one hardly settled through a grounding identity, Deleuze views Kant's project of critical philosophy as heralding Nietzsche's fractured ego. What characterizes Nietzsche's Eternal Return, inspiring Deleuze's third synthesis of time, is time's "going out of joint." What I will here argue is that a new type of mise en abyme, qualitatively different from that of Bergson, underlies this new type of time.

Nietzsche's Eternal Return—"by itself the third time in the series, the future as such"[140]—marks a "caesura," a leap from the duration of time. With Nietzsche, "no future to come could come to compose with or be grafted on this time; . . . be an addition or a supplement to the originary and the fundamental."[141] Although Bergson introduces difference into time, writes Widder, his duration serves to ground representation, and his insistence on its continuity "works to safeguard the coherence of the ego."[142] This is a debatable assertion, given the fact that Deleuze has *just* chosen Bergson's duration—with its past that has never been present and cannot be presentiated—for the sake of ruining the doctrine of representation and the totalitarianism it implies. The leap from time as a coherent whole indeed marks a breaking through of the boundaries of representation, of hierarchized, homogenized time and space, but the duration contains such leaps at its very heart. In Bergson "contracting the whole in each present, each present takes up another level of the whole, and each life takes up another life, which is also at another level."[143] Each "thread" of memory, each "slice" of the cone, embodies past events *contracted upon an entirely new, "unimaginable" ground*, hence comprising an utterly new "life" heterogeneous to all others. Bergson's duration is indeed an "indivisible" space, but "the continuity of duration is also discontinuity, divergence and scission."[144] Difference in Bergson's duration, as in mise en abyme, *precisely* consists in a double articulation, an interplay of the equal and the unequal, of pure difference *and* that difference objectified or represented. In fact, reading de Man, Patricia Lawlor invoked the retro-prospective mise en abyme—which we have shown to ground the Bergsonian, second, synthesis—in a context rather similar to Deleuze's third synthesis, namely de Man's view of the "modernist project" as the endeavor to "distance [one]self from a historical continuum."[145]

Is the third synthesis therefore fairly redundant to the second one? Does it bear a mere didactic role of accentuating one of the two slopes already developed in the second synthesis? Dorothea Olkowski provides us with a clue for another possibility:

> Each is thrown back into the past, the past of Laius's vexing of Iocaste doomed by fate and the past of Claudius's act of murder and Gertrude's complicity. Like so many pasts—that of the abused child, that of impoverishment . . .—for all of them the image of action out of the a priori past is experienced as too great. The hold of the past is too great for Oedipus to search for the truth behind the taunting to which the Corinthian youth subjects him, for Hamlet to believe the ghost and save himself, for the abused, the poor . . . to experience the image of action as anything but too great, too much, unbeatable. Too often they fall back into the Idea. But if an image can be contemplated and drawn from memory the past will be repeated, except as something totally new . . . If the whole of memory can be contracted into an image for action . . . then we have arrived at the present as it moves to the future, the interval that is the capability for action, the "becoming" capable, which is only an instant.[146]

The emphasis here is on the *instant*, a segment of the whole, detached and in "service of" no whole or ideal, discharged of any "ideology" or totalitarianism to reaffirm. Overcoming a sexual trauma, writes Tamsine Lorraine, entails a process of self-transformation that resists majoritarian forms of subjectivity and invites new ways of understanding what it means to be human. The subject is not a thing with an ego that can be damaged, but rather a process that is sustained through social, psychic, and physiological processes.[147] The "truth" of the experience of rape lies as much in its intensities and the potential connections of those intensities to as-yet unactualized modes of being as it does in what actually happened. Reducing her experience to what "actually" happened would be to reduce it and herself to snapshots that could be filed away under extant categories without getting at the singularity of the experience itself in all its layers of complexity.[148]

But what Olkowski suggests is that to overcome "majoritarian forms of subjectivity," to gain a perception of ourselves as open-ended systems always on the verge of becoming-other, the process of therapy should entail not only a minoritarian revision of the past, but a practice, namely engagement with the minoritarian or "micro" level of signification: "we must look at a photograph we love, look at the desired object, the beloved body," as no "ultimate image, no model or standard" but as "a signifier which is also the signified."[149] What one engages with in order to be open for the future, to be capable of transformation and action, of repetition, is an emblem which one embraces at an intimate level which Deleuze terms "molecular," an emblem for itself. To recall, the generative novel, seeking liberation from the "ideology" entailed by the referential level, allowed the molecular, literal level of the work—the level of interplay between sentences, words, and even letters—to generate the narrative. Similarly, here it is only through contemplating a deterritorialized sign, sign as sign, sign as *body*; through "attention to what is theoretically most familiar,"[150] devoid of meaning ascription, that the ego can become *subjected* and passive, a *receptive* affectivity.

We now return to Deleuze to find that like Kant, where the "determined" and "undetermined" are logically preceded by, and defined in terms of, the mediating schema, Deleuze's emphasis is less on the synthesis of future but rather on *its representation*, on the "literal" rather than "referential" level of the idea. Widder wrote that Bergson's duration is "a mysterious ground that is unrepresentable."[151] But in truth the duration *is* representable—by Bergson's famous cone for instance. The third synthesis, on the other hand, consists in fractured ego and non-presentation. Like the schema, the "determinable," it is a dimension where things are only *becoming* and the signs that designate them are inherently mis-representing.[152] Metaphors such as "to make the sun explode" or to "throw time out of joint" or "to kill God"—which Deleuze employs in order to illustrate the synthesis of the future—indeed bear such quasi-representational status. They do not express anything but fracture. Each of these images "is itself divided, torn into two unequal parts,"[153] or to employ McHale's words: "permits no identifiable center of consciousness through which we may attempt to recuperate the ... paradoxical changes of level and other inconsistencies."[154]

McHale's words concern, to recall, the Klein form which the *nouveau nouveau romanciers*, as we saw in chapter 1, substituted the Gidean shield for as a new emblem of mise en abyme. There indeed exists extraordinary historical parallelism between Deleuze's articulation of the third synthesis in his 1968 *Difference and Repetition*, and the rise of the *nouveau nouveau roman* around 1970. Like Deleuze's future breaking with the mise en abyme of Bergson's duration, the *nouveau nouveau roman*—aiming to eradicate "the doctrine of representation"—broke away with the type of mise en abyme prevailing in the (classical) *nouveau roman*. Like Deleuze's future, which despite leaping from the Bergsonian duration, nonetheless precedes that duration—"with the backward move of an 'après coup,' it will have to come first, be the first repetition that retroactively repeats all the others"[155]—in the Klein form as employed by the *nouveau nouveau roman* it is impossible to distinguish between cause and effect.

Klein forms fine-tune our understanding of non- or mis-representing emblems, as well as the relation between things and words, and between time and the metaphors and concepts used to articulate time, found at the basis of the difference between the third and the second syntheses of time. If duration "serves as a mysterious ground that is unrepresentable but that still functions to ground representation," it is only in the sense that continuity occurs in the *comprehension* of this duration. Despite the paradoxes and discontinuities which duration comprises, the reader or philosopher can stably engage with the representation and symbols that stand for that duration. Correspondingly, a fracture of the ego occurs less by the leap of the future, than by what philosophically represents that future: the Klein form, the symbol which leads but betrays whoever "engages" with it.

What we here suggest is a mise en abyme in Deleuze's *very writing*. Like the primordiality Deleuze ascribes to the "schema" in Kant, Deleuze's philosophy of time refers to its own representational devices no less than what those devices, concepts and metaphors "stand for." Deleuze, indeed, as we shall see in chapter 7, suggested that certain symbols and books serve as *mises en périphérie* of reality, as reflective segments situated within a whole, real life, but at the same time generate the whole: "What we see in the crystal," in the philosophical symbol or metaphor of time, he writes—"is time itself."[156]

This pursuit of self-referring metaphors is similar to Derrida, who puts metaphor "into *abyme*" in order to figure "the metaphoricity of the concept, the metaphor of the metaphor, the metaphor of metaphoric productivity itself."[157] The metaphor according to its "metaphysical" concept, believed Derrida, denotes a reality derivative of proper meaning, so that the literal level is "in service" of the figurative one. The provisory loss of meaning, the metaphoric displacement "is seen as a moment of loss anticipating a future recuperation or only as an ornamental and exterior supplement to proper meaning."[158] However, one metaphor, he believes, the metaphor of the concept of metaphor, "a mise en abyme of the philosophical concept of metaphor,"[159] escapes the enterprise of metaphysics. It is no longer derivative of a concept or an ultimate signified and is thus sufficient to shatter the reassuring opposition of the metaphoric and the proper. It indicates instead that the metaphoric and the proper are "breached and broached . . . cut each other at infinity, recut and confirm each other";[160] that in all metaphors the metaphoric is found "originarily" in the proper, intriguing the latter's pursuit of a supplement. Any metaphor is always already conditioned by a more primordial one, so that any provisory loss of meaning which the metaphor entails "ruins itself in a mise en abyme."[161] If for Heidegger language is the "house of Being" through which it unveils and retreats, for Derrida Being is the "retreat of retreat," an unveiling of the retreat, so that the "house of Being" is a metaphor autonomous to the target to which it serves as a vehicle. That is, the course of movement of this image is not from a familiar "house" to the unfamiliar "Being," but rather by its retreat, Being "would give or promise us more about the house than the house does about Being."[162]

Deleuze comments on Heidegger similarly. Being shows itself only inasmuch as it withdraws. But it hence shows itself not merely in beings, but in "something that shows its inevitable withdrawal,"[163] something that embodies an anachronism, a communicational gap between the viewer and the displayer, so that the displayed is a multiplicity of possibilities rather than a presentiated, ontic, entity. This something, or the Thing, is the sign.[164] The Thing in Heidegger, as we shall see in chapter 5, designates a fourfold, a labyrinth, of mirrors, a mise en abyme where each "reflects itself in its own way into its own."[165] It embodies the sign as sign, the sign as a universe of its own. Deleuze views symbolist novelist and playwright Alfred Jarry to be Heidegger's precursor. Like Heidegger's endeavor to "overcome metaphysics," Jarry's "Pataphysics," is the science of that which is superinduced upon metaphysics, "extending as far beyond metaphysics as the latter extends beyond physics."[166] Antimetaphysical, Jarry's thought is above all "a theory of the Sign where the sign neither designates nor signifies, but shows . . . it is the same as the thing, but is not identical to it; it shows the thing."¹⁶⁷ In the verb "show," Deleuze alludes to a distinction he ascribes to Jarry between appearance—dependent on a consciousness that conceives it—and a phenomenon, which "shows itself in itself."¹⁶⁸ The Being of the phenomenon, the "epiphenomenon"—the object of pataphysics—is rather "nonuseful and unconscious."¹⁶⁹ It is a displaced sign, bound to no pre-established semantics. If it refers to a signified, that signified and even that referring function did not preexist the sign: "pataphysics will be, above all, the science of the particular."¹⁷⁰ The "pataphor," the type of metaphor deduced from Jarry's "pataphysics" is correspondingly "generative" in Ricardou's sense; it embodies rather than designates the universe of meaning. It describes a figure of speech that exists as far from metaphor as metaphor exists from non-figurative language. Pablo Lopez provides the following example:

NON-FIGURATIVE

Tom and Alice stood side by side in the lunch line.

METAPHOR

Tom and Alice stood side by side in the lunch line, two pieces on a chessboard.

PATAPHOR

Tom took a step closer to Alice and made a date for Friday night, checkmating. Rudy was furious at losing to Margaret so easily and dumped the board on the rose-colored quilt, stomping downstairs.¹⁷¹

Whereas a metaphor is the comparison of a real object or event with a seemingly unrelated subject in order to emphasize the similarities between the two, the pataphor uses the newly created metaphorical similarity as a reality on which to base itself: "in going beyond mere ornamentation of the original idea, the pataphor seeks to describe a new and separate world, in which an idea or aspect has taken on a life of its own."¹⁷² Like Roussel's stories, which dramatize the literal level of the narrative, the very interplay between letters, the above pataphor of two chess pieces, rather than serving to convey a figurative level, acquires "possibilization," a diegetic level, "a life of its own." It is incarnated as humans and events without ceasing to be signs, two chess pieces. In the world embodied by the pataphor:

> ... the most disparate of things and signs move upon it: a semiotic fragment rubs shoulders with a chemical interaction, an electron crashes into a language ... There is no "like" here, we are not saying "like an electron," "like an interaction," etc. The plane of consistency is the abolition of all metaphor; all that consists is Real. . . . It's just that they have been uprooted from their strata, destratified, decoded, deterritorialized.[173]

Being by essence a misrepresentation of the synthesis of future, and denying its recipient a center of consciousness through which he may recuperate the paradoxical changes of level which the dimension of future consists of, the Klein-bottle calls attention to the sign as sign, to its pataphorical level. It is in this level alone—where the sign bears "a life of its own"—that the difference between Deleuze's second and third syntheses lies. The two differ in almost nothing with regard to the *referential level* of Deleuze's words and metaphors aimed at distinguishing them, since both the duration of time and the Nietzschean Eternal Return refer to a scission in time sustained paradoxically by a coexistence between the two sides of the scission. On the other hand, the two syntheses differ substantially as representations-for-themselves, detached from a referential function. The very representations of these syntheses, their metaphorical rather than figurative levels, embody, or "show" in Jarry's sense, different dramas; they incarnate as different universes. Merely reconceptualizing difference, writes Olkowski, "is not enough to restore difference as difference," rather, "the ruin of representation can be accomplished only on the level of *actual practices*."[174] The establishing of the pataphorical level in his philosophy of time is one of Deleuze's ways to generate rather than designate the difference-in-itself. For Deleuze, time illuminates the metaphors used for explicating that time rather than vice versa. Like the dice roll in Deleuze's Divine Game which brings "tailor-made" game-rules along, the sign brings its referential level along, one that did not preexist the sign.

The pataphoric level of the words and images invoked in Deleuze's syntheses of time by no means marks a textual introversion. To the contrary, it implies a radical extroversion. As we shall see in chapter 7, Deleuze would associate the pataphorical signification with the radical pragmatic signification that characterizes the "rhizomatic book." Unlike normal cases of reading, the rhizomatic book, far from "internalizing" or bracketing out empirical reality (the variety of empirical factors found in the immediate context of signification, such as the empirical reader) is an "assemblage with the outside."

CHAPTER 5

MISE EN ABYME AS A PARADIGM SHIFT I

FROM MIRROR TO "LABYRINTH OF MIRRORS"

THE "MIRROR OF NATURE" AND THE PRINCIPLE OF ADEQUATIO

Aiming to define the difference between continental and analytic philosophy, Rorty follows Heidegger in observing a long tradition in Western thought of viewing philosophy's central concern to be a general theory of representation. Analytic philosophy, he believes, continues that tradition. For Heidegger and other continental philosophers, the notion of knowledge as accurate representation, made possible by special mental processes, and intelligible through a general theory of representation, needs to be abandoned. For them, the notion of "foundations of knowledge" and of philosophy as revolving around the Cartesian attempt to answer the epistemological skeptic are set aside. Further, these philosophers set aside the notion of "the mind" common to Descartes, Locke, and Kant—as a special subject of study, located in inner space, containing elements or processes which make knowledge possible. The picture or emblem which holds both traditional and analytic philosophy captive is that of the mind as a great (static) mirror, containing various representations—some accurate, some not—and capable of being studied by pure, non-empirical methods:

> Without the notion of the mind as mirror, the notion of knowledge as accuracy of representation would not have suggested itself.

Without this latter notion, the strategy common to Descartes and Kant—getting more accurate representations by inspecting, repairing, and polishing the mirror, so to speak—would not have made sense.[1]

Our "glassy essence" was a picture which "literate men found presupposed by every page they read."[2] The mirror metaphor was first used by the Neoplatonists to convey the relationship between the world of the senses and the realm of ideas.[3] Since Augustine, the terms "mirror" and "speculum" have been used "to entitle massive encyclopedias and edifying works where the proposed examples imitate an ideal perfection: *Speculum Mundi*, . . . *Speculum doctrinale*, . . . *Speculum historiale*, . . . *Speculum naturale*, and also a *Speculum morale*."[4] Scholastic philosophy referred to *speculum* "in order to emphasize speculation's capability of indirect cognition of the Divine."[5] With post-Cartesian philosophy, the mirroring aspect of speculation takes on a new and additional meaning. Since Kant, and especially in German Idealism, "speculative" designates "that kind of pure, or purely theoretical, knowledge free from all subjective and practical ingredients that is also the knowledge of itself."[6]

Heidegger distinguishes between two definitions of truth. The first is *adequatio*, that is, correspondence or agreement between representation and state of affairs. This is an objectified type of analogy, where similarity between the analogue and the target is determined, as in allegory, through *formal* reasoning: A is to B as C is to D. Thus *judged* from without, Heidegger views this static relation as compatible with the onticization of Being throughout the history of metaphysics. According to Rorty, the paradigm of the static mirror epitomized and promoted this static relation of similarity. It consists, as we shall specify, in a rigid opposition between the actual and the virtual, and hence (in accordance with our analysis of binary logic in previous chapters) in a rigid predominance of one of the poles (usually the "actual"). Once monocentrism is implied, judgment is established too: relations of similarity between variants are given to a pre-established, transcendental perspective. It was this picture which Heidegger had to abandon if he was to introduce *aletheia*—the shining forth of the Being of a being out of concealment—as the new conception of truth, and it was this picture which continental philosophers had to shatter if they were to establish a philosophy devoid of presupposed totalizing ideals.

Heidegger, in his postwar essay "The Thing"—though Rorty fails to note so—indeed hints toward an alternative paradigm. In this essay, he borrows the nonrepresentational language of mystics such as Meister Eckhart to conceptualize Being in terms of the mirror-play:

> Earth and sky, divinities and mortals—being at one with one another of their own accord—belong together by way of the simpleness of the united fourfold. Each of the four mirrors in its own way the presence of the others. Each therewith reflects itself in its own way into its own, within the simpleness of the four. This mirroring does not portray a likeness. The mirroring, lightening each of the four, appropriates their own presenting into simple belonging to one another. Mirroring in this appropriating-lightening way, each of the four plays to each of the others. The appropriative mirroring sets each of the four free into its own, but it binds these free ones into the simplicity of their essential being toward one another. The mirroring that binds into freedom is the play that betroths each of the four to each through the enfolding clasp of their mutual appropriation. None of the four insists on its own separate particularity. Rather, each is expropriated, within their mutual appropriation, into its own being. This expropriative appropriating is the mirror-play of the fourfold. Out of the fourfold, the simple onefold of the four is ventured.[7]

The thing emerges into being as a thing by bringing near earth, sky, divinities, and mortals. The four facets of Being are a united fourfold since each of the constituents "mirrors in its own way the presence of the others," and therewith "reflects itself in its own way into its own." This "appropriation," and the all-embracing totality it gives rise to, differs from the "self-subsistence" of the negative in Hegel's dialectics, and the "self-solving" it entails, because "this mirroring does not portray a likeness." While the self-subsisting negative is a mere cliché of a conceptual difference—of the *ideal* of contradiction—any duplication of the fourfold or of any of its constituents is performed on an entirely independent ground and hence is "free into its own." As in Blanchot's mechanism of worklessness, where the true subject of the work is the "line of flight," the (inherently futile) leap toward its origin; and as in Iser's theory of reading where the true subject of the work is the very act of fictionalization, the true subject in the infinite mirroring is neither the actual mirror nor the specular image but the "middle," the very act of reflection, apart from which the image and the object reflected do not seem to have real prior existence—"none of the four insists on its own separate particularity." As in Deleuze's space of "intensities" and Simon's *Triptyque*, the four are not "pre-existing pieces," but pieces that are created "by the conglomeration"[8] and "have no other relation save those correspondences."[9]

With its endeavor to overturn metaphysics, post-Heideggerian thought both drew on and broke with Heidegger. It followed his endeavor to formulate a non-conceptual difference, but criticized his "ontico-ontological" difference as bound to a fixed form. Heidegger's "mirror-play" as invoked in "The Thing" is a prominent manifestation of the affinity between Heidegger and his critics, as the latter—Deleuze, Derrida, Blanchot, and others—would also use the double mirror—though far more explicitly than Heidegger—as an ontological paradigm shift.

THREE PARADIGMS OF IMAGINATION

Kearney might reprove Rorty for declining to pursue the alternative picture which served those philosophers in overthrowing that of the mirror: "One must understand that deviation . . . could not arise in a total paradigmatic emptiness,"[10] he cites his teacher Ricœur. His analysis proceeds in terms of a number of what he calls "paradigm shifts" (alluding statedly to Kuhn) which have signaled decisive mutations in the human understanding of imagination during different epochs of Western history: the *mimetic* paradigm of the premodern (i.e., biblical, classical, and medieval) imagination, the *productive* paradigm of the modern imagination, and the *parodic* paradigm of the postmodern imagination. Each historical paradigm privileges some metaphor characterizing the dominant function of imagination at a given time—i.e., "the 'mimetic' privileges the referential figure of the *mirror*; the 'productive' the expressive figure of the *lamp*; and the 'parodic' the reflexive figure of a *labyrinth of looking-glasses*."[11]

The first, the paradigm of "mirror," has already been introduced. It is important, however, to note that while Rorty's study concerns the history of philosophy, Kearney's concerns only that of imagination. Rorty's paradigm of mirror therefore does not strictly overlap with that of Kearney: philosophers which Kearney classifies under the rubric of the second figure, the "lamp," Rorty views as still adhering to the mirror.

The "lamp" paradigm became effective once mind was no longer viewed as an intermediary agency imitating some truth beyond man, but was rather deemed capable of inventing a world out of its human resources, answerable to no power higher than itself. As an effect of his Copernican Revolution, Kant and subsequently Romanticism and German Idealism viewed imagination as an *original* power of production, in whose absence neither sensation nor understanding could have meaning; imagination "ceased to function as a mirror reflecting some external reality and becomes a lamp which projects its own internally generated light onto things."[12] Heidegger himself acknowledges a profound debt to Kant's theory of transcendental imagination. Comprising a projection of possibilities, Heidegger hailed Kant's theory as a decisive anticipation of the analysis of Dasein outlined in his own *Being and Time*. However, if Heidegger's reading of Kant is "notoriously tendentious," entering "with force of arms into the Kantian system in order to subjugate it,"[13] it is because Kant's philosophy, according to Rorty, never abandoned the notion of knowledge as accurate representation. In fact, writes Rorty, we owe the notion of philosophy as a "tribunal of pure reason, upholding or denying the claims of the rest of culture,"[14] and its implication that getting more accurate representations "depends on inspecting, repairing, and polishing the mirror,"[15] to the eighteenth century "and especially to Kant."[16] The principle of *adequatio*, characterizing the mirror, prevails regardless of whether mind is passive or active, a "mirror" or a "lamp."

The third paradigm, the labyrinth of mirrors, which Kearney, like Ricardou, Foucault, and Deleuze, associates with mise en abyme right from the outset,[17] criticized both the mirror and the lamp as safeguarding totalizing ideals in philosophy. A central feature of "post-modern" philosophy, writes Kearney, is the "undermining of the humanist imagination understood as an 'original' creation of meaning."[18] Language, as an open-ended play of signifiers, is no longer thought to refer to some "real" meaning *external* to language, i.e., some "transcendental signified" called truth or human subjectivity. Instead, meaning is deconstructed into an "endless play of linguistic signs, each one of which relates to the other in a parodic circle,"[19] which the labyrinth of mirrors epitomizes.

Kearney fails however, to attend to the actual, *empirical* labyrinth of mirrors, using it instead as a *fable*. His description of the labyrinth as a "*parodic* circle," if bearing any ontological sense at all, is a value imposed upon the symbol—the labyrinth of mirrors—from without, and is incompatible with the "ontological density" which many "postmodern" philosophers rather attributed to it. Additionally, out of the five scholars who adhere—according to Kearney—to the paradigm of "labyrinth" only one—Derrida—actually alludes to it.

Derrida denies that any metaphysical system, however idealist or subjectivist, has ever succeeded in dispensing with the old distinction between the original and its imitation and with the attendant habit of according primacy to the former over the latter. Regardless of whether reality is taken as the original and imagination as the copy (Platonism) or vice versa (Romantic Idealism), the old origin-imitation model prevails.[20] It is just such a double deconstruction which occurs, Derrida believes, in Mallarmé's text "Mimique." Here we are confronted with pure mimicry, a mime which has no original, a representation without presence:

> The mime imitates nothing. And to begin with he does not imitate. There is nothing prior to the writing of his gestures. Nothing is prescribed for him. No present has preceded or supervised the tracing of his writing. His movements form a figure that no speech anticipates or accompanies. They are not linked with logos in any order of consequence . . . we here enter a textual labyrinth panelled with mirrors.[21]

Derrida's description of Mallarmé's "Mimique" as a labyrinthine play of mirrors is paradigmatic of the postmodern concept of the imaginary. The "Mimique" is a form of writing "which imitates nothing which pre-exists it—neither author, event nor world."[22] In accordance with the logic according to which "there have never been anything but supplements," the mime operation "does allude, but alludes to nothing, alludes without breaking the mirror, without reaching beyond the looking glass."[23] The postmodern figure of the labyrinth of multiple mirrors serves not only to deconstruct Platonic models of *mimesis*, but also modern attempts to posit the transcendental imagination as an original production of meaning in its own right.

The lesson Derrida draws from the labyrinth of mirrors is also a positive one. The speculum in Mallarmé's writing

> . . . [r]eflects no reality; it produces mere "reality-effects." . . . In this speculum with no reality, in this mirror of a mirror, a difference or dyad does exist, since there are mimes and phantoms. But it is a difference without reference, or rather a reference without a referent, without any first or last unit . . . Mallarmé thus preserves the differential structure of mimicry or mimesis, but without its Platonic or metaphysical interpretation, which implies that somewhere the being of something that *is*, is being imitated.[24]

In this mirror of a mirror, "a difference or dyad *does exist*." In the space of simulacra "*there is* mimicry"[25] though we are faced with mimicry imitating nothing. What Derrida here stresses—though only Deleuze would fully develop—is that, despite its "broaching and breaching" any "origin" or monocentric "actual," the labyrinth of looking-glasses does retain the dyad of actual/virtual, only that this time, the two variants are devoid of "consubstantiality" and hence of a (predetermined) predominance of one of the poles.

DELEUZE ON BERGSON: CRYSTALLINES, CONVEX MIRRORS, AND DOUBLE MIRRORS

In *Cinema 2*, Deleuze alludes to the mise en abyme by name. In this book, Deleuze returns to *Difference and Repetition* and his study on Bergson in order to show how film embodies the multiplicity of times and their relationships. In *Matter and Memory*, Bergson proposed the scheme of a world with two centers, one real and the other virtual. From this scheme emanate on the one hand a series of "perception-images" and on the other a series of "memory-images," two series "collaborating in an endless circuit."[26] Like the paradox of the past according to which there must always be another time in which time can occur, the actual always already repeats upon a preceding double which is the virtual. Perceptual recognition takes a material object as its point of departure, but for perception to be accomplished the opposite movement must also occur—"the circuit must be completed, so that we have the projection, outside ourselves, of an actively created image, identical with, or similar to, the object on which it comes to mold itself . . . this is the 'virtual image.'"[27]

The cinematic image similarly involves the coexistence of these two modes of reality. It consists—"a bit like the epicurean atom"[28]—in the "indivisible unity of an actual image and 'its' virtual image."[29] What is actual is always a present, "but then, precisely, the present changes or passes."[30] The image has to be present and past, still present and already past, at one and the same time, "the present is the actual image, and its contemporaneous past is the virtual image, the image in a mirror."[31] The metaphor of the mirror here in Deleuze is adopted from Bergson, who contends that our actual existence, whilst unrolled in time, "duplicates itself all along with a virtual existence, a mirror-image."[32] This contention is to be understood in the context of Bergson's identification of the actual-virtual amalgam with "an actor playing . . . [while] beholding himself playing,"[33] an image which immediately recalls Gide's reflection on double mirroring:

> I am writing on the small piece of furniture of Anna Shackleton's that was in my bedroom in the rue de Commailles. That's where I worked; I liked it because I could see myself writing in the double mirror of the desk above the block I was writing on.[34]

Only a double mirror can enable one to both write and see oneself writing, thus comprising a discontinuous space, an anachronism between the reflecting and the reflected. Alia Al-Saji accordingly remarks that Bergson's metaphor of mirror cannot stand for a static mirror:

> The appeal to the mirror image presents Bergson's account with difficulties . . . For this metaphor suggests that the virtual image is to the actual perceived object as copy to original—that the virtual image resembles the object and is derived from it as effect from cause.[35]

The static relation, that of correspondence between the opposing variants in a static mirror, is incompatible with the indeterminable and situational nature of the virtual image, its being "already pregnant with other memories, even the whole of memory."[36] It opposes the fact that the actual and the virtual in Bergson's thought, far from being reduced to a contradiction (which in practice homogenizes the space which the variants populate) coexists as heterogeneous, asymmetrical threads of time. "We are therefore to understand Bergson's mirror image differently," writes Al-Saji, alluding to Bergson's term "mobile mirror." Every moment of our life, writes Bergson,

> . . . presents two aspects, it is actual and virtual, perception on the one side and memory on the other. Each moment of life is split up as and when it is posited. Or rather, it consists in this very splitting, for the present moment, always going forward, fleeting limit between the immediate past which is now no more and the immediate future which is not yet would be a mere abstraction were it not the moving mirror (*miroir mobile*) which continually reflects perception as a memory.[37]

We should allow the (still) mirror image, writes Al-Saji, "a certain spontaneity and power."[38] But by this very statement she hands over her belief that by "mobile mirror" Bergson refers to the same old static device, only laden with new meanings. She fails to understand that Bergson modifies here the very metaphorical level, that by "mobile mirror" he refers to an utterly different type of (concrete and empirical) mirror. The metaphor of "mobile mirror," Bergson explicitly states, is to avoid abstraction, and is therefore not an abstraction itself.

Deleuze, commenting on Bergson, tests three empirical objects fulfilling this "mobile mirror" metaphor. The first is the crystal. Multifaceted, surfaced with diversified angles so as to cause diffuse rather than specular reflection, the crystal symbolizes time always "split in dissymmetrical jets." Furthermore, hosting *simultaneous* reflections, the facets of the crystal embody an "exchange" between the actual and the virtual, the fact that "there is no virtual which does not become actual in relation to the actual, the latter becoming virtual through the same relation."[39] Diffuse reflection in crystallines involves in fact not the surface, but particles a fraction beneath the surface. Phenomenologically speaking, the crystal shares this "depth" with the double mirror. Like the latter (though much less visibly) the crystallite reflection lays bare the pragmatic, infrastructural mechanism of reflection: the "process" insisting throughout the structural or aesthetic "product." More startling is the fact that, like the double mirror, the diffuse reflection is multiplied, generated at each interface of a particle. Like mise en abyme, each of these particles, each crystal which the polycrystalline is composed of, reproduces the entire diffusion of light. Such reproduction is further symmetrical to the process of the crystal growth. Like mise en abyme—and the double mirror—where the whole and the segment are interchangeable, a crystalline is made up of a periodic arrangement of atoms repeated at each lattice point. It looks the same when viewed from any point of the lattice. That is, each chunk of the crystal produced by a mechanism of translation of one unit cell, functions itself as such "motif," or a generative "first time."

Deleuze's second symbol of the time-image is the convex mirror, which "leaves the character with only a virtuality and pushes him back out of field,"[40] so that the character's image, virtual in relation to that character, becomes actual in the mirror. This laconic explanation Deleuze provides needs development. A convex mirror, writes Stephen Miller, creates images that are obviously distorted and that, therefore, cannot render the same kind of mimetically "correct" images that a flat mirror does. But its main characteristic is that it captures everything before it, "no one can stand at an angle too oblique from a convex mirror's perimeter to avoid being observed by another occupant of the same room."[41] Van Eyck, for instance, as in his famous *Arnolfini Marriage*, uses mirrors to compensate for the limits of our field of vision. This condensation of perspectives, write Shetley and Ferguson, enables a paradoxical perspective:

> Occupying the vanishing point of the painting, van Eyck's mirror offers a reflection of our own role as viewers of the depicted scene, and because it is convex, it is able to condense within itself, in reverse, almost the entire field of vision that is presented on the canvas. Close examination of the mirror enables the viewer to see a pair of figures who stand before the couple depicted in the portrait, at the point from which the painted scene has been observed; the mirror allows the painter to perform the paradoxical feat of including observer and observed together in the painting.[42]

A convex mirror reflecting an observer will reflect at the same time observers who do not belong to the observer's focal point or even spectrum. If the observer is "actual" and his mirror-image "virtual," that out of spectrum observer functions as a *third party* which challenges the actual-virtual dichotomy (and the hegemony of the actual). Albert Cook, commenting on Panofsky, also points to the convex mirror—functioning in Netherlandish painting—as challenging this dichotomy. The mirror in Van Eyck's *Arnolfini*:

> . . . counts among the objects of the picture, but along with them also; it constitutes a class by itself, in its power at once to resume and to transcend the strong plenum of the picture. The mirror by its displacement and its distortions, supplements, contains, and also transcends the painting, which is nothing if not otherwise pointed and direct in its centering convergence.[43]

The convex mirror both "resumes" and "transcends" the actuality it is pointed at. On the one hand, "pointed and direct in its centering convergence," the mirror affirms the priority of the reflected as a centralizing axis. On the other hand, "by its displacement and distortions," the mirror allows *another* point of view. Cook's term "supplement" describing the mirror's positioning against the reflected object, seems to allude to Derrida, according to whom an "origin," a plenitude, is interlaced "*originarily*" with a supplement, the other-than-plenitude. What the convex mirror embodies is a realm which comprises the Same and the Different at one and the same time. The convex mirror for these writers, as for Deleuze, symbolizes heterogeneous, incompatible points of view, which yet populate one and the same realm.

The third metaphor Deleuze employs, the "two facing mirrors," is however "all the more active."[44] The Bergsonian image is pronounced, he says, in Welles's *Citizen Kane*, when Kane passes between two facing mirrors,[45] as well as in *The Lady from Shanghai* where "the multiple mirrors have assumed the actuality of the two characters."[46] David Rodowick, on Deleuze, also mentions the salon in Duras's film *India Song*—which Deleuze invokes for other purposes—as epitomizing the difficulty "to decide what is an 'actual' image and what is a 'reflection.' "[47] Though the scene comprises only a still mirror, the spectator views that mirror and the object it reflects (with the difficulty to discern between the two) from without, so that the reflection employed there is in practice a reflection of reflection, mirroring-of-mirroring.

In choosing the double mirror to account for memory, Bergson, like Blanchot, might have drawn on Gide or even Goethe: Applying the phenomenon of repeated mirroring to the question of memory—the figure of Friederike as she was reflected back and forth in his life—Goethe was careful, in contrast to various philosophers and commentators, to contemplate on the empirical double-mirror itself, the "physical symbol taken mainly from the field of entoptics."[48] As in entoptics, where images—reflected back and forth—far from fading away, become rather enkindled, repeated reflections in the psychical sense "not only keep the past in lively memory, but actually enhance, intensify it to a higher degree of vitality."[49] In this way, we obtain a symbolic picture of what has been, and is being repeated daily. As in a double mirror, where a reflection *generates* the surface upon which it emerges; where the subject and object of reflection incessantly change, reflections in Goethe "do not only appear on parallel surfaces, but they are produced by them. Each reflection has an effect on the next one, namely that of an ever increasing intensity."[50] As in Bergson's duration, the past comprises multiplicity and "vitality," and "repeat[s] daily in the history of the arts and sciences and even in the world of religion and politics."[51] It does not exist, writes Deleuze, "but it insists."[52] Each present is "contemporaneous" with the entire past, and far from being a cliché, the virtual in light of which the present occurs repeats with a "high degree of vitality," it is productive rather than reproductive.

The metaphor of facing mirrors symbolizes the indiscernibility between the actual and virtual far more bluntly than the crystal and the convex mirror; parallel mirrors, due to optically factual infinite reflections, render the hierarchy between the actual—the object depicted—and the virtual—its image—ineffective. Bergson, like Gide, pursues a type of mirroring where an actor can view himself acting *while* acting, an empirical device which enables a *simultaneity* between the content and the framing of mirroring, which "absorb[s] the entire actuality of the character, *at the same time* as the character is no more than one virtuality among others."[53] In a play between two facing mirrors, A reflects B while being reflected by it at the same time. This means that B reflects not A but rather a series such as (A *as already reflecting* B), that is, C. In turn, A reflects not B but rather a series such as (B as already reflecting C), that is, D. Retroactively it is of course also the case that B rather reflects (D as already reflecting C), that is, E, and A reflects F and so on. A is (recurrently) transformed by the very action of reflection, from A to C to E, etc. It is here that Deleuze employs the term mise en abyme explicitly, citing Ricardou on the relation between mise en abyme and mobile mirroring: "The mise en abyme does not redouble the unit, as an external reflection might do; insofar as it is an internal mirroring, it can only ever split it in two."[54] Every subject of reflection is always already "cut into two," but therefore also comprises an *aggregate* of the reflected and reflecting: A *as already reflecting* B, B *as already reflecting* C, etc. Put otherwise, as in Blanchot's mechanism of worklessness (which Foucault and Blanchot analyze in terms of infinite mirroring), the act of mirroring is stretched between a subject and an object that did not preexist the act. The actual—the "real world" from which one gazes at the mirror—and the virtual—the specular world embodied by the mirrored image—are derivatives of an ad hoc event, and therefore have no other relation save this interdependence. Each side "is taking the other's role in a relation which we must describe as reciprocal presupposition."[55] An observer, gazing at the double mirror, grasps *simultaneously* the object of reflection and the process or subject of reflection. In a famous photo, depicting Deleuze posing between parallel mirrors, one can observe in the mirror both Deleuze *and* the mirror which enframes him. This is a case very distinct from the static mirror, where one observes the virtual—the image or the "specular play"—and the actual—the framing or the empirical mirroring device—only one at a time.

Hubert Damisch, commenting on Filarete, fails to notice this *primordial* splitting in two, that is the fact that the double doubles no simple but what is always already double. Filarete states that "If you have two [mirrors] reflecting in each other, it will be easier to draw whatever you want to do."[56] Damisch writes:

> The essential thing remains the place, the mirror . . . by means
> of which one can judge not only the diminution of figures, but
> also the distribution of light and shadow, but the mirror, more
> important, whose image of the reality it faces will be implicitly
> understood as analogous to the one the painter has constructed
> on a plane, *con ragione*. Save for the face that a single mirror is
> insufficient, since its image of the things in front of it is reversed,
> or turned around, and can only be set right if one repeats the
> transformation—nullifies it—by means of a *di-montratio*, a
> double showing.[57]

If the static mirror—as both a philosophical emblem and architectural tool—served in the reinvention of artistic perspective and consequently in that of "representation," of hierarchically ordered time and space, the double mirror, according to Damisch, "guarantee[s] nothing but more perfect perspectival representation."[58] If the rules of representation in painting maintain that "the image must appear within the boundaries of a rectangle . . . that maintains the image at a distance from the viewer who views it as if through a window,"[59] the double mirror, reduced to setting the reverse image of the single mirror right, boosts their fulfillment. However, this carved-out aspect (Filerate himself provides no such illusion-rectification function as a rationale) in fact opposes the true ontological "issue" of the double mirror, the fact the second-degree image in the double mirror, the image of image, does not repeat any "first time." The process of mirroring does not revolve around—nor reaffirm—the original subject or object so as to guarantee more perfect perspectival representation. It is rather the case that the second degree is "originary," that the origin itself—always already "split in two"—comprises heterogeneous, coexisting points of view: the image and its reflection. The second-degree image—repeated upon a ground of its own—is heterogeneous to the first, and the third heterogeneous to the second: Any reflection of an nth power operates upon a qualitatively different ground than an $(n-1)^{th}$ one. Like the Go-game pellet whose properties "are subject to continuous change depending on what sort of configurations appear on the board,"[60] the mirrored image bears a situational rather than coded identity.

It is not with explicitness that Olkowski—citing Damisch—acknowledges the double mirror paradigm which Deleuze and Bergson employ. However, by citing Merleau-Ponty, arguing that "seeing and being seen, touching and being touched, are like two mirrors facing one another, an infinite series of images set in one another, a couple more real than either,"[61] she does acknowledge the fact that the image in the double mirror, the image of image, is heterogeneous, that it comprises the image and its reflection, the seeing and the being seen—*at one and the same time*. The double mirroring paradigm seems useful to her endeavor to extend Deleuze's and Bergson's "ruin of representation" and to apply it to the feminine body. The body is not a medium and does not designate substance. Rather, "body is a term that expresses the relationship between forces,"[62] and the ruin of representation consists accordingly in assemblages "with the outside"— the actual assembles with the virtual, the psychological memory with the ontological, and the psychic component of human life with the cosmos.[63] I shall expand upon the relation between mise en abyme, the "outside" of the text, and corporality in chapter 7. This is, however, a relation which the double mirror already demonstrates: It comprises an assemblage of the specular play with its framing, so that the pragmatic and semiotic aspects of the reflected image are indiscernible.

Emphasizing the principle of simultaneity as that which governs the mise en abyme and the double mirror interrelatedly, Deleuze is in line with Dällenbach, Ricardou, Rimmon-Kenan, Le Poidevin and others according to whom mise en abyme comprises a "conjunction" of mutually exclusive narrative-levels. Deleuze alludes, furthermore, to Ricardou's "liberation" and "description" analysis, which applies to a specific form of mise en abyme abundant in "new wave" cinema, where "an image in a mirror, a photo or a postcard came to life, assumed independence and passed into the actual,"[64] or where, inversely, an actual image is discovered to be a mere nested art. This transition implies a double segment, "a superposition of one scene (the events are supposed real) and its proper mise en abyme (the events considered in the meantime as represented)."[65] Due to the discontinuity between the two moments, the transition is doubled and belongs to two series—"The fictive segment belongs first to one sequence then to another." These sequences, however, are *simultaneous*, "there is a retroaction: the elements which are supposed more real were *already* represented."[66] As in Bergson's duration, an element discovered to be virtual rather than actual is retroactively considered to be thus *from the outset*. As a result, two series, two "threads of memory," *coexist*, one where an element is considered real, one where it is considered fictive.

It is in the most immediate sense, the sensory one, that we argue that gazing at a play of mirrors, one perceives the framing—the empirical mirror—and the content—the specular image—simultaneously. Such immediate simultaneity assists in judging between what Hobson (1982) calls "bipolar" and "bimodal" aesthetic views. According to "bipolarists," one can either focus on the framing of art or on its content, but *never* at one and the same time. They follow Coleridge's well-known principle of "willing suspension of disbelief" to argue that the aesthetic illusion consists in a recipient's flickering between two mutually exclusive points of view: the critical one, which acknowledges the real (for example the fact that a prop-sword is just a piece of wood) and the playful which gives in to the virtual (the prop-sword as real-sword within the make-believe context). The picture Gombrich (1960) invokes is Jastrow's rabbit-duck where, unlike mise en abyme, one can perceive only one of the "disjuncts" at a time. Drawing on Genette, Ricardou establishes literature's "bipolarity" otherwise. A narration, he says, comprises two basic levels, the referential—which alludes to an extra linguistic reality, real or imaginary—and the literal or material, which concerns the medium itself—the *written* words, letters and their interplay. The two, writes Ricardou, are inversely proportionate: "The reader can perceive one only at the expense of the other, by effacing it at least temporarily."[67] Citing a scene from Flaubert's *Herodias*, where the outfit of a young girl entering a room is depicted in detail, Ricardou comments:

> If the reader wishes to understand this scene referentially, that is a young lady present *completely* upon entering, he must reject as much as possible the step by step exposure offered by the literality of the text. If [on the other hand] he wishes to comprehend the literal aspect of the text, the "scriptural striptease" of the lady, it is the fully present girl which he must recede from.[68]

In mise en abyme, on the other hand, the work is a "dramatization of its own working." The referential level is modeled on the literal one rather than vice versa, comprising a "close-up" (to use Deleuze's metaphor) on the literal level which turns it into the very diegetic level, a "landscape" or space to dwell in, so that the two levels—the literal and the referential—are perceived simultaneously.

Against Gombrich, "bimodalists" such as Gregory Bateson,[69] Erving Goffman,[70] and in some ways Hutcheon and Waugh, as we saw, argue for the principle of simultaneity as prevailing in *any work of art*, non-reflexive ones included. They argue that frames—artistic, sociological, or specular—by structuring experience, directing actions, and giving meaning to them, in fact *accompany* each and every action and contemplation; that events "are built up in accordance with principles which govern events."[71] Benjamin Harshaw, for instance, argues that every fiction consists in a "double decker" structure of reference, a depiction of Paris in Balzac "refers at the same time both to the real Paris in the External Frame of Reference and to the selection from Paris presented in the internal frame of reference."[72] It refers at one and the same time to a "real world" which engulfs fiction, and to a virtual one which engulfs the real. All fiction comprises "separate but parallel planes" and "each of these planes has its own continuation."[73]

However, nothing in this *reasoned* or speculative accompaniment matches the immediate, sensory, clear and distinct simultaneity between frame and content which one finds—or indeed experiences—in mise en abyme alone. The contemporaneity between series—which Harshaw assigns to *any fiction*—parallels Ricardou's analysis of "liberation" and "description"—which concerns mise en abyme. However, while one finds a *manifest* coexistence between disparate levels in Ricardou's example, is it not forced to apply it to non-reflective fiction—nineteenth-century realism included?

McHale, on his part, commits the double error of adhering to Harshaw's theory and articulating its antimimetology in terms of static mirroring: "The mirror of art must stand apart from and opposite to the nature to be mirrored. A mimetic relation is one of similarity, not *identity*, and similarity implies difference—the difference between the original object and its reflection, between the real world and the fictional heterocosm."[74] Any mirror reflection, according to McHale, participates in two "worlds," both the real and the heterocosm, so that the fictive coexists with but is not defined in terms of the real. But is such dissimulation (rather than simulation) really what a static mirror performs? Discussing mirroring in Borges, I shall later argue in the negative.

GASCHÉ ON DERRIDA: THE TAIN OF THE MIRROR

We have laid down the hypothesis that mise en abyme, in the form of mirroring-of-mirroring, formed a paradigm shift against the figure of the static mirror prevailing throughout the history of philosophy. But with Gasché we are confronted with a problem. It is from *the very beginning*, argues Gasché, that Western philosophy has viewed "reflection" as a concept which requires that the action of reproduction also be thrown back upon itself, hence functioning like a "mirror mirroring itself":

> The Stoics, and later the Neoplatonists, came to understand the nous as a self-reflecting and self-illuminating light, which sees itself by mirroring objects. As soon as consciousness is said to reflect the world and itself by turning upon itself, and thus to be conscious of itself in this act of coiling upon itself, this metaphysics of light, or photology, is transposed to it. Unlike the common notion of reflection, reflection as a philosophical concept requires that the action of reproduction also be thrown back upon itself. Recognizing the convergence of the word *reflection*'s etymological meaning with the metaphoricity of light, one could venture a preliminary definition: reflection is the structure and the process of an operation that, in addition to designating the action of a mirror reproducing an object, implies that mirror's mirroring itself, by which process the mirror is made to see itself.[75]

This is particularly true, writes Gasché, of Hegel's absolute reflection, a "reflection contained within reflection":

> To achieve the totality of all the movements of reflection, it is not sufficient to point to the dialectics of self and Other which take place between mirror and object. This dialectic is possible only on condition that the mirror of self and Other is itself only a form of absolute reflection. Reflection's reflection requires that reflection be contained within reflection, that mirroring itself include the mirror's mirroring.[76]

I am not convinced however, that in posing this difficulty Gasché is familiar with the actual device of "mirror's mirroring" and its philosophical meaning. The "self-illuminating" mirror, the mirror's mirroring he ascribes to Hegel, is a mere conceptual construct which has lost contact with the *empirical* object of two facing mirrors. Hegel, writes Gasché, "set out to ground reflection in the homogeneous ground of the reflection of reflection."[77] But self-reference, as we saw in Russell's semantics, does not necessarily entail mise en abyme, or double mirroring. The double mirror, governed by the mechanism of retroaction which renders every reflection always already displaced, performed upon a different logical level, and differing from itself, is far from embodying a "homogeneous ground." It was in fact for this very anti-Hegelian sake, the heterogenization of ground, that many writers recounted in the present chapter—*including Derrida in the name of whom Gasché criticizes Hegel's absolute reflection*—have rather *embraced* the double mirror paradigm.

Hegel defines contradiction as exclusively meaningful difference, so that difference, or the relation to otherness, becomes a "relation to the negative," and this negatively characterized otherness allows for reflexive determination in a developing dialectical system. Derrida "takes reflection's exigencies seriously," but his logic of supplementarity, writes Gasché, avoids falling prey to the "fictions" on which the absolute reflection is based.[78] He sets out to introduce difference into this totalistic reflexivity, and his questioning the very possibility of a source of reflection, of a constituting homogeneous principle, opens that source to the "heterogeneity of the ground as the radical Other, and to the heterogeneity of the noncontradictory Other."[79] Reflection no longer bears a simple origin, "what is reflected is split in itself,"[80] incessantly referring to another double. The fact that every origin already implies a double—the supplement it shares its originality with—is what prevents total reflection from becoming a self-sufficient ground, and such double exposes any origin in the form of productive imagination, intellectual intuition, or other to be a myth, a fiction.[81] What Gasché failed to notice was that speaking of a reflection "split in itself," Derrida was referring to an actual object, the very double-mirroring which Gasché has mistakenly associated with Hegel's Absolute Reflection.

Instead, Gasché embraces another metaphor of Derrida, the "tain of the mirror." If the breakthrough toward radical otherness in Hegelian and other "metaphysical" philosophies always already takes place in homogeneity, within the defined boundaries of the Same; if philosophy is incapable of comprehending what is outside it otherwise than through the appropriating assimilation of a negative image of it into the specular nature of philosophical reflection, then scission and dissemination "is written on the back—the tain—of that mirror."[82] This metaphor aims at depicting the fact that unity rather relies on what this unity cannot hope to reflect, on what lies beyond the mirror, "on the other side of the speculum, in the beyond of the presuppositions of the philosophy."[83] On this lining of the outside surface of reflection "one can read the 'system' of the infrastructures that commands the mirror's play and determines the angles of reflection."[84] Deconstruction is what "breaks through the tinfoils" of the mirrors of reflection to demonstrate "the uncertainty of the speculum."[85]

Mirroring-of-mirroring, as we saw, consists similarly in a coexistence of two incommensurable orders: The mirror's image, which comprises a "specular play," a plenitude, and the mirror's framing, which comprises the *parergon* of that play, that which is merely "adjunct"—the contingent element which as such escapes assimilation into that plenitude, but which is as originary as the former. With its multiple subjects and objects of duplication, the double mirror further comprises an infrastructural pluralism—"swarms of differences"—found beyond or rather beneath unity, whilst—like the tain of mirror—conditioning it.

Interestingly enough, these two figures—the tain and the double mirror—are proposed by Derrida in the *very same study*. As against Gasché, I believe that the latter of these two, the mirroring-of-mirroring—is preferable. First, contrary to the tain, the mirroring-of-mirroring is a metaphor shared by various poststructuralist philosophers and poeticians, and consensus is a prerequisite for a picture, model or pattern to serve as a paradigm. Second, while the double mirror is a *symbol* of the new (poststructuralist) reflection, the tain is its mere allegory and as such inadequate.

True paradigms, writes Kuhn "can guide research even in the absence of rules."[86] This maxim resonates with Ricœur's "hermeneutics of faith," according to which the type of metaphor fitting to serve as an ontological paradigm is the *symbol*, a "self-presenting" metaphor that rather than being instrumental in the explication of the Being of beings directs and delimits the enquiry. The allegory's figurative meaning, to recall from chapter 1, is always external to, and not directly accessible from, its literal one. Allegory is signified only by means of *formal* reasoning: A is to B as C is to D. By contrast, symbolic signs are opaque "because the first, literal, obvious meaning itself points analogically to a second meaning which is not given otherwise than in it."[87] In the symbol, I cannot objectify the analogical relation that connects the second meaning with the first. Like the paradigm, the symbol leads "in the absence of rules," and at no stage is the analogue dispensable. Rather than judgment—a comparison of the two sides of the analogy—the symbol consists in "faith," in "engagement" with one of the two sides or levels: the "literal" level. It is by "giving in," by "living in the first meaning" that a reader is led by it beyond itself, into the target meaning. It is through constant enquiries into the analogue itself, not in any generality it might stand for, that one conceives (and reconceives) the target.

The mirroring-of-mirroring can function as a symbol because that which it is meant to designate, the space of simulacra and its properties—notably the simultaneity between incommensurable variants—are unmediatedly perceived; not with their fully articulated philosophical meaning, of course, but with nonetheless a sufficient level to *suggest* this meaning, or in any case to *stimulate the question* that shall intrigue an ontological revision. Moreover, comprising infinite repetitive reflections which are heterogeneous yet coexisting, incommensurable yet populating a single "intensive" space, the symbol of the double mirror is a "saturated" phenomenon which generates an inexhaustible hermeneutic activity, and therefore an "oracle" to consult when forming the response.

Nothing of this applies to the metaphor of the "tain of the mirror." The tain is an allegory because its philosophical meaning is purely ascribed to it from without. Gazing at the tain one would only view an object *in the world*, within a plenitude, *not anything that contests a plenitude*, that is, exposes it to be "inevitably imperfect and limited."[88] If—as is the case in a static mirror—one can gaze at the image and the tain only in inverse proportion, than both claimants for predominance—the specular play and the empirical world, the virtual and the actual—remain secluded from one another and hence intact, unaffected by one another. The tain is gazed at in a context where reflection is not *in action* at all. The two therefore succumb to and reaffirm the Law of the Identity of Indiscernibles, and, consequently, binary logic, where an oscillation between the two variants can only mean "a renewal of the hierarchy or the substance of values," never "a transformation of the very value of hierarchy itself."[89]

BORGES AND THE "MONSTROSITY OF MIRRORS"

Inspiring the philosophy of difference of Deleuze, Foucault, Blanchot, and others, Borges himself rather adheres to the figure of the static mirror. In "Tlön, Uqbar, Orbis Tertius" and "The Library of Babel," shows Beatriz Urraca, the mirror functions as a mise en abyme, mostly of the "transcendental" type. But Borges's mirrors are plain, "he never says that they are curved; instead, what we have is a statement that they faithfully duplicate appearances."[90] The controlling role of the mirror in these two stories begins with its strategic placement, such as by the doorway into the library or in the opening page of each story as a "threshold" that must necessarily be crossed if we are to enter Borges's fantastic, imaginary worlds. But passage through the mirror not only takes us into a fictional world, it forces us to observe the laws that make reflection work. Urraca believes that Gasché's (following Derrida's) concept of the "tain of the mirror" develops what is suggested in Borges's fiction, and complements Dällenbach's idea of mise en abyme.[91] What the metaphor of the tain and the transcendental mise en abyme share in common is an exposition of "an inside vision of what makes reflection possible."[92] According to Eco:

> Vertical mirrors themselves do not reverse or invert. A mirror reflects the right side exactly where the right side is, and the same with the left side. It is the observer . . . who by self-identification imagines he is the man inside the mirror and, looking at himself, realizes he is wearing his watch on his right wrist. But it would be so only if he, the observer I mean, were the one who is inside the mirror. On the contrary, those who avoid behaving as Alice, and getting into the mirror, do not so deceive themselves.[93]

For Borges, too, mirrors neither distort nor interpret reality. To the contrary, they are unnerving and monstrous precisely because "they mark the uncanny separation between the human sphere of activity and consciousness and something unfathomable, uncontrollable, with its own laws that challenge our means of knowledge and interpretation."[94] What Borges sees in the mirror is an image of himself so exact that he is afraid of "not being able to tell the copy from the original."[95] He views the specular distinction of the copy from the origin as a self-distinction, a "pure" difference, "made" rather than derived from a presupposed form of difference. Correspondingly, he views the distortions of mirror reflections as imagined, a defense mechanism against the "terrible truth" that is our inability to distinguish the specular copy from the origin. In truth, when I move my right hand, the mirror reflects the movement accurately, as the reflection occurs on the absolute, empirical, right side of the device.

The problem, however, in Borges's ascribing principles of difference to the static mirror—his contention according to which humans, on some primordial level, find mirror images "monstrous"—is that it bears no everyday indication. People do not view their mirror image as indiscernible from themselves, as *doppelgangers* claiming authenticity. They do not view the virtual as *challenging* the actual, but as subjected to it through the relation of correspondence. This fact falsifies, in particular, Borges and Eco's view of mirror illusions as indicating the observer's imagining himself to be "the man inside the mirror"; their belief that falling prey to a left-right mirroring optical illusion indicates an extrapolation of the self. Because a trainee truck driver who mistakenly steers left instead of right in an attempt to shift the rear of the truck rightward does not do so by force of an illusion that he drives forward in an inverted cabin situated in the rear of the truck. He cannot be said to have allowed expression to hidden ontological truths in a moment of "sleep of reason"; he is highly concentrated, and knows exactly where the cabin is and in which direction he is headed (i.e., backwards). Instead, the novice uses the mirroring device with premature habit, with unskilled use of a device, in no different a manner to how hammers or flutes are sometimes used. This type of illusion deriving from premature use of the device is qualitatively different from the peculiarities perceived while gazing at the double mirror. Here, the paradox according to which realms that logically exclude each other nevertheless ontologically coexist takes over the beholder regardless of his level of acquaintance with the device.

Eugen Fink, a friend and disciple of Heidegger on whom Deleuze significantly relies in developing his Divine Game, also ostensibly draws heterological meanings from the still mirror. Fink, as we shall later explore, views play as "an ontological symbol," a realm from which Being—in its Heideggerian sense—"springs."[96] Play comprises an interlacing of reality and unreality:

> The doll is a product of the toy industry . . . But seen with the eyes of a little girl who plays, the doll is a child and the small girl is its mother. It is not as though the child thought the doll were actually a living child . . . She possesses, on the contrary, a *simultaneous* knowledge of the doll as such and its meaning in play. The child who plays lives in two worlds.[97]

Such simultaneity also exists in nature, "in the reality of curious things which, without doubt, are in themselves something of reality and yet contain an element of unreality."[98] An example is "a poplar on the shore of a lake projecting its reflection over the mirroring surface of the water":[99]

> The reflections themselves, make up part of the whole of the optic phenomenon, which consists of real things and the light which envelopes them . . . The trees on the bank are reflected in the lake, a smooth and highly polished metal surface reflects the objects around it. What is a reflected? As an image it is real; it is a real reproduction of a real tree, its source. But it is "in" (or "as") image that the tree is represented. It appears to be on the surface of the water, but in such a way that it springs from the medium of the reflection and is not there in reality . . . The

reflection of the poplar does not hide the surface of the water which it covers and which serves it as a mirror. The reflections of the poplar are there as reflection, a real thing known in itself, and an unreal poplar in the sphere of reflection.[100]

But Fink hence invokes in fact no still mirror. Mihai Spariosu correctly observes that Fink's mirror "is not a platonic one" but should be rather thought of as a lighting that allows beings to emerge into presence,[101] a generative rather than reflective mirroring. It is indeed a double mirror. What one observes when gazing at a poplar's reflection is an *image* of a reflection, not an unmediated one. He therefore observes a reflection of reflection. It is only due to this mirroring-of-mirroring that, gazing at a reflection of a tree in water, one views *simultaneous*ly both the image of the tree and the surface of the water which "hosts" that image and which, being a reflecting device, is a "thing in reality."

CHAPTER 6

MISE EN ABYME AS A PARADIGM SHIFT II

FROM PLAY TO "DIVINE PLAY"

THE PLAY OF THE WORLD AND THE PLAY OF BEING

Play in ancient Greek thought has often been employed in the form of a game metaphor that imagines the relationship between divinity and man as one between a player and a plaything. This metaphor, originating in Homer, is used for the first time in a philosophical context by Heraclitus, and is then transformed into a rational principle by Plato.[1] Play as a major philosophical topic resurfaces, writes Spariosu, with the rise of German Idealism, predominantly in Schiller who "explicitly calls the heuristic fictions of philosophy 'play,' relinking art and the aesthetics with the nonviolent, rational play concepts in their Platonic version."[2] Nietzsche will break with this Schillerian tradition by no longer subordinating aesthetics to ethics and rationality but vice versa. Heraclitus for Nietzsche is the most innocent and most just thinker, because Heraclitus was able to think the difference in quantity that generates quality:

> If everything is fire there is nothing opposite to it. Even as it appears that opposite qualities diverge out of a single force, still light and dark, bitter and sweet are attached to each other and interlocked at a given moment. And while one or the other may momentarily ascend, such ascendancy is not permanent; it is not the establishment of a stable substance.[3]

Difference is neither contradiction nor even contrariety; it derives in fact from univocity. Likewise, Nietzschean evaluations are not simply values, but the modes of existence of those who evaluate. The judgment "good" does not emanate from those to whom goodness is shown. Instead as noble and powerful, the high-minded judged themselves and their actions as "good." In so doing, they created "good" as a value, an evaluation which is both critical and creative, both ethical and aesthetic. They thus constituted "an active difference at the origin."[4] Like instances of Deleuze's repetition which repeat upon an exclusive ground, "endemic" to each of the instances, the moral value is constituted upon no presupposed web of values but rather assimilates those values to serve retroactively as its justification and necessitation. Nietzsche points out the bond between Hellenic philosophy and the Hellenic mode of life, which is based on play as *agon*. The Greek individual fights as though "he alone were right," his fight is performed upon a ground that bears no existence other than that fight, in a "world," or rather a series of "worlds," contracted and appropriated by, and created retroactively for the sake of that individual fight alone. Lacking moral substances, the construction and destruction concerned with the strife are "innocent," and innocent existence is a game of chance:

> If ever I have played dice with the gods at their table, the earth, so that the earth trembled and broke open and streams of fire snorted forth: for the earth is a table of the gods, and trembling with creative new words and the dice throws of the gods.[5]

God as Reason (or Reason as God) offers "blessed security" only to the mediocre. The golden mean or measure whereby risk-taking or chance is minimized, or at least given the appearance of being regulated and therefore under control, is a static concept of power, which Zarathustra opposes to the nobility of hazard's eternal play of forces, "with no ultimate judge or absolute ruler, but only an infinite number of players, losers and winners indifferently."[6] However, existence as a game of chance is a serious game. Just as any moral value is creative rather than critical, in the Divine Game, as Deleuze would develop, a roll, unconfined to presupposed organizing principles—such as probability theory or a win/lose system—is nevertheless not free floating. It does form part of a coherent whole and does succumb to a generality, only that this whole and generality are "endemic" to and paradoxically generated by the roll itself. The rules of the game come "tailor-made" to the roll, so that the player experiences every moment as good and valuable.

Despite a complex and ambivalent relation to Nietzsche, Heidegger views the will to power as a mode of reducing Being to beings, as a determination in which the metaphysics of subjectivity attains the peak of its development. Accordingly, while for Nietzsche the world-play gains meaning only in relation to the will to power, for Heidegger "all being as such could occur essentially as a game in which everything is at stake."[7] Heidegger's philosophical use of play becomes more and more operative and frequent in his later thought, where play "invariably crops up whenever the author attempts to describe Being."[8] For example, in "The Origin of the Work of Art," Heidegger suggests that the strife between world and earth—of which the work of art is a locus—is more accurately an *agon*. In "The Essence of Ground," Heidegger defines Being itself as play, or as an "interplay of Ground and Groundlessness, of sending forth and withdrawal, which cannot be rationalized or thought of in terms of any particular being."[9] The play of Being in Heidegger also comes into presence as an "epochal sequence," that is, as history: "Being plays with Dasein its game of advancing and retreating in different ways in different epochs. Epochal sequence . . . is sudden, spontaneous, and arbitrary unfolding."[10] In *On the Essence of Language*, language which is seen as the house of Being also plays a game of venture with Dasein. Man does not define Language or Being, but Language or Being defines man so that even Western metaphysics is not some kind of avoidable human misprision, but "an arbitrary turning in the hide and seek game that Language-Being plays with Dasein."[11]

In his book on Nietzsche, Eugen Fink raises the question that is designed to separate his own interpretation of Nietzsche from that of Heidegger: Is Nietzsche only the end of metaphysics—or is he the harbinger of a new experience of Being? The answer to this question, Fink insists, can be found only in an examination of Nietzsche's concept of play as *Weltspiel*, and Nietzsche's cosmological view of play does go beyond Western metaphysics.[12] With Nietzsche, human play, especially the play of the child and the artist, becomes a "key concept for the universe" or a "cosmic metaphor." This does not mean that the human ontological modality is uncritically applied to being in its entirety, "rather vice versa: the human essence can only be conceived and determined through play if man is conceived in its ecstatic openness towards the existing world and not simply as a thing among other things within the cosmos."[13] The essence of man derives from the totality of beings, conceived as the play of the world. Where Nietzsche conceives Being and becoming as play, he is no longer caught in the trap of metaphysics: Man as player who ecstatically opens himself to the formless, Dionysus, the playing-god, is himself "a playmate in the game of the world."[14]

GADAMER:
PLAY AND THE HERMENEUTIC CIRCLE

Though in Nietzsche and Heidegger play is a first principle, which remains groundless while it grounds their thought, play itself does not receive sufficient critical attention in their work. The latter task is assumed by Heidegger's friends and disciples Eugen Fink and Hans-Georg Gadamer.[15] Gadamer transposes Heidegger's relation between Being and beings onto play-player relations. As against Kant and Schiller, who reduced play to the player's subjectivity, Gadamer contends that play does not have its being in the player's consciousness or attitude, but, on the contrary, play draws the player into its dominion and fills him with its spirit. The player experiences the game "as a reality that surpasses him,"[16] all playing is "a being-played," and the attraction of a game, the fascination it exerts, "consists precisely in the fact that the game masters the players."[17] However, intentionality is not to be entirely exempted from the ontology of play. The "essence of play"—whether animate or inanimate—is a "to-and-fro" movement without any extrinsic goal. When it comes to human play, such recurrent transformation bears a specific subject: "Play itself is a transformation of such a kind that the identity of the player does not continue to exist for anybody. Everybody asks instead what is supposed to be represented, what is 'meant.'"[18] What the being of play consists in is *a recurrent displacement of intentionality from being constitutive of play to being an effect of play*, already part of a "script," in fact, a make-believe intentionality.

In literature, whose mode of being is inferred from that of play, understanding a historic or fictional text does not entail a judging subject, a person who holds himself back and refuses to take a stand with respect to the claim made about him: "The freedom of self-possession necessary for one to withhold oneself in this way is not given here, and this, in fact, is what applying the concept of play to understanding implies."[19] Rather than self-possessing, the understanding reader is "always already drawn into an event through which meaning asserts itself."[20] But, once more, the subjectivity of the reader is not entirely debarred:

> Just as we were able to show that the being of the work of art is play and that it must be perceived by the spectator in order to be actualized, so also it is universally true of texts that only in the process of understanding them is the dead trace of meaning transformed back into living meaning.[21]

A literary work does not have a "being in itself that is different from its reproduction or the contingency of its appearance."[22] Rather, only the reader's decoding of a historical or fictional text can transform "something alien and dead into total contemporaneity and familiarity."[23] Such "contemporaneity" occurs due to the reader's investing his own beliefs, preferences, and prejudices. Posing a question as to the text's correct interpretation, he is always already involved, outlining the answer.

In truth, however, Gadamer's to-and-fro movement between the ontic and the ontological is dissymmetrical. It is *always already* in service of the ontological:

> Play itself is a transformation of such a kind that the identity of the player does not continue to exist for anybody . . . The players (or playwright) no longer exist, only what they are playing. But, above all, *what no longer exists is the world in which we live as our own.*[24]

During play, the empirical world in Gadamer "no longer exists." If it plays a role in the to-and-fro movement which governs play, that role is merely instrumental—the concealment out of which the being of play unveils. It is not in fact an empirical player who is engulfed by play in Gadamer's ontology, but rather an implied one, a player already structured by play. The oscillation between the ontological and the ontic in Gadamer's idea of play *does* stabilize at some point, converging into but one of the two poles—the ontological, and the same is true of his conception of literature, as we shall elaborate in chapter 7. Deleuze's Divine Game would set out against precisely such a bias.

EUGEN FINK: PLAY AS THE "SYMBOL OF WORLD"

In "The Ontology of Play," Fink proposes a cosmological interpretation of the world which is already implicit in Heidegger's thought, but which "clearly spells out Dasein's dual role of player and toy in the play of the world."[25] Human play is an intertwining of reality and appearance. The doll is a product of the toy industry, it is a mannequin made up of material and a piece of wire or of plastic. We can buy it at a certain price; it is merchandise. But seen through the eyes of a little girl who plays, the doll is a child and the little girl is its mother. It is not as though the child thought the doll were actually a living child, "for she is not under a false impression, not apt to confuse the nature of things," she possesses, on the contrary, "a simultaneous knowledge of the doll as such and its meaning in play."[26] The child who plays lives in two worlds. The "world of play" or the "community of play" is accordingly an imaginary sphere or even a "magical creation" within the real sphere. We play in the world which we call real, but in so doing, we create for ourselves another world, a mysterious one. This world is not just nothing and still it is not something real either, "in the world of play we act according to our role; but in this world imaginary persons live, as the 'child' which takes on body and life, but which is nothing more than a doll or even a piece of wood in reality."[27] The world of play is not suspended in a domain of pure imagination nor objective illusion. Rather—as real objects are indispensable to it as props—it always possesses a real theatre. Though the world of play, as Huizinga wrote, has neither place nor duration but operates in the interior space and time proper to it, when we play we use real time and have real space besides.

The most ancient games, writes Fink, are magical rites in which man represents his destiny, and commemorates the events of birth, death, weddings, war, etc. However, play, or even a plaything, does not symbolize a segment of the ontic world. Rather, in the limited space-time of play, world totality shines forth—"to play is to take an explanatory attitude toward being at all times."[28] If play gains priority over the other fundamental human phenomena—death, love, strife, and work—it is because it expresses Dasein's essential relationship to the world-totality, while the others express only "intraworldly relations between Dasein and other beings."[29] Play symbolizes world's totality because whilst all other human phenomena imply a distinction between reality and unreality (appearance), play implies an interlacing of the two through the "appearing-to-be." Fink here reverses the Platonic dialectic of reality and unreality, showing that the "appearing to be" transcends the causal chain of ordinary reality. It is in fact more "real," being a mode of knowledge that comes much closer to Being than so-called natural objects and phenomena.[30] Like Being, it is "obscure and indefinable" yet it is that within which we move when we play,[31] and it has a presence and suggestive force more powerful and impressive than everyday affairs.

Above all, like Being with regard to entities, the appearing-to-be is neither defined in terms of the real, nor stands in *contrariety* to it. Though disparate to one another, the actual and the virtual occur simultaneously: "we do not pass by continuous transition from the space of the world of play to that we ordinarily occupy."[32] Man not only knows how to make artificial objects generally, but he knows how to produce things which properly belong to an "appearing-to-be-that." To say that play and world do not stand in a relation of contradiction or even contrariety to each other, that no pre-established constraints define their juxtaposition, is to say that their juxtaposition forms the only ground of their juxtaposition. Like Derrida's origin with regard to the supplement, the world of seriousness distinguishes itself from play while containing the latter "originarily," at its very heart. Play is a spectacle "which might represent the whole as in parable, producing a clarifying and speculative metaphor of the world,"[33] it represents that whole by also representing the very gap from that whole, namely the *very play of actuality and virtuality*. Therefore, if play is a case where "the whole of being can be found by reflection in a single isolated being,"[34] it should be thought of "not as a platonic mirror of world,"[35] but a mirror immanent to the world it reflects, a mirror reflecting reflection, a mise en abyme of reality.

It is also a radical case of mise en abyme—a *mise en périphérie*—generating the whole within which it functions as a section. The interlacing of reality and imagination which the actual world consists in and which play depicts is generated *by the very assemblage with the depicting play*. This is why in the history of thought, writes Fink, there have been not only those who tried to conceive of the being of play, but also those daring at an "unheard of inversion of the process," where the meaning of being springs from play.[36] It is now clear why Deleuze, developing his Divine Game as a symbol of his synthesis of future, alluded extensively to Fink. Like the caesura in time in Deleuze's third synthesis, which retroactively precedes time, play precedes the reality in which it functions as a segment. Like the pataphoric level in Deleuze's synthesis of future, play—rather than a medium of conceiving Being—is the source out of which the meaning of Being springs, and in this sense *the primary object of ontological investigation*.

But is play (in general) truly a mise en abyme? Fink argues that the real space-time which play occupies is "different yet indiscernible" from the fictional one; that like the actual and virtual of the double mirror, the two come as an aggregate, a bimodality of an indivisible unity. He proves this bimodality by arguing that at any given moment the player can renounce his role, "even at times he is necessarily engrossed, the consciousness of his double existence does not abandon him."[37] But is this argument valid? Does play indeed imply the principle of simultaneity? According to Gadamer, only by utter surrender to play or game, by a complete giving up of one's subject, can a player play. Play indeed consists in oscillation or to-and-fro movement between the being of play and the subject of the player, but such oscillation does not in itself infer that a player bears the ability to renounce play *while playing*, that he bears the consciousness of his double existence. Any renouncing from the side of the player, when performed, belongs *already* to the realm of seriousness—any decision to renounce his role can only come post-factum following actual abandonment, so that the realm of play and that of seriousness are never simultaneous. Roger Caillois would likewise maintain that a case where a player is conscious of playing, is one where play has already become "corrupted."

CAILLOIS AND LEVINAS: PLAY AND THE OTHER-THAN-BEING

Roger Caillois's *Les Jeux et les Hommes* (1961) opens by dividing play into four categories: Agon (competition and skills), Alea (chance), Mimicry (simulation and drama), and Ilinx (vertigo and destruction of stability). Caillois then demonstrates how cultures diversify according to the types or amalgams of types of play that dominate their *Geist* and institutions. Viewing play as grounding culture, Caillois thus follows Nietzsche and his descendants—Heidegger, Fink, Huizinga, and others. But here comes Caillois's twist, he turns to discussing play that oversteps its boundaries, lasts too long, or to which a life is over-dedicated. In such situations, "What used to be pleasure becomes an obsession . . . what was a pastime is now a compulsion and source of anxiety."[38] Each of the types is destined to transform into a counterpart, obsessive and pain-inflicting mode: Alea turns into superstition, Ilinx into drug addiction, etc. Phenomenologically speaking, play turns from being ontological to being ontic; from grounding culture to being objectified, consumed, and abused within culture; from being self-presenting to being represented within the world of reality and aims. Caillois here highlights the transparent and supposedly trivial fact that play cannot last forever, *that play ends*.

Following Huizinga, Gadamer underlined the seclusion of play—the fact that human play requires an isolated space, a playing field for example, and that setting off such physical space also "sets off the sphere of play as a closed world, one without transition and mediation to the world of aims."[39] Such seclusion (and consequently exclusion) is in line with Heidegger's concept of death as the limit in relation to which I am constituted as a subject. Caillois, on the other hand, laying bare the very boundaries of play, is rather in line with Blanchot's concept of death. Like the latter, the "death" of play is an event *in its own right*, "in service" of no ludic plenitude. Purely contingent, debarred from being part of the "essence of play," it is non-transformable into structure. In line with Blanchot, the end of play also marks the ambiguity of play as bearing two irreducible modes. On the one hand, play bears an ontological valence, functioning—as Fink says—as the "symbol of world" and even the ground "from which Being springs." On the other hand, play functions as an entity, an *object* in the world, only that this ontic is pure, the ontic as ontic, in service of no "daylight of being."

To rephrase, Caillois's theory unveils the fact that what underlies Heidegger's, Gadamer's and—to a large extent—Fink's ontology of play is an ideological choice. In their framework, the (transparent) "death" of play embodies the ontico-ontological difference, and the empirical reality or pragmatic circumstances that surround play embody the Heideggerian "earth" vs. "world"; they assume a mere instrumental role in the shining forth of the pre-comprehended "being of play." By contrast, in Caillois, the death of play—overlapping with its "outside"—functions as the "night itself" rather than the "night of the day." It is the "night before the night" which, despite serving as a foundation of play, is discontinuous with play, thus—like Blanchot's death—exists "before" in as much as it exists "after." It renders play oscillating between symbolizing Being and the beyond Being.

Caillois, we might say, "deconstructs" the traditional paradigm of play. He shows the necessity with which what this paradigm secludes is systematically related to what it excludes. Levinas, likewise, criticizes the paradigm of "play" for epitomizing monocentrism. He "goes out of his way"[40] to distinguish his heterology from the "game of arts" and the "play of the world" of his colleague at the time of his studies under Heidegger in 1928–29, Eugen Fink:

> In opposition to the vision of thinkers such as Eugen Fink who require, among the conditions of the world, a freedom without responsibility, a freedom of play, . . . [we discern] a responsibility that rests on no free commitment, a responsibility whose entry into being could be effected only without any choice. To be

without a choice . . . sets up a vocation that goes beyond the limited and egoist fate of him who is only for-himself.[41]

Levinas's concept of an "innate" otherness, and hence responsibility, at the origin of the self—prior to any empirical one—stands in contradiction to the self-sufficiency of play and the "egoist fate" of the player, his being a "cheerful exuberance that takes life lightly and withdraws from every care and responsibility"[42]; play "withdraws from the strict conceptual sobriety of philosophy."[43] In Levinas, where the ethic precedes the metaphysic, and where responsibility is the primordial metaphysical state, the "play of being" is also a misleading philosophical illusion:

> Prior to the play of being, before the present, older than the time of consciousness . . . the oneself is exposed as a hypostasis, of which the being it is as an entity is but a mask . . . In itself, the oneself is the one or the unique separated from being.[44]

Play consists, according to Gadamer, of a self always already "drawn into" the being of play. According to Levinas, however, that being-of-play which the self succumbs to is a totalizing ideal, and the player, as unique and specific, a "pure ontic," retains a gap between himself and this ideal, even while assuming the "mask" of fulfilling it. This is a subtle gap which the ontology of play cannot hope to detect.

Like Levinas and Caillois, Deleuze too would break with "the cult of origin" in approaching the paradigm of "play." However, whilst Levinas remains antiludic and Caillois retains a methodological ambiguity toward this paradigm, Deleuze would opt for a third path. He would develop the ontological and ethical significance of a specific, "anomalous," type of play—the Divine Game.

DELEUZE: THE DIVINE GAME AND THE ETHICS OF BECOMING

Mise en abyme is a structural device that is not the prerogative of literature, writes Dällenbach,[45] and scholars would extend the concept to art, theater, and even music.[46] Deleuze—drawing on Nietzsche—shows mise en abyme to be embodied as a unique dice game: a game within a game. This game is "divine" because it is with the Earth as their table—says Nietzsche—that the gods play dice. But the game is therefore also extraordinarily earthy: whereas the regular, "human" player surrenders to chance only the events prevailing within the boundaries of the dice-play, the divine player surrenders also the contingent events that surround him as a person in the empirical world. Deleuze demonstrates this play within play—play having itself as an object—citing from Borges's "The Lottery in Babylon":

> If the lottery is an intensification of chance, a periodic infusion of chaos into the cosmos, would it not be desirable for chance to intervene at all stages of the lottery and not merely in the drawing? Is it not ridiculous for chance to dictate the death of someone, while the circumstances of his death—its silent reserve or publicity, the time limit of one hour or one century—should remain immune to hazard?[47]

The gambler's actual interaction with the game, his attitude toward the results of the dice roll—all are a further circuit of rolls and results.

In Gadamer, during play, the empirical world "no longer exists." It plays a role in the to-and-fro movement which governs play, but that role is merely instrumental—the concealment out of which the being of play unveils. By contrast, in the case of Deleuze, the here-and-now circumstances of play, the ontic as ontic (such as the empirical player), are incorporated into play *without ceasing to be specific and empirical*; without being assimilated into structure. If play was determined by Gadamer (following Huizinga) as "distinct from ordinary life both as to locality and duration," that is resulting from bracketing out the empirical world, in Deleuze the game comprises not only the possibilities within the board. What is played, gambled on, and given to chance is also the outside, the "ground," the very framing of that board. The Divine Game incorporates, or rather assembles with, the pragmatic circumstances that prevail beyond the spatiotemporal boundaries in which play secludes itself. In other words, the empirical reality bracketed out from the Divine Game is nonetheless a participant: "Nothing is exempt from the game."[48] The outside of the game, its pragmatic, empirical aspects, bears yet a signification within the game, *as empirical*, without being assimilated by, or described in the terms of, the "inside"; the game's *very differentiation* from its outside prevails within the game—a mise en abyme.

The Divine Game thus offers an ontological paradigm symbolizing both Being and the other-than-Being. Moreover, far from assuming the "egoist fate" which Levinas ascribed to the play as an ontological symbol, the divine play entails an active ethical meaning. Deleuze and Guattari "are not known for promoting the kind of concern and sensitivity to the other that Levinasian-inspired forms of poststructuralist [philosophy] have advocated."[49] Yet if, for Levinas, the self—always already stamped by otherness—is hence defined in terms of responsibility, bound to ethics before asking the Heideggerian question of Being, then a (Deleuzian) game, comprising a "grafted on function," a juxtaposition with its outside, is by (a Levinasian) definition always already bound to ethics as well—that which Loraine has called the "ethics of becoming."

In the "ethics of becoming" responsibility is directed not toward people, but rather processes of self-transformation, oppressed by majoritarian forms of subjectivity which treat the self and the other as things with ego. It is directed toward becoming subjects, situational entities populating the "middle" between taxonomical rubrics, and embodying as such "that which has just happened and that which is about to happen, but never that which is happening."[50] Only the unfolding capacities and potentialities of these becoming-subjects has been blocked, and their power of connecting, affecting and being affected has been cut off. If for Deleuze what is real are becomings, "assemblages" between incommensurable, situational, and yet essentially contemporaneous variants, then "it is through joining forces with others that we can enhance our own enjoyment of life."[51] Inversely, if the self is a becoming, less that which differs from otherness than the very *middle* between the two, then an impaired openness to the outside which the other experiences impedes my own power:

> Being surrounded by others who are traumatized and thus cut off from their own ability to affect and be affected, their joy dampened, their openness impaired, I am surrounded by others unable to respond to me and unable to provoke, through responsive attentiveness, responses in me that enhance my own becoming. It can only enhance our own joyful becoming to be in connection with systems that are as open-ended as possible. A situation in which most lines of flight are blocked will most likely be a situation in which my own lines of flight will be blocked as well.[52]

The double becoming-other of genuine encounters—where each allows self-transformation through being open to (affecting and being affected by) the other—not only allows new assemblages to form, but also gives rise to the participating variants in the first place. It is through a participation in a process of becoming—being engaged with the Divine Game—that I both receive a call for responsibility and answer it.

This is to say that Deleuze's ethics is devoid of ideology. According to Schiller, human beings gain from play an "experience of formality," structure which does not vitiate freedom but which "prepares them for the consummate point of moral existence: spontaneous but lawful agency."[53] Deleuze—breaking with mimetology—can by no means view play, like Schiller, as instrumental to totalizing ideals such as "real life." However, his ethics does in fact answer to Schiller's call for a morality that "does not vitiate freedom." If in Schiller the ethical attribute of "freedom" pertains to the essence of play, in Deleuze it is embodied as the very *line of flight* between play and its outside, two situational variants that did not preexist the line stretched between them. It is with its "texture" rather than content, the very here-and-now "assemblage" between the game and the variety of pragmatic factors found in its immediate pragmatic context—not any allegorical meaning this encounter might bear—that the game acquires ethical meaning. If the player receives a call for responsibility—due to the game's outside being stamped at the game's very origin—the call is answered by the very call, a mise en abyme. It is upon a space already made up of an assemblage with its outside that play exercises a responsibility for becoming-subjects, that is, for assemblages of this sort.

The responsibility toward becoming-subjects should in particular be distinguished from a responsibility toward otherness as prevailing in current multiculturalist discourse. If "we should perhaps mistrust all this talk about multiculturalism,"[54] writes Rudi Visker, if multiculturalism is often "another way of labeling and controlling others,"[55] it is because it often falls into the pit of "negation," the amalgam of contradiction and totalitarianism. True multiplicity, we have seen, does not presuppose difference, but rather allows it "to be made." Multiculturalism, on the other hand, presupposing multiplicity, implies a preexisting unity, a substance underlying the variants, assigning them an internal, "nucleotide" identity, and a binary value: "One is the positive and the other the negative, but the former as a positive which is such within, and the latter as a negative which is such within."[56]

Specifically, pursuing pluralism, multiculturalist discourse ends up judging reality according to a pre-established dichotomy: The (totalizing) "self" and the (oppressed) "other," two identities assigned for substance-agents, persisting in them throughout all circumstances and contexts. Fulfilling a pre-established ideal—"the paradigm of an otherness that is supposed to shake the foundations of Western philosophy"[57]—this quasi-Other is objectified, shackled to a representation, and assumes a monolithic idol—not a "face"—of otherness. On the other side of the injustice, he is licensed to an act of violence while yet retaining, even reaffirming, the status of a victimized, apotheosized otherness. It was to eradicate (pre-established) ideals from multiculturalism, and to render this discourse susceptible to (here-and-now) facts and nuances that Visker writes: "It is true that the Other's alterity is not a consequence of his characteristics, but it seems a mistake to make alterity precede these characteristics and detach it from them."[58] Multiculturalist discourse substitutes the totality of the self for that of the "other," thus "idolizing" otherness, reducing it to a substance, an identity that remains continuously present throughout all change.

Deleuze's ethics of becoming stands in contrast to this idolization of otherness. It is directed toward neither the Self nor the Other, but instead toward *true otherness*, a middle, or rather a coexistence between incommensurable entities that as such fits into no representation.

Philosophically and sociologically speaking, multiculturalism and postcolonialism seem to have been strongly linked to a type of contemporary ludic discourse which I shall here present. It is first important to stress that "ludic" here refers to play in its broad sense as launched in romanticism, identifying between art, play, and the lyrical, as all "involve the freedom, the autonomy, and the originality of the individual."[59] This conception continues in Huizinga, arguing that poetry (and therefore play) "lies beyond seriousness in the primordial domain peculiar to the child, the animal, the savage, the visionary, in the domain of dreams, of ecstasy, of intoxication, of laughter."[60] Play and literature, argue later scholars, also interact through literature taking a ludic form (as, for example, in the literature of nonsense and humor), or containing explicitly playful content: Lewis Carroll as a writer, for example, "plays an agonistic game with the reader, perhaps not unlike a writer of mystery novels."[61] A more radical account of the role of the ludic in texts and their study comes from Jacques Derrida. Criticizing literatures of criticism, theology, Marxism, and structuralism he finds language to be constantly reinterpretable with no central, essential, or final meanings, and written texts as "a play of signifiers, always susceptible to multiple interpretations, always susceptible to 'deconstruction.'"[62]

Victor Turner associates the ludic with the "liminal." Society is a process in which any living human group alternates between fixed and "floating worlds," the world of aims and the world of play, which is "more serious than we, the inheritors of Western Puritanism, have thought."[63] In order to generate novelty, human beings have created anti-structural, "liminal," areas of time and space which are neither here nor there, "they are betwixt and between the positions assigned and arrayed by law, custom [and] convention."[64] In these areas, "people 'play' with the elements of the familiar and defamiliarize them. Novelty emerges from unprecedented combinations of familiar elements."[65] Rituals, carnivals, dramas, films, etc., open to the "play of thought," are the settings in which new paradigms and models, often fantastic, arise, some of which may have sufficient power and plausibility to eventually replace the force-backed political and judicial models that control the centers of a society's ongoing life.

Liminality as a "between and betwixt" position, according to Turner, is embodied not only as playful and aesthetic forms, but also as the destratified type of subgroups—the "communitas"—which sustains them, and which "cannot be legislated for or normalized since it is the exception not the law."[66] The implication of this contention is that the virtual and ludic is materialized not only as art, literature, plays, and games, but also the ludic elements of society—writers, actors, artists, etc.—"fiction is both a pragmatic and a semantic notion, since the organization of cosmological space has pragmatic undertones."[67] They not only write and perform works of fiction but also generate what Pavel has called "ontological landscapes"—"different domains, populated by different kinds of beings."[68] If the ludic gives rise to counterfactual worlds it also gives rise to counterfactual, real-life constructions, a multiplicity of private or peripheral realities within the hegemonic reality of everyday social experience. This is particularly true, believes McHale, with regard to "postmodernist fiction," whose "dominant" is ontological rather than epistemological, foregrounding questions like "What kinds of world are there?" rather than "How can I interpret this world of which I am a part?"[69] The ludic not only holds the mirror up to reality, but also infuses diversification by generating communities of readers caught by these counterfactual worlds, and engaged—as gap-fillers—in their creation. As Barthes writes, a novelist "is inscribed in the novel like one of his characters . . . his inscription is ludic . . . his life is no longer the origin of his fictions but a fiction contributing to his work."[70]

But is this postmodernist promise fulfilled? Do these ludic subgroups indeed embody communitates functioning as the seabed of cultural creativity, and infusing society with pluralism? Let us open this discussion with a paragraph from William Gass citing W. H. Auden in the context of the Vietnam war:

> Why writers should be canvassed for their opinion on controversial political issues I cannot imagine. Their views have no more authority than those of any reasonably well-educated citizen. Indeed when read in bulk, the statements made by writers, including the greatest would seem to indicate that literary talent and political common sense are rarely found together.
>
> . . .
>
> Israel makes war, and there are no symposia published by prizefighters, no pronouncements from hairdressers, . . . from the dentists . . . But critics, poets, novelists professors, journalists—those used to shooting off their mouths—they shoot . . . and those used to print, they print; but neither wisdom nor goodwill . . . are the qualities which will win you your way to the rostrum . . . just plentiful friends in pushy places and a little verbal skill.[71]

This revived Platonian suspicion toward writers seems to be motivated not by their political power per se, but by the ironical stance they hold while maintaining this power, namely their ostensible political weakness and deprivation. Let us demonstrate this point, pointing to the prominent Israeli writer Amos Oz's fable of the "teaspoon," delivered in a recent interview:

> The fire, the flames are big and horrific. Everyone of us has to choose confronting a big fire . . . You can write an angry letter to the editor blaming those who started the fire. But you can also take a bucket of water and pour it on the fire. And if you don't have a bucket, use a glass or a cup. And if you don't even have that, use a teaspoon . . . The teaspoon is very small and the fire is very large but there are many of us and everyone of us has a teaspoon . . . I do what I can as a teacher, as a writer, as a neighbor, as a citizen to pour some water on the flames of hatred and incitement and fanaticism and bigotry and prejudice. I have words and I use words. My words are my teaspoon.[72]

The disturbing element in this fable is less the triviality of the message, than the fact that it was never a mere "teaspoon"—nor even a "bucket"—that Oz had in his hand. Like many Israeli post-1967 writers, artists, and intellectuals, Oz formed part of a powerful network inspired by the then trendy New Left, debarring and delegitimizing any opposing or even non-ideological writing, and enjoying enormous public budgets and emphatical media coverage. His works soon became part of the Israeli literary canon.

His ludic power thus consists in imposing a simplistic dichotomy: Whereas "bad politicians" make war and spread hatred and bigotry, critics, poets, novelists, actors and other liminal—and ostensibly "marginalized"—groups express the voice of reason and consciousness, and heroically extinguish "horrific fires" using mere "teaspoons."

Brian Sutton-Smith would view this *topos*—still prevalent in media and academia—as part of contemporary, pejoratively narcissistic, ludic ethics. Caillois, we previously saw, analyzes the latent potential of the ludic for stagnation and "corruption." Huizinga argues similarly that as civilization proceeds "play becomes increasingly professional and therefore doesn't contribute to civilization."[73] Sutton-Smith, despite accusing Huizinga for falling here into "romanticist nostalgia," argues himself for strata and power implied in contemporary "rhetoric of play":

> Those who have lauded the imaginary kinds of play are the social and intellectual elites, always concerned to differentiate their own sophisticated social or solitary playfulness from that of the masses . . . We hear of plays peak experience, as flow, as autotelic, as authentic experience, as spiritual experience . . . as infinite games, not finite games; as playing with boundaries, not within boundaries; as being playful but not serious . . . ; as playing by heart. These are increasingly said to be better ways of playing for oneself. But it is probable that that self will have to be somewhat fortunate in having wealth, education, special training, or spiritual guidance, in order to have access to these "better" forms of play. We are living at a time when the concept of the "good" player, one who was probably a member of the new games movement[. . .] is beginning to emerge as a person of higher ethical status.[74]

The "rhetoric of play" is a function of power. That which is celebrated by contemporary ludic subgroups, their "issue" or the ideal incarnated into them, is not this or other new fantastic paradigm or model—as was expected from a liminoid communitas—but rather the *very philosophical apotheosis of play*, its very rhetorics. Accordingly, far from being a function of difference, the very "liminal" value of play is exploited to gain economic power and exercise political exclusion. Turner does mention "normative" or "ideological" type of communitates, a perduring social system attempting to foster and maintain these relationships on a more or less permanent basis.[75] This is not however the case here, where the very ideas of change, innovation—and even "liminality," "communitas," and "ludics" are transformed into monolithic substances thus pertaining to representation and totalitarianism.

Far from infusing pluralism into art, writing, politics, and societies, contemporary ludic ethics substitute one totalizing ideal for another. Levinas has previously denounced the ludic for safeguarding the priority of Being over ethics. However, governed by the "liminal"—this time transformed into a totalizing ideal—contemporary ludic subgroups sustain an ethics which, more than falling in the pit of "egoist fate," falls—like multiculturalism and postcolonialism—into idolizing otherness. It uses the logic of play to render otherness a substance, bestowing upon it the status of "marginality" which paradoxically entails a monocentric power. To rephrase, contemporary ludic ethics as previously expressed by Oz—idolizing the marginal and denouncing the center (as such) in the same breath—resonates with the discourse of otherness as conveyed by multiculturalism and postcolonialism. If the countereffect of colonialist marginalizing of the Other was his idolization by postcolonialism and multiculturalism, then the countereffect of marginalizing the liminal, virtual and ludic by mimetology has been a discourse idolizing them.

Moreover, if multiculturalist (and postcolonialist) discourse consists in "negation," that is of a pre-established dichotomy between the (oppressing) "self" and the (victimized and apotheosized) "other," then its overwhelming embracing by "critics, poets, novelists, professors, journalists"—and of course Hollywood actors—is hardly surprising. It was due to embracing the ludic in the first place—consisting in a monocentrism of the virtual such that excludes the *pragmatic* level that surrounds play—that multiculturalist and postcolonialist discourse excluded pragmatic thinking from their worldview and action, opting instead for a "massive," dogmatic and intellectually feeble conception. They lost the art of conceiving a given reality with its specifity; with giving attention to the difference this reality "makes" versus a pre-held ideal and ideology.

As reactionary as Gass's remarks might look, Gilles Deleuze, associated usually with the political left, might have well embraced them. If ludic ethics lost the art of conceiving reality in its specifities, the Divine Game, whose (essentially contingent) pragmatic level insists within the semiotic one, "calls on us to attend to the situations of our lives in all their textured specificity."[76] It gives rise to an ethics premised on immanent criteria and rules rather than transcendental ideals. It invites us to track the subtleties of meaning emerging in a given context; and it encourages responses that "go beyond a repertoire of comfortably familiar, automatic reactions."[77]

The inherent completeness of Deleuze's act of responsibility—the fact that a call of responsibility is answered by the very call, should finally be opposed to Levinas himself. According to Levinas, responsibility is rather infinite, ever growing, "the more I answer the more I am responsible; the more I approach the neighbor with which I am encharged the further away I am."[78] Like Derrida's concept of "iterability," postulating that we have no choice "but to mean something that is already, always other than what we mean," Levinas's "infinite responsibility" postulates that "the intention toward another, when it has reached its peak, turns out to belie intentionality,"[79] that one cannot ever hope to be intentional toward the other, thus saturating the Other's need, and each failure to fill in this gap results in further attempts, inherently futile.

We have previously criticized Derrida, arguing that his concept of iterability indicates a fall into the pit of "negation." His postulating an incompleteness, we have argued, implies a pre-established epistemological boundary, an organizing principle governing the instances of repetition, thus fitting badly with his pursuit of pure repetition or repeatability. Daniel Smith finds a similar structural closure implied in Derrida's "infinite idea of justice," consisting, like iterability, in an unrealizable justice, "decisions" incapable of being determined to be just, and finally a call to justice continually reborn due to this very incapability. Seeking to go "beyond" and "otherwise" than Being, Derrida, writes Smith, is a philosopher of transcendence, but his transcendence "represents my slavery."[80] A call to justice that I can never satisfy is an imperative "whose effect is to separate me from my capacity to act."[81] It does not pertain to ethics, whose fundamental question is "What *can* I do?" and hence the repetition it entails is not of a moral agent but of a purely artificial construct, set in advance within a purely artificial closure. The same criticism now applies to Levinas's "infinite responsibility": The logical impossibility to saturate the Other's needs implies instances of repetition reduced to representations, pre-established loci upon a unity; a totalitarianism which fits badly with Levinas's pursuit of otherness.

Levinas's "proximity" between the self and the Other, as we argued in chapter 3, is mise en abyme: "something in me has already been stirred by [the Other's] appeal before I could even decide to study the legitimacy of its claims."[82] The Self gazes at the Other only by force of this Other always already being stamped at the heart of the Self. For Levinas

> the holes in my skin are not openings that precede the encounter with the Other as its conditions of possibility; quite to the contrary, they presuppose an Other looking at me. My skin is thus no ordinary bag, but a twisted surface where the inside is an outside, in the manner of a Moebius Strip.[83]

But his concept of Moebius Strip, or rather mise en abyme—like Derrida's—is therefore "lacunal" as well. We have previously shown the "lacunal" to be a misconception of mise en abyme. This conception implies that instances of mise en abyme are consecutive and linear; that they are added onto a monolithic substance, a whole that precedes them both qualitatively and temporally. However, in true mise en abyme, as we have argued all along, an instance is rather added to a whole which did not preexist it.

In the Divine Game in particular, the very infrastructure of the game is given to a mechanism of repetition and difference. That which repeats—with difference—is not only the roll but also the ground from which it sprang and from which it gains its meaning and justification, not segments of dissected Being but (univocal) Being in its entirety. Whilst in the "human" game of dice, outcomes are separated "according to the distribution of the hypotheses which they carry out,"[84] governed by extrinsic organizing principles, notably those of causality and probability, outcomes of the rolls in the Divine Game "distribute *themselves* in the open space of the unique and non-shared throw."[85] Each roll is distributed according to a here-and-now regularity which the roll has brought along. This is why the coming to rest of the throw is not played upon the same table as its setting in motion;[86] the roll always already displaces the very setting upon which it emerged. The game which has occurred in pragmatic setting A occurs retroactively in setting B, "endemic" to the particular dice result. If Deleuze's is a game "you cannot lose," if it is not subject to "the winning and losing hypotheses,"[87] it is not because it lacks rules, but because each roll "entails the reproduction of the act of throwing under another rule."[88]

Like a circuit of mise en abyme, transforming the very object and subject of the mise en abyme to which it was added, the roll is the axis of a coherent whole, a "tailor-made" ground upon which the roll repeats, and which comprises a contraction of all previous throws, set in a constellation which the roll has brought into existence by its sheer emergence: "the whole of chance is affirmed in a necessarily winning throw."[89] Correspondingly, in Deleuzian ethics the act of attending to the Other's needs is fated to succeed. It is performed upon a plentitude, a fullness, and toward an Other—or rather a becoming—which the line of flight, the act of responsibility, has generated in the first place.

CHAPTER 7

THE RHIZOMATIC BOOK AND THE CENTRIFUGAL *MISE EN ABYME*

"MINOR LITERATURE" AND THE SEMIOTICS OF "EXPRESSION"

Gadamer—following Huizinga—showed art and literature to be ludic. The "subject" of the experience of art, that which remains and endures, is not the subjectivity of the person who experiences it but the work itself, and "this is the point at which the mode of being of play becomes significant. For play has its own essence, independent of the consciousness of those who play."[1] Like play, art and literature consist in a to-and-fro movement, the mechanism of transforming the recipient and its intentionality into an effect of the work itself. If Deleuze (unlike Levinas) refrained from direct criticism of the paradigm of play, he does criticize art and literature for often promising (like the ludic) to "break through the wall" of representation by disaggregating functions of power into "autonomous aesthetic traits," that is, turning art into an "end in itself."[2]

By promising so, these art forms hand out their "ideological" endeavors, that is, their following and reaffirming pre-established ideals, so that one totalizing ideal (real life) is substituted for another (that of art). Bracketing reality out and turning into a totalizing ideal instead, art deprives its characters, plot, and textuality of their specifity, transforming them instead into representations, clichés of pre-established determinations. By their very endeavor to oppose Platonism, art and literature become "critical of life rather than creative of life."[3]

There exists, however, "another type of literature" that does not consist in "fleeing *into* art, taking refuge in art," and "reterritorializ[ing] on art,"[4] a type that does "cross the wall of representation." Rather than following ludic ethics in idolizing and exoticizing the other-than-given (launching literary "voyages to the South Seas"[5]), this literature generates "active lines of flight or of positive deterritorialization,"[6] stretched upon no ground that preexists the line. This literature is non-ideological by nature, freed from the writer's "concern."[7] Its breaking through the structural closure "isn't a question of liberty as against submission, but only . . . a simple way out . . . as little signifying as possible";[8] it fulfills no ideal that transcends the here-and-now textuality of the work, no (fictive) reality to which the text functions as a mere "semiotic channel."[9]

In *Moby-Dick* for instance, Captain Ahab, inaccessible, detached from humanity even while surrounded by people, "has an irresistible becoming-whale."[10] "Becoming animal" denotes a series of organs succumbing to no organizing principle, a question of "composing a *body* with the animal";[11] a here-and-now entity, unthinkable in terms of a preceding form, but as a contingency that only bodies can epitomize. It comprises no synthesis, but links entities which did not preexist the line stretched between them, it is an "unimaginable" entity *always* falling between "rubrics," thus evading representation. But for Blanchot the "becoming animal" is but a manifestation of another coexistence, between the book and its "outside":

> To bring Ahab and the whale . . . together in one space—this is the secret which turns . . . Ahab into Melville.[12]

The encounter of Melville with the origin of the work is indistinguishable from Ahab's meeting *his* point of pure exterior. In fact, the "space of literature" in Blanchot—as we have previously seen—comprises the very set of crossings and recrossings of the boundary between literature and its exterior, "nothing happens except this very crossing."[13] The space or diegesis in which Ahab—and Melville—encounter Moby Dick, is not a heterocosm to which the text refers, but one pertaining to the work's *pragmatic level*, its processes of production. If the work encounters its origin, or absolute exterior, "before the encounter is possible," it is because the work assembles with the outside as such, without the latter being "internalized" by the inside, a crude pragmatic level in service of no aesthetic "ideology."

In Kafka's "minor literature," likewise, where to become animal is "to stake out the path of escape in all its positivity, to cross a threshold,"[14] textual contents "free themselves from their forms as well as from their expressions, from the signifier that formalized them."[15] Yiddish, a language "filled with vocables that are fleeting, mobilized, emigrating, and turned into nomads,"[16] opens for Kafka the path to make the German language "take flight on a line of escape."[17] By deterritorializing language, detaching signifiers from preexisting signifieds, he will pull from German "the barking of the dog, the cough of the ape, and the bustling of the beetle."[18] He will abandon sense, rendering it no more than implicit. He will render all signs undone, nonsignifying,[19] or rather signifying in a code (language) that did not precede the work and which is not necessarily human—"I do not see the word at all, I invent it."[20] Far from bearing a vehicular role and referential function, Kafka's literature comprises a "collective assemblages of enunciation."[21] Enunciation, to recall, differs from utterance, "as structuring differs from structure and fabrication from the object fabricated."[22] It pertains to the pragmatic level of the phrase, its very body, or textuality, which is why "it is so awful, so grotesque, to oppose life and writing in Kafka."[23] Whilst a majoritarian, or established, literature "follows a vector that goes from content to expression," minor literature "begins by expressing itself and doesn't conceptualize until afterward."[24] Concepts in minor literature do not precede their expression either temporally nor qualitatively. To the contrary, they are generated by their expression:

> It is not the law that is stated because of the demands of a hidden transcendence; . . . it is the statement, the enunciation, that constructs the law . . . the writings precede the law, rather than being the necessary and derived expression of it.[25]

In Kafka (as in the *nouveau nouveau roman*), expression, unconfined to signifiers, "breaks forms, and encourages ruptures and new sproutings."[26] In English Nonsense Literature, likewise (as "surface sense" and "surface nonsense" are not opposites but oppose the absence of sense, and the "nonsense of difference constitutes sense in terms of divergence"[27]), a word "denotes what it expresses and expresses what it denotes; it expresses its denotatum and designates its own sense. It says something, but at the same time it says the sense of what it says: it says its own sense."[28] It designates nothing that precedes logically or temporally the act of designation, so that a recipient must "take over, anticipate, the material,"[29] that is, reconstruct the content of the message as well as its very code.

The generative novel introduced in chapter 1 is a more explicit case of literature whose primary diegesis consists not of the referential, but of the literal-material level of the text: the letters, syllables, and even the typographical aspects of the page itself. Deleuze invokes this genre by following Foucault's fascination with Roussel and by alluding to Ricardou's poetics of the genre in *Cinema 2*. Deleuze's pursuit of a literature that "has nothing to do with ideology"[30] seems in fact to echo Ricardou's as presented previously, where "ideological forces" in the work are manifested via the dominance of the referential level. In a literature committing a true "line of flight," writes Deleuze, nominal, coded resemblance come into action only by becoming indistinguishable from the differential character which separates two words or even two letters, such as "b" and "p" in "Parmi les Noirs."[31] Generative structures "enable the novel or film to exist independently, aside from ideology or sociological issues and without serving even as an instrument of propaganda for any concept of avant-garde,"[32] be it even the Deleuzian concept of difference. For Deleuze, the *nouveau roman* was "the attempt to create a new, immanent form which entails a maturity of perspective, the possibility of having done with 'judgement' [which] depends upon pre-existing, fixed values, and precludes the invention of the new."[33] The generative novel, a specific branch of the *nouveau roman*, "invents the new" in a unique manner. It allows the story to be modeled on the body of the text, its literal-material level, and two bodies can never be identical.

THE RHIZOMATIC BOOK AND ITS READER

Ricardou, however, envisioned more, a future mise en abyme reproducing the story "not in an allusive manner but in its entire literalness";[34] a book whose mise en abyme reproduces not a book "such as this," but its very materiality. Mallarmé in *Livre*, a colossal work never completed, envisioned likewise "a numerous book, multiplied in itself by a movement unique to it."[35] What Deleuze has termed the "rhizomatic book" seems to have achieved this goal, challenging Literary Theory with a genre it believed to be impossible, where each specimen is a new creation in the most immediate sense, the material: In the rhizomatic book, the text is a function of the empirical body of an empirical (rather than implied) reader.

In *A Thousand Plateaus*, where Deleuze projects his principles of difference and repetition onto inquiries into culture and science, the rhizome—symbolizing the difference in itself, or paths between heterogeneous counterparts—and the tree—symbolizing centered systems and pre-established paths—serve as pivotal metaphors. In the domain of literature and semiology, Deleuze distinguishes between the rhizomatic and the arborescent books.

Binary logic is the "spiritual reality" of the tree-book, setting a dichotomy between the actual and the virtual. As "there is no dualism without primacy,"[36] one of these variants functions as "the One as subject or object," which "plots a point, fixes an order,"[37] and the other as a corrupt version, a fall away from the "One." It is usually the virtual, the book, which is a fall away from the actual, the world. Such a relationship defines the "bad concept" of mimicry,[38] which presupposes the temporal and qualitative precedence of the reflected over the reflecting. However, acknowledging that the virtual might also become "tyrannical," Deleuze brings cases such as the Bible (of the Reformation) and such as Marx and Freud, all "still Bibles,"[39] where the book becomes "a body of passion" which "internalizes reality." It forces the world to assimilate into its "territories and genealogies," that is, ideals which the book embodies or conveys.

The rhizome—botanical or other—is a nonhierarchical system "without a General and without an organizing memory."[40] A stranger to any idea of genetic axis, it operates by "variation, expansion, conquest, and offshoots."[41] It comprises only secondary roots, "grafted" onto one another, in the sense that no pivotal taproot, no preexisting principle, governs their juxtaposition. Consequently, roots in a rhizome are not "points or positions," unit-like constants with "tidy" boundaries; no viable focal point is enabled in a rhizome. Like the Deleuzian difference, each root instead functions in multiple constellations, an organ of a variety of series, each of which borders the rest upon a "ground" that did not preexist their juxtaposition. In this sense, any point is "connected to anything other,"[42] but also to its Other: The rhizome "in its entirety" is not a constant, it does not preexist its parts, "it may be broken, shattered at a given spot, but it will start up again . . . on new lines."[43] Like the rhizomatic book, it is "an assemblage with the outside."[44]

In his quasi-historiographical account of "regimes of signs," Deleuze provides an example of such "assemblage with the outside"—the oral book. Set against the "passion book," the oral book is characterized by "circulation" and "deterritorialization." Rather than reproducing a prototype, thus presupposing an origin, each copy of an oral book—like the Deleuzian difference—brings its own "endemic" ground with it: The book is "a movement from one *territory* to another."[45] Rather than a cliché, the copy is an independent creation differing from all others by mutations input by a specific reciter. In the context of the oral pre-Homeric epic, for example, copies differ according to "rivalry between several cities for the birth of a hero."[46] Each encounter with a recipient produces a different book, different in the most immediate sense—the material. The actual "inscription" changes due to an encounter with a new recipient.

Such differentiation is enabled because the rhizomatic book is an "*imbrication* of the semiotic and the material,"[47] a grafting between incommensurable variants rather than a stable configuration where the latter is subordinated to the former. As in Deleuze's linguistics, the semiotic level of the book is susceptible to the pragmatic one, to a variety of factors present in the immediate context of the act of reading hence differing from act to act, rendering the book pluralized. These contingent elements of book and reading which are parallel to what J. L. Austin—in the domain of speech—has termed "appropriateness conditions," include the ink, the ornamentations, the paper or leather sheets, the cover, and—above all—the specific empirical reader. They have traditionally been considered within philosophy, Derrida teaches, to be the *parergon* of language and reading. However, the contingency of the pragmatic elements, their specificity as here-and-now circumstances, and even the dismissal of their variety throughout history as "mere otherness" (differences in matter rather than form according to Aristotle) brings Deleuze to rather allow them ontological significance. The *crucial* ontological difference for Deleuze passes between the inessential, as an inherently singular occurrence, and the structure it escapes absorption into.

If Heidegger's ontico-ontological difference is transposable to Gadamer's play-player or reader-text relationship, Deleuze's difference takes expression in the Divine Game and the rhizomatic book. For Gadamer, as we saw, during play, the ontic, empirical world "no longer exists." It is assigned an instrumental role in a mechanism of *aletheia*, functioning as the concealment, the "night," through which Being "shines forth." It is not in fact an empirical player who is engulfed by play in Gadamer's ontology, but rather an implied one, a player already structured by play. In accordance with his ontology of play, Gadamer's ontology of literature, where the reader who "transform[s] something alien and dead into total contemporaneity and familiarity"[48] is always already "drawn into an event through which meaning asserts itself";[49] it is not in fact an empirical reader who is drawn into that "event," or into the "living reality" of the text, but merely an implied one, a reader already structured by that book. The play of language "*itself* proposes and withdraws, asks and fulfills itself in the answer."[50] The work Gadamer attempted to establish comprises a play between two "horizons," that of the reader investing his "prejudices" in interpreting the text, and the text, transforming this interpretation into a diegesis, a "universe" within which the reader always already dwells. In reality, however, these horizons do fuse, so that the to-and-fro movement between them is in fact but a predicate in the understanding of a "first signifier," Heideggerian Being.

Gadamer opens by arguing that a literary work does not have a "being in itself that is different from its reproduction or the contingency of its appearance,"[51] but in truth the "contingency of appearance" of the text is debarred from or bracketed out of the work. What interests Gadamer, to extrapolate from Dällenbach

> . . . is not the response of a given explicit reader, impossible to generalize about, but that of the reader-subject, exposed to the supraindividual pressures of an episteme, ideology, or unconscious desire, and, even more, the response of the implied reader, understood as the reading role inscribed in the text.[52]

By contrast, in the case of Deleuze, the "pragmatic" circumstances of play, most notably the empirical player, are incorporated into the play without ceasing to be specific and empirical. Correspondingly, in Deleuze's ontology of literature, the text becomes hybrid. It incorporates empirical reality without either being internalized by the other.

Eco argues against Ingarden, Iser, and, implicitly, Gadamer, that whilst every work of art indeed demands that the reader modify the original artifact according to his personal inclinations and "existential credentials," only the type of contemporary art where such "reinvention" is overtly thematised is a true "open work." The "Wandering Rocks" chapter in Joyce's *Ulysses*, for instance, "amounts to a tiny universe that can be viewed from different perspectives," thus suggesting constantly shifting responses and interpretative stances. In his *Finnegans Wake*, the opening word of the first page is the same as the closing word of the last page of the novel, so that—as in a rhizome—"each occurrence, each word stands in a series of possible relations with all the others in the text."[53] If the theory of the open work is "a poetics of serial thought,"[54] it is because open possibilities are established not only horizontally, but also vertically; because like Deleuze's instances of repetition, successive occurrences belong to heterogeneous organizing principles, "each message establishes its own code; each work appears to be its own linguistic foundation, its own poetics."[55] While a classic work of art respects the laws of probability, of "pre-established principles that guide the organization of a message and are reiterated via the repetition of foreseeable elements,"[56] the open work—like Deleuze's "Divine Game"—"draws its main value from a deliberate rupture with the laws of probability that govern common language."[57] Consequently, while a general work of art proposes an "openness" "based on the *theoretical, mental* collaboration of the consumer,"[58] the receiver of the open work, breaking with pre-established codes, is required to do some of the organizing and structuring of the literary discourse himself, and thus actually (as in the case of the musical composition "Scambi") "collaborates with the composer in *making* the composition."[59]

Is it true, however, that the receiver of Eco's "open work" "performs" (rather than receives) the work in a sense more immediate and less "mental" than any other work? Hutcheon, as we saw, whose poetics draws heavily on Eco's, admits that it isn't. Her "narcissistic work," which like the open work lays bare the role of the reader, is mimetic of a process—that of its own receiving—rather than an object, and accordingly comprises resources invested by the recipient. But these resources are eventually intellectual rather than empirical, the process generic rather than specific, and the reader implied rather than empirical:

> The reader is . . . a function implicit in the text, an element of the narrative situation. No specific real person is meant; the reader has only a diegetic identity and an active diegetic role to play.[60]

Eco, like other reception theorists, adheres to a Gadamerian framework where the true contingent and specific is debarred, where the role of the recipient is restricted to virtual encoding, filling "spots of indeterminacy" on the level of reference alone.

By contrast, the recipient of Deleuze's rhizomatic book actually inscribes, *on the literal level*. He enters at a stage where the work is still not ready for display. It becomes so only as hybrid, only through assembling its semiotic signs with the reader's empirical body and actions. Any integration of an empirical reader into the narrative, believes Dällenbach, "is an illusion which will surely sooner or later be undone."[61] The rhizomatic book challenges this axiom. Empirical reality assembles with the rhizomatic book without ceasing to be disparate, without "being internalized" by the book. The empirical level of bodies and actions that serve in the text of the hybrid work is not "concealed," in Ricardou's words, during the process of reference.

THE RHIZOMATIC BOOK AS MISE EN ABYME

Any rhizome, writes Deleuze, comprises a peculiar "map" that is "itself a part of [that] rhizome,"[62] reflecting its very reflection, a mise en abyme. Being incommensurable, lacking a presupposed shared ground, the book and its outside can only encounter upon a ground made up of their ad hoc encounter; any encounter has already taken place upon its mise en abyme. Foucault has expressed this in *The Order of Things*. The Renaissance, like the rhizomatic book, is characterized by coexistence rather than hierarchy between signs and nature: "Language reside[s] in the world, among the plants, the herbs, the stones, and the animals."[63] Similitude between a signifier and its signified takes place ad hoc, with no "table of representation" to mediate and underpin it. Like the rhizomatic book, "there is no difference between marks and words in the sense that there is between observation and accepted authority."[64] Due to the lack of ground for any similarity, and the lack of "accepted authority," the only criterion of similitude is the encounter itself. Consequently, "a resemblance becomes double *as soon as* one attempts to unravel it,"[65] any resemblance is *always already* split in two, a mise en abyme. Mise en abyme, in the hybrid work, is the "genotypic" level responsible for the paradoxical simultaneity between inversely proportionate aspects of these works. Empirical actions vs. semiotic signs, the literal level vs. the referential one, all "shine forth"—to use Heidegger's terminology—without either of each pair "concealing" itself before the other.

The mise en abyme underlies yet another trait of the rhizomatic book. Despite its compounding of the fictional and the real, the hybrid work has nothing to do with distantiation à la Brecht, an ideologically-driven unmasking of the artistic framework. Not only does the latter ascribe self-reflexivity a didactic role (be it even intra-literary, such as "treatises on art, Poetry of poetry")[66] that as such fits badly with generative endeavors, but the reality distantiation supposedly lays bare is nothing but a presupposed ideal. The fact that the state of defamiliarity, of reality laid bare, succeeds that of familiarity in a *linear* fashion, implies a *presupposed* substance upon which they are set as distinctive points preexisting the difference between them. Defamiliarity follows a state of familiarity, the surrender of a recipient to an aesthetic illusion. Yet such surrender, a concealment of the text in favor of its referential level, is not one the hybrid work has allowed at any stage. Reality during the concretizing of the hybrid work is not *laid* bare: *It is bare from the outset.* Distantiation dismantles the work's boundaries *after* the recipient experiences a façade of plenitude. By contrast, the leap from the hybrid work's boundaries precedes that very work. The hybrid work consists, from the outset, of an assemblage between the text—as plenitude—and the empirical reader—a singularity that leaps from that plenitude. Thus, the transgression of boundaries has always already taken place beforehand. In the rhizomatic book, the "future always exist[s] before it can exist,"[67] it is equivalent to "being punished before having committed a fault, or crying before having pricked oneself."[68] The dismantling of the hybrid work's cohesion and integrity paradoxically occurs prior to its being complete, or prior to its being at all.

The mise en abyme—the genotypic level which is responsible for such causal and temporal inversion—is of a unique type, a "composite mise en abyme" or a *mise en périphérie*. It reproduces a juxtaposition between "found objects," thus serving as an "iconic double" which bears, as we saw in chapter 1, a coherence that the patchwork it doubles lacks by definition. Consequently, the mise en abyme, a segment of the work, nevertheless occupies a primary narrative level that precedes that work. Assembling with a wasp to form a rhizome, writes Deleuze, the orchid at the same time, "forms a map with the wasp, in a rhizome."[69] Likewise, the mise en abyme of the hybrid book stands for an assemblage which did not come to existence prior to such reflection. While mise en abyme usually only *reflects* the work it is embedded in, in the case of the rhizomatic book, the mise en abyme, despite being a diminished model, precedes and generates the macro-level. Mise en abyme, we saw in chapter 1, "breaches and broaches" the work's boundaries, however, in the rhizomatic book it does so *before the text has even gained boundaries*, a violation of the laws of entropy which was previously invoked in Deleuze's synthesis of future.

Consisting of a diminished double which precedes the embedding, reflected whole, the mise en abyme prevailing in the rhizomatic book yet assumes another designation, namely, it is a radical case of a centrifugal mise en abyme. An aporetic mise en abyme, both embedding and being embedded within the narrative, suggests not only a centripetal movement that induces the mise en abyme to close in on itself but also a "dynamic centrifugal mode of infinite expansion."[70] In Albee's *Tiny Alice*, in a room in Miss Alice's castle, there is an exact model of the castle which even includes a "model of the model of the castle." But this inevitably brings the characters to wonder whether or not Miss Alice's castle serves itself as a replica of an absent meta-level castle. In truth, we shall immediately stress, one cannot determine what form that meta-level would bear, in other words, that what Alice's castle serves as a replica of is itself a castle. While in other works, even the generative novel, centrifugal radiations converge to the outmost circuit of the emblem, never crossing it, in the rhizomatic book—encompassing the *empirical reader itself*—they break through the boundaries of the work altogether. Consequently, the generating mise en abyme is embodied as the *rhizomatic book itself*. The book—like a map "drawn on a wall" or "constructed as a political action"[71]—becomes a "naturalistic" mise en abyme, a "trace of creation in the created."[72]

Deleuze has already deployed such a mise en abyme in developing his synthesis of the future. An active Kantian EGO_0 synthesizing $WORLD_0$ is transformed into a passive one by this very action, becoming an effect of a new active EGO_1 synthesizing $WORLD_1$. Likewise, if Bergson's duration of time is a mise en abyme, Nietzsche's eternal return embodies an outermost circuit of this mise en abyme, which causes the latter to duplicate upon an "unimaginable" territory: "with the backward move of an 'après coup,' it will have to come first, be the first repetition that retroactively repeats all the others."[73] The caesura in time occurs when time "undoes" the outermost circle of the mise en abyme so that an "eternally excentric circle" opens:

> [W]e rely upon the overly simple circle which has as its content the passing present and as its shape the past of reminiscence. However, the order of time, time as a pure and empty form, has precisely undone that circle. It has undone it in favor of . . . an eternally excentric circle.[74]

The centrifugal mise en abyme of time transgresses the boundaries of the form of time, so that the form of time is there "only for the revelation of the formless."[75]

Deleuze alludes again to the centripetal-centrifugal distinction in *Cinema 2*. The crystal image, that which symbolizes the duration of time,

> . . . has these two aspects: internal limit of all the relative circuits, but also outermost, variable and reshapable envelope, at the edges of the world, beyond even moments of world. The little crystalline seed and the vast crystallizable universe: everything is included in the capacity for expansion of the collection constituted by the seed and the universe. Memories, dreams, even worlds.[76]

We have previously remarked that like mise en abyme, each chunk of the crystalline functions itself like the crystalline seed, as *the* "motif" or generative "first time." But here Deleuze speaks of the "crystallizable universe" as itself a "little crystalline seed," prior to there being a universe, or rather an "outermost circuit" of that crystalline universe, "at the edges of the world," just beyond the "moments of world," which is "variable and reshapable," that is to say, no longer confined to the form and even concept of mise en abyme. Before elaborating on that "yet to come" which the edge circuit of mise en abyme becomes a mise en abyme of, let us discuss an empirical example of the rhizomatic book—the *sefer*.

AN EMPIRICAL EXAMPLE: THE JEWISH SCRIPTURE AS A RHIZOMATIC BOOK

The oral book, doubtfully a book, is but a semi-empirical example of the rhizomatic book. Jewish scripture, on the other hand, namely the *sefer* (book), a halakhic (legal) term designating a specific medium, a genus applied to books which share distinctive physical and metaphysical features, is more than an example of the rhizomatic book. Being its only empirical example and a highly elaborated one, it is in light of the rabbinic book that one can adequately understand Deleuze's idea of "rhizomatic book" in the first place, and can acknowledge that the latter designates a genre rather than an abstract concept. Deleuze himself does not differentiate the Jewish from the Judeo-Christian book—both, he argues "internalize" reality.[77] He commits this mistake due to considering the content of the Hebrew book, but failing to take into account its morphology and practices, which in (rabbinic) Judaism count no less.

The sages of the Babylonian Talmud granted the status *sefer* to the Torah (Pentateuch), and to four other texts, similar to the Torah in terms of ritualistic format, material, and use: the *tefillin* (phylacteries), the *Scroll of Esther*, the *get* (ritual divorce bill), and the *mezuzah* (a parchment hung upon doorposts). What distinguishes the *sefer* are halakhic requirements with regard to its format, material, preparation, and use. First and foremost, it is to be written up (except for the borderline case of the *get*) on a parchment scroll—not upon paper or any other material:

> He writes neither on a [wooden] tablet, nor on paper, nor on a partially-finished hide, but only on parchment, as it is said, "In a book" (*m. Sotah* 2:4, quoting Num 5:23).

In addition to the requirement that the *sefer* take the form of a scroll, its parchment should be processed from the skins of kosher animals only, which should usually be reserved for this purpose before tanning. The writer should undergo ritual purification before setting up to write. He must use a quill and only certain types of ink and follow sanctified formats and letterforms.[78] Once prepared, the *sefer* acquires sanctity. It is used for ritual reading on the Sabbath and festivals and requires mourning and burial rituals when it is removed from use. Unlike other inanimate objects, it sometimes is even capable (despite its sanctity) of transferring impurity to the hands that touch it.[79] Necessitating ritualistic preparation, having its pragmatic level, counting—ritualistically and phenomenologically—as much as the content, the *sefer*'s material level and empirical surrounding cannot be bracketed off from its semiotic one.

The *tefillin* (phylacteries) are perhaps the most instructive example. This apparatus comprises of two cubic leather cases, made to be worn, or "lain," upon the arm and forehead by means of leather straps to which they are attached. Into the cubes are inserted scrolls of parchment upon which passages from the Pentateuch are inscribed. Consisting of scrolls and parchments, the *tefillin* comprise a "book":

> There is no difference between books and tefillin and mezuzot, only that books may be written in any script whereas tefillin and mezuzot must be written in [Hebrew] Ashurit [script]. (*m. Meg.* 1:8)

This text is received not by bracketing out the pragmatic aspect of the signs in favor of the semiotic one, but, on the contrary, by making it manifest; by literally wearing the signs on the body.

The *mezuzah*, similarly, is an article constituting a scroll inscribed with biblical passages, usually inserted in a case (which is not halakhically obligatory), and hung upon the doorpost, or placed in a niche inside it. Thus, like the *tefillin*, the *mezuzah* is a "book" fulfilled by physical placement rather than reading.

With regard to the *get*, the Bible says: "When a man takes a wife and marries her, if then she finds no favor in his eyes because he has found some indecency in her, and he writes her a book of divorce (ספר כריתת) and puts it in her hand and sends her out of his house, and she departs out of his house" (Deut 24:1). The sages consequently establish legal analogies between the book of Torah—an archetype of "book" and the *get*: "[From the word] *sefer* I understand [that the husband must give the wife] a 'book,' " writes the Talmud, and Rashi's canonical commentary spells out that "book means a scroll" (*b. Giṭ.* 21b).[80] Like the Torah, *tefillin* and *mezuzot* (though not to the same degree of severity), the *get* is furthermore invalid unless ink is used.[81] The dominance of the pragmatic level of the *get* gives rise to a unique generative quality: The *get* constitutes rather than documents the divorce. It is distinguished from other legal bills in the Talmud (as in other codes of law) in that while commercial and legal actions can take place without inscription—a document, if signed, only serves as an indication of the deal made, a proof before the court when needed—a divorce can take place only with an actual bestowal of the *get*:

> R, Judah . . . held that . . . the reason why the *get* is valid is because he has inserted the words "and this," which show that he was divorcing her with this *get*, but if he did not insert these words, people will say that he divorced her by word of mouth, and the document is merely a corroboration. (*b. Giṭ.* 85b)

The words of the *get* themselves perform the divorce. A *get* that does not "do the talking," that does not bestow itself, is not a *get*.

The book of Torah, as the halakhic archetype of *sefer*, a book whose body counts as much as its sense, and where empirical reality overlaps with textuality, acquires as such, writes Barbara Holdrege, an "ontological status." In the Midrash, the rabbinic corpus of homiletic interpretation, it is considered as the blueprint or plan that the Creator employed in fashioning his creation:

> In the accepted practice of the world, when a mortal king builds a palace, he does not build it out of his own head but follows an artisan. And the artisan does not build out of his own head but he has designs and diagrams, so as to know how to situate the rooms and the doorways. Thus the holy One, blessed be He, consulted the Torah when He created the world. (*Gen. Rab.* 1:1)

This is why the writing of the Torah according to the Talmud should be "accurate by a hair's breadth": "Should you perchance omit or add one single letter, you would thereby destroy all the universe" (*b. 'Eruv.* 13a).

In addition, various *minhagim* (customs) personify the Torah as a living organic entity capable of entering into a dynamic relationship with the people of Israel. In the customs of the festival of Simhat Torah (Rejoicing of the Torah), for instance, the symbolism of Torah as the bride of Israel predominates. On this day, the annual cycle of reading of the Torah is completed and a new cycle of reading is immediately begun. The man who is called to the lectern to read the concluding portion of the Torah is called Hatan Torah, bridegroom of the Torah, while the man who is asked to begin the new cycle by reading from the first portion of the Torah is called Hatan Bereshit, bridegroom of the beginning, that is, of Genesis.[82]

Finally, the scroll of Esther is a *sefer* as well: "R. Hama b. Guria said in the name of Rab: The Megillah is called 'book' . . . to show that if it is stitched with threads of flax, it is not fit for use" (*b. Meg.* 19a). As in the case of a book of Torah (*b. Mak.* 11a), threads made of linen are forbidden in the scroll of Esther. Consequently, the corporeal, material level of the scroll—not only the semiotic one—generates meaning. For example, the ritual reading of the scroll cannot be done by heart, but must be performed directly from a written text.[83]

Being rhizomatic books, the five books are the only Jewish scriptures that bear mise en abyme. This mise en abyme conditions the *sefer*'s hybrid nature, the fact that its *very text* comprises both semiotic signs and the empirical factors surrounding these signs.

The *get*, as a legal bill, is distinguished for its narrative style, namely for recounting the gathering of the court, the circumstances under which the spouse bestows the writ of divorce. It then ends with the following statement: "And this shall be to you from me a writ of divorce and a letter of release and a *get* of dismissal" (*b. Giṭ.* 85b). Unlike any other rabbinic legal documents, the *get* thus refers to itself, comprising a mise en abyme. The reflexive formulation of the *get* has been coined so as to meet the requirement that the *get* generates rather than reflects or corroborates reality. A mise en abyme, the utterance of the *get* depends upon no "external" intention. It is performed upon a double of itself, thus comprising a self-subsisting reality.

The *tefillin* (of both the arm and the forehead) contain four biblical passages similar in content, that contain, according to the sages, the very commandment to wear *tefillin*:

> You shall therefore lay up these words of mine in your heart and in your soul, and you shall bind them as a sign on your hand, and they shall be as frontlets between your eyes. (Deut 11:18)

The commandment of *tefillin*, namely to lay "these words" on arm and forehead, is fulfilled precisely by wearing the commanding words. The work comprises its outside at its very heart. The *tefillin* cannot encounter their recipient without having always already done so—a mise en abyme.

The *mezuzah* is likewise inscribed with passages which command one to place "these words" on the "doorpost" (lit. "*mezuzot*") of the house (Deut 6:4-9 and 11:13-21). Thus, like the *tefillin*, the commandment of *mezuzah* is fulfilled by placing on the doorposts the very words that command the *mezuzah*.

In rabbinic thought, out of the five "scrolls," only the scroll of Esther, comprising mise en abyme, preserved the scroll form. For the other four "scrolls"—*Ruth*, *Eikhah* (Lamentations), *Shir ha-Shirim* (Song of Songs), and *Kohelet* (Ecclesiastes)—a regular codex may be used when they are publicly read on festivals.[84] The scroll tells that Mordechai "wrote these things and sent books to all the Jews who were in all the provinces of King Ahasuerus, both near and far" (Esther 9:20), informing them of the fall of Haman and providing instructions for the future. According to Rashi these "things" and "books" "designate the scroll of Esther as is." Rashi, ascribing to the book of Esther a reflective property, seems to rely on an ancient exegetical tradition, because the so-called First Targum (Aramaic translation) of the scroll provides the same interpretation, this time to the verse "Then Queen Esther, the daughter of Ab'ihail, and Mordechai the Jew gave full written authority, confirming this second letter about Purim" (Esther 9:29). The Targum interprets "written authority" as "this entire scroll" (ית כל מגלתא הדא).[85] It is perhaps due to its sharing with the book of Torah both the category of *sefer* and the status of mise en abyme, that which "allows past, present and future to become interchangeable,"[86] that the book of Esther—alone among the Writings and the Prophets—is compared to the book of Torah with regard to its place in kairological time:

> The scroll was stated to Moses at Sinai, for there is no consideration of posterior and anterior in the Torah . . . The prophets and the writings are destined to be annulled, but the Five Books of the Torah are not destined to be annulled . . . Also the Scroll of Esther and the laws are not destined to be annulled. (*y. Meg.* 1:5)

The legal provisions in Deuteronomy concerning the future office of the king, writes Jean-Pierre Sonnet, entail a mise en abyme. They decree that "when he sits on the throne of his kingdom, he shall write for himself a copy of this Torah in a book . . . and it shall be with him and he shall read in it all the days of his life" (Deut 17:18–20). But what the king will read, writes Sonnet, is precisely what the people are currently hearing, and "what the king will be perusing is a duplicate of a written record of 'this Torah.'"[87] However, Sonnet objects to the idea that the "book of Torah," referred to various times in Deuteronomy, is Deuteronomy itself, and refrains from the question of what text the reflective utterances "book of Torah" or "words of Torah" *do* refer to. For the sages of the Babylonian Talmud, by contrast (and for the reader of the book of Torah, that is the Pentateuch as *already received by the rabbinic tradition*), it went without saying that the "book of Torah," alluded to in Deuteronomy, begins in Genesis.

A second mise en abyme, according to the rabbis, is found in the revelation at Mount Sinai:

> What is the meaning of the verse: "And I will give thee the tables of stone, and the Torah and the commandments, which I have written that thou mayest teach them" (Exodus 24:12)? "Tables of stone": these are the Ten Commandments; "Torah": this is the Pentateuch . . . It teaches [us] that all these things were given to Moses on Sinai. (*b. Ber.* 5a)

Some *midrashim* view the tablets as inscribed with the entire Pentateuch: "Hananiah, son of the brother of R. Joshua said: 'Between each of the Ten Commandments were written all of the passages and details of the Torah'" (*Songs Rab.* 5:14). Some even stress their scroll-like format: "R. Joshua b. R. Nehemiah said: 'There was a miracle involved [in the tablets]. For they were made of hard stone and yet rolled up'" (ibid). The book of Torah therefore embeds a double: the book in its entirety as received at Mount Sinai. If the mise en abyme in Deuteronomy—as Sonnet noted—belongs to the type which Dällenbach has termed "enunciative," the one in Exodus mainly embodies—due to the universal and unmatched significance of the revelation of Sinai—the "transcendental" type, which reflects within the narrative "what simultaneously originates, motivates, institutes and unifies it."[88]

However, being a double of a *sefer*, the mise en abyme in the Torah pertains to a type which Dällenbach's typology could not have imagined. If the very material level of the *sefer* generates meaning, then the *sefer* is necessarily a single specimen, a here-and-now existence, that cannot be doubled without changing its identity. But the consequence of this regarding the mise en abyme is extraordinary. The double that the book of Torah, and the *sefer* in general, embeds is not a virtual one. If the Jerusalem Talmud requires the reader of the Torah in synagogue and its translator to be different persons, arguing that "just as it was delivered by a mediator [i.e., Moses] so it is to be delivered by a mediator" (*y. Meg.* 4:1), it is because what the Israelites received at Sinai was not a book "such as this." It is rather *the very actual book* read at a Sabbath or festival.

It is because they contain a poetical mise en abyme that the five texts were granted the status of *sefer* in the first place. This mise en abyme, in turn, governed by the principle of coexistence, guides the *sefer*'s pursuit of a coexistence between the semiotic and the pragmatic levels of its signification.

Consequently, acquiring a pragmatic level, a morphology, whose weight in the process of reading is not less important than the semiotic level—the *sefer* consists of another mise en abyme, corporeal, pragmatic, yet unknown to literary theory, emerging from its empirical use by an empirical recipient. The pragmatic mise en abyme in the *sefer* does not double a story. It rather doubles or in fact generates the story's pragmatic assemblage with its (pragmatic) outside. The text thus alters from recipient to recipient. Not due to changes in the domain of words and letters—indeed, "even one imperfect letter can invalidate the whole" (*b. Menaḥ*. 34a), but due to here and now factors, present in the pragmatic context of each reception, predominately the very body of the recipient. Rather than being bracketed out—as in ordinary texts—this body becomes part of a text, turning it into a hybrid, which is why the use of the *sefer* is not properly speaking a ritual at all, an event segregated from reality. It is, rather, performed (or should be performed) naturalistically, a point illustrated by the fact that the Talmud views the tefillin not as a ritualistic device but as integral to the Israelite cranium.[89]

We must finally remark that the form of the scroll itself renders a book hybrid. Contrary to the codex, the "*logoi en biblios*," says Derrida, are "deferred, reserved, enveloped and rolled up," and thus "force one to wait for them."[90] If the text of the codex, where a desired location is reachable instantly, epitomizes the Heideggerian "daylight" of presence, the scroll's, where the finding is deferred, epitomizes the other-than-presence.

José Faur follows Derrida in ascribing heterology to the scroll:

> The scroll of the Hebrews is unbounded and unframed . . . Therefore, it can be rolled inwardly, towards the recto, the verso serving as its boundary. Because the book is written on the verso and cannot be rolled in, it requires an outside element, the frame: as does an art object, every book requires a *parergon*. The inward movement of the scroll indicates that the text is thoroughly cross-referential and therefore self-referential.[91]

Breaking with binary divisions, the scroll of the Hebrews renders the inside and the outside distinct but not according to the Law of Identity of the Indiscernibles; mutually exclusive logically, yet coexistent ontologically. The Hebrew book, says Faur drawing on Derrida's extensive use of mise en abyme, is "cross-referential" in the sense of coexisting with its outside, with a domain it cannot internalize, and "self-referential," a mise en abyme, in the sense that the two encounter each other upon no ground other than the primordial "aggregate" made up of their very encounter.

"DIAGRAMMATICAL" REALITY AND THE "SHEAF" OF TRANSCODATION

In the latter part of "Language to Infinity," Foucault also reflects on the ontological meaning of the centrifugal mise en abyme. He detects and analyzes a quasi-historical shift between the form and function of language in antiquity and those of modernity emerging at the end of the eighteenth century with Sade and the Novels of Terror. To the language of antiquity, which Foucault terms "rhetorics," applies the analysis in chapter 3, according to which the leap toward death generates exponential, centripetal circuits of mise en abyme which render the space of literature "thick," "amplified," "indivisible," and "ontologically condensed," so that language can reside safely "surrounded by a circular mirror" and "completed in a beautifully closed form."[92]

The language of modernity, on the other hand, consists in a "disease of proliferation," a "ceaseless speech" which endeavors to "exhaust all that can ever be"; a language which is "always excessive and deficient[,] . . . always . . . a supplement."[93] If rhetorics placed death or the infinite "outside of itself," modernity shadows death to become its "loyal enemy." Foucault here seems to echo Heidegger's 1954 treatise, "Question Concerning Technology." Heidegger views technology as objectifying or presentiating future moments, the symbol for that being turbines accumulating energy. Events and artefacts are thus deprived of "alethean" qualities. Rather than "shining forth" out of concealment, they are bound to being clichés of pre-established determinations. Foucault likewise views modern language as anticipating all future divergences in language so as to defeat death, to render the temporality it implies ineffective:

> We must ceaselessly speak, for as long and as loudly as this indefinite and deafening noise—longer and more loudly so that in mixing our voices with it we might succeed—if not in silencing and mastering it—in modulating its futility into the endless murmuring we call literature.[94]

Attempting to subjugate every possible language, every future language,[95] the language of modernity reduces them to pre-established representations in a shared "table of representations." Far from being a heterogenous space, and as such "indivisible," the language of modernity becomes "excessive and of so little density" that it "sheds . . . all ontological weight."[96]

If the classical language for Foucault bore the form of accumulating reduplications of mise en abyme, the modern one comprises their dispersion. The metaphor Foucault provides for this "disease of proliferation" is a centrifugal mise en abyme: Borges's "Library of Babel." Since a book which aims to include all books must also include itself, a second book appears, then a third, then infinite books and "shelves." The library itself is only "shelved among so many others—after all the others, before all the others."[97] This openness of the book to its outside results, as in Derrida's iterability, in an incompleteness of signification. Books and languages are "always excessive and deficient," and language—as in Derrida—"only speaks as a supplement."[98]

Such inherent "deficiency" in the "modern" act of signification stands in opposition to Deleuze, where an act of signification—reconstituting language—is "fated to succeed." This "affirmative" approach is at work even with the centrifugal mise en abyme. A circuit of the centrifugal mise en abyme becomes—like that of the centripetal one—an axis of an ad hoc plenitude, a coherent "sheaf" in Deleuze's terms, only that this time it summons, we shall see, not previous circuits of a poetical mise en abyme, but future ones, incarnated as instances of living and physical nature.

Like the actions of the spy Tsun in Borges's "The Garden of Forking Paths"—killing Dr. Albert only in order to indicate to his German handlers the location of the British artillery park, the town of Albert—the rhizomatic book, we commented previously, becomes a "naturalistic" mise en abyme. Its "narrative level" overlaps with the empirical world, and the next level up from this, the "created" which that book is a "map" of, is rather found at "the edges of the world, beyond even moments of world."[99] Being a centrifugal mise en abyme (and a *mise en périphérie*), the book is a "diagram" that "does not function to represent . . . but [to] construc[t] a real that is yet to come, a new type of reality."[100]

The "real yet-to-come" is "variable and reshapable," as any narrative would be, had we access only to its mise en abyme. The mise en abyme of *Hamlet*—depicting the murder of a king and the seduction of his widow—could just as well serve to reflect an entirely different story, for example one which thematizes the succession of philosophical paradigms. The book of

Torah—a rhizomatic book—served, according to the sages, as a "diagram" as well: God's, as an architect, in creating the world. But in the very same *midrash*, the sages argue that this diagram—preexisting even some attributes in the person of the divine—also gave rise to many other worlds.[101] The diagram is *transformational, it "fosters* connections between fields."[102] It is the threshold to an absent, foreign semiotics.

Though any literary text can be defined as "a crossroads of absences and misunderstandings: the absence, for the receiver, of the sender and his context and, for the sender, of the receiver and the context of reception,"[103] the absence in question is so extreme that rather than encoding, the rhizomatic book is in a "perpetual state of transcoding."[104] Its signs serve *only* the people to come, or even "cosmic things." They are received only in ways "unthinkable," in the sense that birds, marking their territory, are perceived as "singing" by human ears.

Indeed, nature, like the book, transcodes too. It comprises a semiotic activity "residing in the world," thus susceptible to ever changing pragmatic conditions. A natural entity signifies with its body, a level *already* found in the "middle" between the given and its outside, a line of flight, a "path," to which the addresser and an addressee—but also the very code upon which the message was "inscribed"—are "strictly subordinated."[105] Neither preexisted the moment of signification.

From the lack of preexisting codes and subjects, Deleuze infers an extraordinary interplay between transcoding creatures. There is no privileged code—ethologist or other—that serves as a "higher reality" in interpreting transcoded signs: Applying to the birds' song the attribute of joy and sadness, or viewing them, like Klee, as a "twittering machine" would not carry "the slightest risk" of anthropomorphism or chauvinism.[106] Neither is there a risk of vulgar, over-reductionist naturalism, should one claim that the book of Torah transcodes to the bacteria upon its leather parchment; that theirs is one of the worlds which that book, according to the *midrash*, served as a diagram for. "The prime quality of the written medium is its ability to be a Torah-beyond-Moses, by overcoming the limitations of space and especially of time,"[107] writes Sonnet. But the *sefer* seems to overcome even the limitations of code. It is addressed not to an anthropological recipient, but an unimaginable species—a here-and-now, irreducible, "assemblage" between written text and a specific body.

Correspondingly, the transcoding subject, rather than a rigid one, repeats "intensively." It is a single subject which yet participates in multiple "planes":

The spider web implies that there are sequences of the fly's own code in the spider's code; it is as though the spider had a fly in its head.[108]

According to Jakob von Uexküll (1982) whom Deleuze invokes here, the subject and object of the transcoding message, and even the *umwelt* or environment containing them, did not preexist this line of communication. That all transcoding creatures share a single, Anaxagorean subject is proved, says Deleuze, by the fact that animals sometimes transcode in a *manifestly* human manner, as in the "mysterious" and "prodigious" cases of pilgrimages to the source among salmon, or supernumerary assemblies of locusts.[109]

Upon transcoding, the book hence "groups all the forces of the different milieus together in a single sheaf."[110] The reality yet-to-come comprises an accumulation of all acts of transcoding—zoological and literary. Thus, the hybrid book challenges not only the division between the semiotic and pragmatic, but also that between nature and culture. It assumes the subject, the self, which *each and every earthy and celestial creature* bears while signifying—inevitably—with its body. Drawing on Klee, Deleuze often calls the vast "receptacle" of all transcoding acts "cosmos": "powered by centrifugal forces that triumph over gravity"[111] the hybrid book "open[s] a cosmos."[112]

This "diagram" or mise en abyme—thus extended—comprises *itself* a "diegesis," an action world; the hybrid work—an assemblage between bodies—nonetheless contains a "plot." Rather than excluding the referential level, the rhizomatic book *assembles* with it. Indeed, when Deleuze argues that fabulation "engender[s] the people to come,"[113] the book which conveys that fabula is a hybrid book, it is in "need of a people"[114] in the sense that "semiotic components are inseparable from material components."[115] Its language is pushed "towards an outside . . . consisting of visions and auditions,"[116] in the sense that it resides, in Foucault's word, "in the world, among the plants, the herbs, the stones, and the animals." The instructive example here would be the book of Torah or the Scroll of Esther, where a story is read, but where one mainly needs to hear the reading, not to understand what is being read.[117] Deleuze also advocates taking up the Bergsonian notion of fabulation, which consists in an *accidental* encounter between a fabula and an event. Bergson brings the example, studied by Ronald Bogue, of a woman who approached her apartment lift with the intention of descending to the ground floor. Hallucinating that a lift operator was pushing her away, the woman was miraculously saved from falling into a void. The lift was not functioning properly, and the gate was open even though the car was stationed on a flight below. If Bogue is correct that the fabualtion which Deleuze pursues is, therefore, not properly speaking a narrative, he is wrong in identifying it with hallucination, which as such causes us to engage "in a critique of the received truths and realities of the present."[118] The hybrid work suggests no opposition of any kind (temporal, ontological, political) between the given and the other. Not only does it not render visible the fictional, the "other" reality, it does not even *lay bare*—as we have already remarked—the empirical one. Comprising a mass of transcoding acts, of messages signifying with their empirical rather than semiotic level, the diegesis of the hybrid book rather comprises crude reality itself. This reality is neither the heterocosm of reader-response criticism, nor the "real life" of mimetology. It is rather the pre-personal reality which Blanchot, as we saw, has termed "il y a," a "sheaf" of bodies, prior to being deprived of their "flesh and blood reality," and prior to being "resuscitated" in language and in the universal signification of Being. To recall, it was also crude metaphors, metaphors as metaphors, metaphors yet bare of a target, that conveyed Deleuze's synthesis of the future.

Any circuit in a centrifugal mise en abyme, like the "night before the night," is an infrastructure of a mise en abyme to come. Whilst in Bergson's duration—a centripetal mise en abyme—every circuit generates a new "thread of memory," a new history, the centrifugal circuit which the rhizomatic book (and the synthesis of the future) consists in always already withdraws into being *prehistorical*; it comprises the *infrastructure* of reality yet to come. Crude reality, or reality-for-itself, is defined by no historical time, "it has neither beginning nor end, but always a middle."[119] It precedes the reality yet-to-come like the prehistorical, the untimely, precedes the historical. It conditions the historical, yet "refrains" from any semiotics (yet-to-come) that would bind the two under one ideal. If Deleuze previously designated the intensive, transcoding subject as "cosmos," he now calls it "earth," or a "geomorphic subject." The author of the hybrid book "no longer identifies with Creation," but "sink[s] deeply into the earth: Empedocles."[120] Empedocles, arguing that "many fires burn beneath the earth;" that "there is no substance of any of all the things that perish, nor any cessation for them of baneful death," represents, according to Blanchot, "the will to burst into the world of the Invisible Ones by dying."[121] He is similar to Orpheus who set out to rescue Eurydice, the "origin of the work," the "profoundly obscure point toward which art and desire, death and night, seem to tend,"[122] from the underworld. For Heidegger, as we have seen, the earth, "the origin of the work of art," is already in service of the mechanism of *aletheia*. It bears an instrumental role, the unconcealment out of which the being of the work emerges into "world" or "daylight." For Blanchot, on the other hand, the "subterranean" or "terrestrial" is the only point "which is worth reaching."[123] If night for Heidegger is the "night of day," night "in service" of day, Blanchot to the contrary pursues the "night as such." That night is however impenetrable to thought in the sense that in the "daylight of language" things are always already annihilated and enter as universals. No word—being by essence iterable, able to function in multiple contexts—can designate a thing *in its here-and-now singularity*. At the moment Orpheus does gaze back upon his beloved he banishes her again to Hades. The outside is not to be reached or seen but only to engender infinite attempts at reaching it.

For Deleuze, however, an "epiphany" of such origin *is* at hand. The hybrid work, a mise en abyme on the level of reality, a diagram of a reality yet-to-come, materializes as one. Transcoding, the book acquires the single, heterogeneous subject which all transcoding creatures of nature—animate or inanimate—share at once. They have no existence apart from the moment of transcoding, and their very acts of transcoding, contracted, form a "cosmos." Such "Dionysian" drama is at the same time "chthonic." Dwelling in a reality which encodes in a language *which has not yet come*, the writer of the hybrid work is granted a license which Orpheus was refused—to gaze at the things which precede the mediation of language.

CONCLUSION

Poeticians of the mise en abyme stressed four interrelated traits, four aspects of a unique pluralism the mise en abyme infuses into the text, for which it would be invoked by poststructuralist philosophy.

The first is the singularity of the mise en abyme. This trait means that no pre-established categories of resemblance between the reflecting segment and the main narrative can apply to it; that mise en abyme only *becomes* such through a here and now juxtaposition between narrative (or logical) levels. Seeking to break with "ideology," that is, presupposed, totalizing ideals governing the creation (and discourse) of the literary work of art, Ricardou deployed this trait to develop a "generative" poetics where the referential level of the work is modeled on the work's (inherently singular) literal level, rather than vice versa. Blanchot, seeking likewise to liberate the work from the "reader's concern," invoked this trait to develop a "space of literature" modeled on "earth" rather than "world," that is, on the infrastructure, or very processes of writing and meaning-making. Deleuze, pursuing like Ricardou a literature that "has nothing to do with ideology," invoked this trait to break even with the idea of a code (a language) that precedes the writing and reception of the work. Indeed, the "text" in his "rhizomatic book" is a hybrid consisting of both semiotic signs and the very body and actions of a here and now empirical (rather than implicit) reader. Like Blanchot's *il y a* (the pre-personal existence), Derrida's metaphor and Jarry's pataphor, the diegesis of the rhizomatic book is "subterranean." It comprises a centrifugal mise en abyme reflecting only a "yet to come" whole. It is a unique "map" or "diagram," discontinuous with the target, thus "zoomed in" or given to a "close up" to embody a universe of its own. Pataphoricity further serves Deleuze in distinguishing his synthesis of the past from that of the future, as the difference between them is reduced to that between their metaphors—the Gidean mise en abyme and the Klein form respectively—rather than vice versa. The Klein form—inspiring the break of the new New Novel from the "old"—does not *stand* for a discontinuity more radical than the Gidean mise en abyme, but it does prevent a "center of consciousness" through which we may attempt to recuperate the paradoxical changes of level within the Klein form *itself*. Fink follows a similar logic. Viewing play as a *mise en périphérie*, both reflective of and generative (by its *very act* of reflection) to the world, he launches an "unheard of inversion of the process," where the meaning of Being springs from play rather than vice versa. In Deleuze's "divine play," a play within play, the pragmatic surroundings of the game—inherently singular—insists within the semiotic. Consequently, as against "ludic ethics," his "ethics of becoming," "calls on us to attend to the situations of our lives in all their textured specificity."

The second is the ambiguity of the mise en abyme. A result of a juxtaposition governed by no logical constraints, mise en abyme is insubordinate to the law of excluded middle. Rather, the reflective utterance operates in two *incompatible* series at one and the same time: the main narrative and the embedded, reflective one. This ambiguity in mise en abyme underlies Dällenbach's "economic" methodology—oscillating between structuralism and poststructuralism—and his typology consisting in "amalgamation" and "sliding" between variants. Blanchot used this trait to establish an "ambiguity" between the "daylight of being" and the "night in itself," without the latter being secondary to the first, and a philosophy of competing hypotheses whose differences cannot ever be reconciled or mediated. Deleuze and Derrida adopted this trait in order to challenge "negation" in philosophy, namely, the doctrine of representation sustained by binary logic. Modeling the "difference in itself" (Deleuze) and "quasi concepts" (Derrida) on mise en abyme (so as to be always already difference of difference, trace of trace, etc.), these writers articulated difference as performed on a multiplicity of logically excluding yet ontologically simultaneous registers.

The third trait is the principle of retroaction. If the small-scale segment that reflects the whole functions at the same time as a segment of the whole it reflects, then it cannot reflect the whole without transforming both the subject and object of reflection by this very act. This principle underlies Dällenbach's mechanism of filling-drilling "gaps of indeterminacy"—filling what retroactively is another hole in need of filling—and Iser's "acts of fictionalization" (which draws heavily on Blanchot), performed retroactively from the side of the fiction constituted. Blanchot's mechanism of worklessness draws overtly on Gide. Due to the discontinuity between the work and its "absolute exterior," every "leap" toward this exterior is retroactively performed at the domain of the latter, this time aimed toward another "exterior," so that the "space of literature" comprises this very series of displacements and recrossings. In Bergson's duration (modeled on mise en abyme), each perception, added to a series of memories, reconstitutes this series to become *ab initio* another "thread" of memory. Accordingly, both Bergson's and Kant's concept of "schema" consists not of a static, linear mediation between the a priori and the sensory-data, but a diminutive double, a mise en abyme of this very dyad. In Deleuze's synthesis of the past, associated with Bergson's duration, time is constituted while passing in the time constituted; time as "ground" is retroactively time as "foundation." In Deleuze's synthesis of the future "with the backward move of an 'après coup,' " an instance breaking through duration will have to be the first repetition that retroactively repeats all the others.

The fourth is the principle of coexistence. If mise en abyme differs from Russell's Theory of Types, Tarski's meta-level/object-level distinction and Hegel's triadic dialectics, it is due to the reflecting utterance participating at the signifying and meta signifying levels at *one and the same time*. There exists a circularity—or should we say, a mise en abyme—in the very poetical determination of mise en abyme. If mise en abyme is the "other in the text," if it disrupts the dominant narrative's claim for totality, it is not so much for embodying the small-scale segment that reflects the whole, but rather for populating *the seam* between the two, for comprising the very "aggregate" (to use Leibniz's terms) between these two incommensurable (yet "compossible") narrative or logical levels. Hutcheon employs this principle to develop a "process mimesis" where descriptions of objects in fiction are simultaneously creations of that object. Doležel and Pavel use it to unconfine possible worlds semantics from Russellian "segregationism." Le Poidevin and Füredy—attempting to reconcile the logic of mise en abyme with Russell's and Tarski's framework—and Rimmon-Kenan—showing the futility of this attempt—articulate the principle of coexistence in terms of simultaneity between mutually exclusive hypotheses which the reader has attained at the end of the reading process.

What Blanchot called the "fatality of light" exploits the fact that incommensurable instances of mise en abyme nonetheless contract, forming what Foucault has called an "ontologicaly dense" space. Deleuze likewise uses the term "affirmativeness" to describe the fact that, like a circuit of mise en abyme which added to a whole retroactively reconstitutes the whole (from reduplicating X to reduplicating (X within X)), an instance of signification reconstitutes language in its favor, rendering that instance "fated to succeed." An instance of difference always brings along an ad hoc and a "tailor-made" plenitude, one which did not preexist the instance that "expresses" it. Derrida, on the other hand (but only in our first, "argumentative," reading), adopting the mise en abyme only to denounce its "logocentric" aspects—remains inattentive to the actual emblem of mise en abyme and to what poeticians had to say about it. He thus seems not to acknowledge this (ad hoc) plenitude at the heart of difference. Banning any coherence in the understanding of difference, he ends up adopting the "lacunal" misconception of the mise en abyme as consisting of radically discrete circuits. But these latently bear an "internal" or "coded" rather than "situational" identity; they imply their allocation to pre-established "rubrics," well distinguished from each other, hence—despite Derrida's heterological endeavors—an organizing principle, a unity that governs (binary) difference. Derrida's Iterability as generated by the incompleteness of signification, his idea according to which every attempt to mean and intend is inherently futile, implies—like the lacunal mise en abyme—static subjects and objects of signification. For Deleuze, the acute difference lies not between the Same and the Different, but rather between two modes of a "univocal" Being: the Same and the Different and the Same and the Different understood as secondary powers. Derrida (unlike Searle) does acknowledge that true repetition repeats no privileged first time but what is always already double, but does not draw the correct lesson from this "splitting into two," namely that incommensurable variants rather come as an aggregate. For Deleuze, it is never by excluding "metaphysics" or "logocentrics" that one gains a grasp of the "difference in itself." His "repetition for itself," repetition of repetition, does not aim to negate "mechanical" repetition (derived from identity). Instead, the two co-depend, or better: the repetition-for-itself is the very "middle" *between these very types of repetition*, "One is bare, the other clothed."

All this was true, however, only in our "transcendent" or "argumentative" reading of Derrida. Guided by "The Law of Genre," we offered a counter, "textualistic" reading of *Limited Inc* and Derrida's conception of intentionality as developed there. In this new reading, the very utterances expressing the incompleteness of intentionality and signification function as prospective mises en abyme for the hosting text, whether *Limited Inc* or the present study interpreting them. They thus signify "analogically," as icons, rather than digitally, as symbols, that is, with their "body" rather than content. Since such signification prevents suspending the variety of contingent factors present in the immediate, "physical" context of the message, the message and its reception come as "conjoined and allied." This is to say, the prospective mise en abyme determines the outlines of its reception, whether that reception agrees with the semantic, or coded meaning of the utterance, or not. Employing thus the principle of coexistence, Derrida maintains that the utterance regarding intentionality, and the act of signification in general, inevitably succeeds.

It was for epitomizing the principle of coexistence that the double mirror, associated by poeticians with mise en abyme right from the start, was chosen by post-Heideggerian philosophy (with Goethe, Bergson, and Heidegger himself as precursors) to replace the traditional paradigm of a (still) mirror which served to sustain the metaphysical "myth of origin." Unlike Gasché's metaphor of "tain of the mirror," the double mirror does not merely represent (or serve as an allegory of) the principle of simultaneity between incommensurable "disjuncts." It also *performs* it, thus fulfilling Kuhn's prerequisite of paradigms "to direct even in the absence of rules." As against the still mirror, where the two are inversely proportionate, in the double mirror one gazes at the semiotic level of mirroring (the reflected image) and the pragmatic level (the mirroring device) *at one and the same time*.

The equivalent paradigm shift, the "divine" dice game, substituting the traditional paradigm of play (criticized by Levinas and to some degree Caillois for epitomizing binary logic and monocentrism), consists likewise in "submitting to chance" not only the results of the roll but also the variety of empirical, or pragmatic factors present in the immediate context of the game. The game's *very differentiation* from empirical reality prevails within the game—a mise en abyme. It was for this "middle" that the Divine Game could substitute "ludic ethics" with an "ethics of becoming." "Ludic ethics" consists in setting a dichotomy between the (inherently oppressing) Self and the (inherently oppressed) Other, thus idolizing the Other, that is, turning it into a monolithic substance and a totalizing ideal. The "ethics of becoming," on the other hand, consist in a responsibility toward neither the Self nor the Other as things with ego, but rather toward processes of self-transformation, objects and subjects that did not preexist the act of responsibility. Consequently, as against Levinas's "infinite responsibility" (resulting from the inherent futility of saturating the Other's needs, which amounts—like Derrida's Iterability—to the incompleteness of intentionality), a Deleuzian act of responsibility is "fated to succeed."

Joseph Carroll expresses what many laymen and scholars mistakenly believe the *raison d'être* of poststructuralist philosophy to be:

> The norm that typically governs poststructuralist political thinking is that of anarchistic utopianism. Poststructuralism affiliates itself with every form of radical opposition to prevailing or

traditional norms. It affiliates itself with Marxist hostility to bourgeois power structures and to the hegemony of Western culture generally . . . I would contend that when one adopts a reflexive, automatic hostility to all normative structures, and combines this reflexive hostility with a hostility to all "logocentric" or rational modes of thought, the result is merely a perverse negativity. The basic poststructuralist position, inverting that of Alexander Pope, is that whatever is, is wrong. I would not agree with Pope that whatever is, is right, but I would agree even less with people who are fundamentally opposed to the very principle of normative order.[1]

Carroll is right in the sense that if Deleuze spoke of "vulgar Leibnizism" there does sometimes exist a "vulgar Deleuzianism," where unity, identity, immediacy, totality, cohesion, and presentness are too readily denounced, whereas distance, difference, deferment, and separation are idolized, that is, blindly, mechanically, and most of all—one-sidedly—affirmed. There is hardly, however, any of this "perverse negativity" in the establishing generation of poststructuralist philosophy. Drawing on the logic of the mise en abyme, the concept of difference of various writers rather consists in an "economy" between the vector of unity and that of separation. Mise en abyme is "the structural revolt" of a fragment of narrative against the whole which contains it, but this whole, the hegemonic text, inevitably "takes revenge." Mise en abyme is the *very apparatus* of "attack" and "counter attack," and it is always by forming an (ad hoc) unity with other circuits that a given circuit of mise en abyme is logically disparate to them. For poststructuralist philosophy, difference is epitomized less by the Other that challenges the totality than by the very "assemblage" between totality and the Other that challenges it, the very coexistence between these two incommensurable variants. Only this "middle," escaping as such representation, embodies true, radical otherness. And it alone should serve in developing pluralistic ethics and politics, highly suspicious of the "logic of state," and yet—as against multiculturalism and postcolonialism—refusing to substitute one totalizing ideal—the Same—with another—the Different.

Carroll further states, that poststructuralist philosophy informs us that "the ultimate nature of reality is linguistic or rhetorical in character . . . forbidding us access to any realm outside a chain of constantly displaced signifiers."[2] To the contrary, however, Deleuze's "rhizomatic book" marks a radical case of extroversion as its diegetic level crosses the culture-nature divide.

Assembling with "the outside"; consisting of an "imbrication of the *semiotic* and the *material*," that is, the very body of the empirical recipient, the rhizomatic book "transcodes" rather than encodes—it signifies in a yet to come code for yet to come recipients. But an act of transcodation, shows Deleuze, being an instance of mise en abyme, summons all others, all transcoding acts in nature, into a single "sheaf." If this "sheaf" of pre-encoded acts and bodies can yet embody a universe or a diegesis, if matter—strictly governed by physical laws—can yet signify, it is because mise en abyme comprises a coexistence of disparate yet simultaneous levels: the metasignifying and the signifying. This is to say that governing (evolutionary) time, mise en abyme causes matter to come always as an aggregate containing itself, an imminent code, as well as an imminent decoding mind.

NOTES

INTRODUCTION

1. Ron (1987, p. 430).
2. Gide 1956 [1889–1949]. It was rather Magny (1950) who coined the noun out of the adverb "en abyme" employed by Gide.
3. See Rinon (2006).
4. Dällenbach (1989, p. 118).
5. Toloudis (1983, p. 30).
6. McHale (2006, p. 176).
7. Kuiken (2005).
8. For example Olkowski (1999, p. 140).
9. Ricœur (1967, pp. 15-16).
10. The term "poeticians" denotes literary theorists or scholars of Poetics, and is employed for example in Bordwell (2008).
11. Ricœur (1967, p. 15).
12. Dolcini (2007, p. 296).
13. Dällenbach (1989, p. 170).
14. May (1994, p. 33).

CHAPTER 1

1. Gide (1956, p. 17).
2. Dällenbach (1989, p. 8).
3. Dällenbach (1989, p. 24).
4. Ricardou (1972, p. 221), translation mine.
5. Carrard (1984, p. 844).
6. Ricardou (1973, p. 73). English citation from Deleuze (1989, p. 82).
7. Cited in Ron (1987, p. 419).
8. Dällenbach (1989, p. 18).

9. Dällenbach (1989, p. 18).
10. Dällenbach (1989, p. 18).
11. Cited in Dällenbach (1989, pp. 14–15).
12. Cited in Dällenbach (1989, p. 16).
13. Shetley and Ferguson (2001, p. 68).
14. Dällenbach (1989, p. 36).
15. Dällenbach (1989, p. 169–74).
16. Dällenbach (1989, p. 35).
17. Dällenbach (1989, p. 34).
18. Genette (1972, pp. 241ff).
19. McHale (1987, p. 113).
20. Ollier (1988, p. 147).
21. Dällenbach (1989, p. 44).
22. Deleuze and Guattari (henceforth "Deleuze") (1987, p. 40).
23. Dällenbach (1989, p. 44).
24. Carrard (1984, p. 848).
25. Dällenbach (1989, p. 44).
26. Ricœur (1967, p. 16).
27. Ricœur (1967, pp. 15–16).
28. Ricœur (1967, p. 15).
29. Gadamer (2004, p. 147).
30. It is important to note here, though without elaborating on this dispute, that Walter Benjamin would have sharply criticized Ricœur's negative view of the allegorical. He would view it as originating in Romanticism, where, pursuing the "unlimited immanence of the moral world in the world of beauty" (Benjamin, 1998, p. 160), thinkers glorified the symbol whose radiance transmits itself spontaneously, without need of poetic convention, and by contrast devalued allegory as mere conventional form, inauthentic, and not grounded in experience. Studying the allegory as deployed in the Baroque, Benjamin, on the other hand, shows the allegory as more than an outward form of expression. It is rather a kind of experience arising from "an apprehension of the world as no longer permanent, as passing out of being: a sense of its transitoriness" (Cowan, 1981, p. 110). Thus, writes Cowan, he foreshadows Derrida's deconstruction of experience and view of intuition as "continually making new beginnings" (ibid. 114).
31. Dällenbach (1989, p. 44).
32. Dällenbach (1989, p. 50).
33. Dällenbach (1989, p. 221n).
34. Ron (1987, p. 426).
35. Ricœur (1970, p. 28).
36. Rimmon-Kenan (1982, p. 28).
37. Dällenbach (1989, p. 44).
38. Dällenbach (1989, p. 206n).

39. Dällenbach (1989, p. 51).
40. Bal (1978, p. 119).
41. Ricardou (1981, p. 328).
42. Dällenbach (1989, p. 44).
43. Ricardou (1981, pp. 328-29).
44. Ricardou (1973, p. 31), translation mine.
45. Blanchot (1999, p. 450).
46. Dällenbach (1989, p. 60).
47. Dällenbach (1989, p. 61).
48. Dällenbach (1989, p. 65).
49. Dällenbach (1989, p. 65).
50. Dallenbach (1989, p. 66).
51. Ricardou (1973, p. 54), translation mine.
52. Ollier (1988, pp. 146-47).
53. Dällenbach (1989, p. 69).
54. Dällenbach (1989, p. 69).
55. Cited in Dällenbach (1989, p. 69).
56. Cited in Dällenbach (1989, p. 14).
57. Ricardou (1977, p. 54).
58. Ricardou (1977, p. 36).
59. Ricardou (1973, p. 29), translation mine.
60. Ricardou (1967, p. 178).
61. Ricardou (1977, p. 52).
62. Ricardou (1977, p. 52).
63. Ricardou (1977, p. 52).
64. Morrissette (1985, p. 4).
65. Ricardou (1977, p. 52).
66. Dällenbach (1989, p. 98).
67. Dällenbach (1989, p. 94).
68. Dällenbach (1989, p. 96).
69. Dällenbach (1989, p. 80).
70. Dällenbach (1989, p. 101).
71. Dällenbach (1989, p. 103).
72. Dällenbach (1989, p. 101).
73. Derrida (1987b, p. 53) alludes to Kant.
74. Carrard (1984, p. 841).
75. For example Jakobson (1990, Passim). In accordance with the paradigmatic/syntagmatic symbiosis in his poetic function, Jakobson advocates the pursuit of a historical enquiry at the heart of the "synchronic" or universal one, putting the latter to test.
76. Bal, seeking to "fit mise en abyme into a semiotic frame" (1978, p. 122), has rejected ambiguities in the definition and methodology of mise en abyme, failing

to acknowledge their constructive role. Consequently, her scientific "standardizing" of the mise en abyme, especially by discarding with the "metaphorical" notion of "mirror," results, as Ron (1987) shows, in a typology where relations of resemblance between the representing and the represented are trivial and sterile.

77. Dällenbach (1989, p. 110).
78. Dällenbach (1989, p. 112).
79. Dällenbach (1989, p. 106).
80. Blanchot (1995, p. 332).
81. Dällenbach (1989, p. 219n).
82. McHale (1987, p. 6).
83. Dällenbach (1989, p. 106).
84. Deleuze (1987, p. 357).
85. Dällenbach (1989, p. 107).
86. Deleuze (1994, p. 17).
87. Dällenbach (1989, p. 118).
88. Toloudis (1983, p. 31).
89. Dällenbach (1989, p. 163).
90. See Toloudis (1983).
91. Hobson (1998, p. 75).
92. Dällenbach (1989, p. 155).
93. Dällenbach (1989, p. 140).
94. Dällenbach (1989, p. 234n).
95. McHale (1987, p. 126).
96. McHale (1987, p. 127).
97. McHale (1987, p. 118).
98. Morrissette (1972, p. 52) cites Brody.
99. Carrard (1984, p. 844).
100. McHale (1987, p. 14).
101. Dällenbach (1989, p. 165).
102. Dällenbach (1989, p. 163).
103. Dällenbach (1989, p. 166).
104. Dällenbach (1989, p. 112).
105. Hobson (1998, p. 75).
106. Ricardou (1973, p. 73).
107. Dällenbach (1989, p. 148).
108. Deleuze (1987, p. 352).
109. Deleuze (1987, p. 353).
110. Deleuze (1994, p. 2).
111. Dällenbach (1989, p. 166).
112. Dällenbach (1989, p. 159).
113. Dällenbach (1989, p. 159).
114. Dällenbach (1989, p. 163).

115. Dällenbach (1980, p. 437), cites Philippe Hamon.
116. Ingarden (1973, p. 247).
117. Dällenbach (1980, p. 439).
118. Dällenbach (1980, p. 444).
119. Ricardou (1973, p. 73).
120. Carrard (1984, p. 848-49).
121. Hutcheon (1980, p. xii).
122. Hutcheon (1980, p. 4).
123. Cited in Hutcheon (1980, p. 54).
124. Hutcheon (1980, p. 54).
125. Hutcheon (1980, p. 5).
126. Hutcheon (1980, p. 42).
127. Hutcheon (1980, p. 88).
128. Hutcheon (1980, p. 117).
129. Hutcheon (1980, p. xi).
130. Waugh (1984, p. 6).
131. Waugh (1984, p. 3).
132. Waugh (1984, p. 18-19).
133. Waugh (1984, p. 36).
134. Waugh (1984, p. 88).
135. Hutcheon (1980, p. 115).
136. Hutcheon (1980, p. 139).
137. Dällenbach (1980, p. 436).
138. Gadamer (2004, pp. 110 ff).
139. Deleuze (1987, p. 127).
140. Dällenbach (1989, p. 80).
141. Doležel (1998, p. 7).
142. Doležel (1998, p. 8).
143. Doležel (1998, p. 8).
144. Doležel (1998, p. 10).
145. Pavel (1986, pp. 13ff).
146. Doležel (1998, p. 20).
147. Doležel (1998, p. 17).
148. Gasché (1988, p. 137), alluding to Schlegel.
149. Deleuze (1994, p. 45), italics mine.
150. Deleuze (1994, p. 28).
151. Doležel (1998, p. 163).
152. Doležel (1998, p. 163).
153. Pavel (1986, p. 70).
154. Pavel (1986, p. 67).
155. Rimmon-Kenan (1982, p. 21n).
156. Rimmon-Kenan (1982, p. 21).

157. Rimmon-Kenan (1982, pp. 21–22), italics mine.
158. Rimmon-Kenan (1982, p. 22).
159. McHale (1987, p. 121).
160. Rimmon-Kenan (1982, p. 22).
161. Rimmon-Kenan (1982, p. 28).
162. Irvine (2009).
163. Rimmon-Kenan (1982, p. 28).
164. Rimmon-Kenan (1982, p. 29).
165. Derrida (1997, p. 158).
166. Derrida (1997, p. 160).
167. Rimmon-Kenan (1982, p. 28).
168. Deleuze (1989, p. 104).
169. Rimmon-Kenan (1982, p. 31).
170. Rimmon-Kenan (1982, p. 31–32).
171. Kowzan (1976, p. 92).
172. Deleuze (1987, p. 12).
173. See Tally (1996).
174. Jameson (1988 p. 353).
175. McHale (2006, pp. 186–87).
176. Kowzan (1976, p. 92).
177. Kowzan (1976, p. 92).
178. Le Poidevin (1995, p. 229).
179. Le Poidevin (1995, p. 230).
180. Le Poidevin (1995, p. 230).
181. Le Poidevin (1995, p. 230).
182. Le Poidevin (1995, p. 231), italics mine.
183. Le Poidevin (1995, p. 232).
184. Le Poidevin (1995, p. 235–36).
185. Le Poidevin (1995, p. 236).
186. Le Poidevin (1995, p. 237).
187. Le Poidevin (1995, p. 237).
188. Füredy (1989 p. 751).
189. Füredy (1989 p. 752).
190. Füredy (1989, p. 753).
191. Füredy (1989, p. 755).
192. Füredy (1989, p. 755).
193. Füredy (1989, p. 758).
194. Le Poidevin (1995, p. 232), italics mine.
195. Füredy (1989, p. 755).
196. Füredy (1989, p. 756).
197. Füredy (1989, p. 767).

CHAPTER 2

1. Foucault (2002, p. 229).
2. Nietzsche (1966, p. 23).
3. Dolcini (2007, p. 296).
4. Heidegger (1998a, p. 128).
5. Heidegger (1996, p. 6).
6. Heidegger (1996, p. 3).
7. Heidegger (1996, p. 4).
8. Deleuze (1994, p. 197).
9. Heidegger (1996, p. 6).
10. Heidegger (1996, p. 140).
11. Heidegger (1998b, p. 248).
12. Heidegger (1996, p. 7).
13. Gasché (1988, p. 301).
14. Derrida (1997, p. 20).
15. Derrida (1981b, p. 41).
16. Gasché (1988, p. 137).
17. Johnson (1981, p. viii).
18. Derrida (1997, p. 20).
19. Derrida (1997, p. 18).
20. Derrida (1997, p. 21).
21. Derrida (1997, p. 70).
22. Derrida (1973, p. 86).
23. Gasché (1988, p. 188).
24. Derrida (1973, p. 86).
25. Hegel (2010, p. 374).
26. Derrida (1978, p. 255).
27. Derrida (1982, p. 13).
28. Derrida (1982, p. 13).
29. Derrida (1973, p. 67).
30. Derrida (1997, p. 112).
31. Derrida (1973, p. 67).
32. Husserl (1983, p. 246).
33. Derrida (1973, p. 104) cites Husserl.
34. Husserl (1983, p. 247).
35. Füredy (1989, p. 756).
36. Derrida (1973, p. 104).
37. Derrida (1997, p. 158).
38. Derrida (1973, p. 88).
39. Gasché (1988, p. 223).

40. Derrida (1997, p. 167).
41. Derrida (1997, p. 215).
42. Derrida (1981a, p. 110).
43. Derrida (1997, p. 145).
44. Gasché (1988, p. 211).
45. Derrida (1997, p. 246).
46. Derrida (1997, p. 215).
47. Derrida (1997, p. 163).
48. Derrida (1982, p. 7).
49. Gasché (1988, p. 88).
50. Dällenbach (1989, p. 170).
51. Derrida (1987a, p. 304).
52. Hobson (1998, p. 75).
53. Gasché (1988, p. 282).
54. Derrida (1982, p. 10).
55. Derrida (1997, p. 47).
56. Derrida (1981a, p. 355).
57. Derrida (1988, p. 12).
58. de Nooy (1991, p. 23).
59. de Nooy (1991, p. 23).
60. Derrida (1987b, p. 27).
61. de Nooy (1991, p. 26).
62. Derrida (1988, p. 62).
63. Bearn (2000, p. 453).
64. Gasché (1988, p. 281).
65. Gasché (1988, p. 212).
66. Foucault (2002, p. xvi).
67. Gasché (1988, p. 212).
68. Searle (1977, p. 199).
69. Derrida (1988, p. 7).
70. Derrida (1981a, p. 206).
71. Gasché (1988, p. 192).
72. Deleuze (1987, p. 168).
73. Deleuze (1987, p. 154).
74. Dällenbach (1989, p. 222n).
75. Dällenbach (1989, p. 111).
76. Füredy (1989, p. 752).
77. Ricardou (1973, p. 73). English citation from Deleuze (1989, p. 82).
78. Ricardou (1972, p. 221), translation mine.
79. Derrida (1987b. p. 291).
80. Bearn (2000, p. 441).

81. de Nooy (1991, p. 24).
82. Dällenbach (1989, p. 44).
83. Gasché (1988, p. 154).
84. Johnson (1981, p. xiv).
85. Gross (1986, p. 29).
86. Gross (1986, p. 29).
87. Derrida (1997, p. 27).
88. Gross (1986, p. 29).
89. Miller (2002, p. 62).
90. Miller (1995, p. 82).
91. Derrida (1981a, p. 7).
92. Miller (2002, p. 75).
93. Derrida (1988, pp. 18, 59, 105).
94. Derrida (1988, p. 114).
95. Miller (2002, p. 60).
96. Derrida (2013, p. 3).
97. Derrida (2013, p. 5).
98. Derrida (2013, p. 7).
99. Miller (2002, p. 76).
100. Ron (1987, p. 424).
101. Bal (1978, p. 124).
102. Derrida (2013, p. 7).
103. Derrida (2013, p. 14).
104. Derrida (2005, p. 59).
105. Derrida (2005, p. 57).
106. Derrida (2005, p. 33).
107. Derrida (2005, p. 27).
108. Miller (2002, p. 69).
109. Miller (2002, p. 75).
110. Miller (2002, p. 79).
111. Miller (2002, p. 66).
112. Derrida (2013, p. 14).
113. Derrida (2005, p. 10).
114. Widder (2003, p. 453).
115. Derrida (2013, p. 6).
116. Derrida (2013, p. 14).
117. Derrida (2013, p. 28).
118. Derrida (2013, p. 27).
119. Such extension would follow Marcel Raymond and the Geneva school, who "in a gesture reminiscent of Husserl in his discussion of epoché, bracket out the world and all subjective interference in order to grasp the consciousness of the

author in its purity" (Holub, 1995, p. 311), that is, not the empirical author, but "that which is immanent in the text, actualized in the materiality of the work" (Carrard, 1984, p. 841).

CHAPTER 3

1. Heidegger (1996, p. 242).
2. Heidegger (1996, p. 223).
3. Heidegger (1996, p. 245).
4. Heidegger (1996, p. 389).
5. Heidegger (1996, p. 234).
6. Blanchot (1986, p. 70), italics mine.
7. Blanchot (1995, p. 323) cites Hegel's *System of 1803–1804*.
8. Blanchot (1995, p. 322).
9. Gasché (1996, p. 51).
10. Blanchot (1995, p. 323).
11. Gasché (1988, p. 200).
12. Blanchot (1995, p. 327).
13. Gasché (1996, p. 65).
14. Hill (1997, p. 114).
15. Blanchot (1995, p. 336).
16. Blanchot (1995, p. 337).
17. Deleuze (1994, p. 112).
18. Deleuze (1994, p. 113).
19. Hill (1997, p. 56).
20. Heidegger (2002, p. 16).
21. Heidegger (2002, p. 26).
22. Heidegger (2002, p. 27).
23. Heidegger (2002, p. 33).
24. Heidegger (1998a, pp. 128–29).
25. Derrida (1987b, p. 290).
26. Heidegger (1998a, p. 134).
27. Heidegger (1998a, pp. 134–35).
28. Schwartz (2000).
29. Heidegger (1998a, p. 135).
30. Derrida (1987b, p. 291).
31. Blanchot (1982, p. 167).
32. Blanchot (1982, p. 167).
33. Heidegger (1998a, p. 134).
34. Blanchot (1982, p. 54).
35. Blanchot (1988, pp. 14–15) with Hill's modifications (1997, pp. 58–59).

36. Hill (1997, p. 59).
37. Blanchot (1982, p. 163).
38. Blanchot (1982, p. 239).
39. Blanchot (1988, p. 27).
40. Blanchot (1988, p. 26).
41. Blanchot (1995, p. 332).
42. Blanchot (1988, pp. 25–26).
43. Cited in Dällenbach (1989, p. 14).
44. Blanchot (1982, p. 89).
45. Blanchot (1982, p. 171).
46. Blanchot (2003, p. 94).
47. Blanchot (1982, p. 168).
48. Blanchot (1999, p. 447).
49. Blanchot (1982, p. 169).
50. Foucault (1998, p. 92).
51. Foucault (1998, p. 90).
52. Marion (2002, p. 35).
53. Blanchot (1982, p. 175).
54. Blanchot (1999, p. 447).
55. Blanchot (2003, p. 236).
56. Blanchot (1982, p. 176).
57. Blanchot (2003, p. 235).
58. Dällenbach (1989, p. 219n).
59. Blanchot (1995, p. 336).
60. Blanchot (1999, p. 447).
61. Dällenbach (1989, p. 219n).
62. Blanchot (2003, p. 234).
63. Blanchot (2003, p. 94).
64. Motzkin (2000, p. 163).
65. Motzkin (2000, p. 163).
66. Iser (1993, p. 1), italics mine.
67. Iser (1993, p. 223).
68. Motzkin (2000, p. 169).
69. Motzkin (2000, p. 172).
70. Motzkin (2000, pp. 171–72).
71. Iser (1993, p. 226).
72. Iser (1993, p. 225).
73. Iser (1993, p. 229).
74. Iser (1993, p. 226).
75. Iser (1993, p. 226).
76. Iser (1993, p. 223).
77. Blanchot (1995, p. 329).

78. Blanchot (1995, p. 329).
79. Blanchot (1999, p. 444).
80. Blanchot (1995, p. 332).
81. Gasché (1996, p. 55).
82. Blanchot (2003, p. 219).
83. Blanchot (2003, p. 219).
84. Laporte (1996, p. 29), cites Blanchot.
85. Laporte (1996, p. 30).
86. Gasché (1996, p. 65).
87. Hill (1997, p. 62).
88. Blanchot (1995, p. 330).
89. Blanchot (1995, p. 330).
90. Laporte (1996, p. 32), italics mine.
91. Blanchot (1995, p. 338).
92. Blanchot (1995, p. 329).
93. Blanchot (1995, p. 334).
94. Hill (1997, p. 140).
95. Hill (1997, p. 62).
96. Levinas (1978, p. 57).
97. Levinas (1998, p. 7).
98. Levinas (1998, p. 25).
99. Gasché (1988, p. 192).
100. Hill (1997, p. 63).
101. Levinas (1998, p. 25).
102. Deleuze (1987, p. 21).
103. Blanchot (2003, p. 94).
104. Blanchot (2003, p. 94).
105. Blanchot (2003, p. 94).
106. Blanchot (2003, p. 94).
107. Blanchot (1982, p. 239), italics mine.
108. Foucault (1986, p. 23).
109. Foucault (1998, p. 91).
110. Gasché (1996, p. 65), italics mine.
111. Blanchot (1982, p. 239).
112. Blanchot (1999, p. 448).
113. Foucault (1998, p. 91).
114. Deleuze (1994, p. 237).

CHAPTER 4

1. Villani (1999, p. 130).

2. May (1994, p. 33).
3. Boundas (2006, p. 6).
4. Hegel (2010, p. 374), italics mine.
5. Deleuze (1994, p. 30).
6. Deleuze (1994, p. 32).
7. Deleuze (1994, p. 28).
8. Deleuze (1994, p. 45).
9. Hegel (2010, p. 374).
10. Hegel (2010, p. 376).
11. Hegel (2010, p. 374).
12. Deleuze (1994, p. 50).
13. Deleuze (1994, p. 49).
14. Williams (2003, p. 71).
15. Hegel (2010, p. 376).
16. Deleuze (1989, p. 104).
17. Widder (2003, p. 461).
18. Widder (2003, p. 452).
19. Deleuze (1987, p. 11 and passim).
20. Deleuze (1990, p. 8).
21. Deleuze (1994, p. 43).
22. Widder (2001, p. 444).
23. Widder (2001, pp. 444–45).
24. Deleuze (1994, p. 28).
25. Deleuze (1994, p. 33).
26. Deleuze (1994, p. 192).
27. Deleuze (1994, p. 2).
28. Deleuze (1994, p. 36).
29. Deleuze (1994, p. 222).
30. Deleuze (1994, p. 295).
31. Deleuze (1994, p. 125).
32. Deleuze (1994, p. 49).
33. Deleuze (1994, p. 45).
34. Leibniz (1989, p. 46).
35. Deleuze (1994, p. 48).
36. Deleuze (1994, p. 237).
37. Leibniz (1979, p. 233), italics mine.
38. Deleuze (1994, p. 47).
39. Deleuze (1994, p. 59).
40. Deleuze (1994, p. 67).
41. Deleuze (1994, p. 60).
42. Deleuze (1994, p. 63).
43. Deleuze (1987, p. 126).

44. Deleuze (1994, p. 46).
45. Deleuze (1994, p. 59).
46. Deleuze (1994, p. 62).
47. Deleuze (1994, p. 66).
48. Heidegger (1987, p. 156).
49. Kuiken (2005, p. 297).
50. Deleuze (1997c, p. 194).
51. Deleuze (1997c, p. 191).
52. Kuiken (2005, p. 304).
53. Deleuze (1994, p. 46).
54. Kuiken (2005, pp. 300–01).
55. Kuiken (2005, p. 304), italics mine.
56. Deleuze (1994, p. 41).
57. Deleuze (1994, p. 17).
58. Huizinga (1949, p. 9).
59. Deleuze (1994, p. 284) cites Nietzsche (1961).
60. Deleuze (1994, p. 283).
61. Bearn (2000, p. 460).
62. Deleuze (1987, p. 56).
63. Bearn (1987, p. 441).
64. Blanchot (2003, p. 233).
65. Deleuze (1987, p. 78).
66. Deleuze (1990, p. 70).
67. Deleuze (p. 1990, p. 24).
68. Deleuze (1997a, p. 102).
69. Deleuze (1997a, p. 102).
70. Deleuze (1997a, p. 97).
71. Deleuze (1997a, p. 103).
72. Deleuze (1990, p. 20).
73. Derrida (1982, p. 10).
74. Bearn (2000, p. 452).
75. Bearn (2000, p. 460).
76. Deleuze (1994, p. 24).
77. Williams (2011, p. 22).
78. May (1994, p. 44), italics mine.
79. Deleuze (1994, p. 234).
80. Deleuze (1994, p. 28).
81. Deleuze (1994, p. 246).
82. Deleuze (1994, p. 124).
83. May (1994, p. 33).
84. Deleuze (1994, p. 75).
85. Williams (2011, p. 29).

86. Deleuze (1994, p. 73).
87. Deleuze (1994, p. 75).
88. Bergson (1920, p. 169).
89. Widder (2006, p. 409).
90. Williams (2011, p. 43), italics mine.
91. Dällenbach (1989, p. 69).
92. Ron (1987, p. 417).
93. Ron (1987, p. 433).
94. Dällenbach (1989, p. 65).
95. Dällenbach (1989, p. 61).
96. Deleuze (1994, p. 79).
97. Widder (2006, p. 409).
98. Bergson (1919, p. 194).
99. Deleuze (1989, p. 81).
100. Al-Saji (2004, p. 208).
101. Bergson (1919, p. 194).
102. Al-Saji (2004, p. 205).
103. Bergson (1920, p. 197).
104. Bergson (1920, p. 198).
105. Deleuze (1989, p. 82).
106. Boundas (2006, p. 5).
107. Deleuze (1994, p. 99).
108. Deleuze (1988, p. 60).
109. Deleuze (1994, p. 81).
110. Al-Saji (2004, pp. 209–10).
111. Deleuze (1994, p. 79).
112. Deleuze (1994, p. 81).
113. Deleuze (1994, p. 82).
114. Deleuze (1994, p. 82).
115. Deleuze (1988, p. 59).
116. Deleuze (1994, p. 83).
117. Bergson (1919, p. 196).
118. Lawlor (2003, p. 47).
119. Bergson (1919, p. 219).
120. Bergson (1919, p. 220).
121. Deleuze (1988, p. 60).
122. Lawlor (2003, p. 48).
123. Deleuze (1997c, p. 195).
124. Deleuze (1994, p. 85).
125. Deleuze (1994, p. 86).
126. Guyer (2006, p. 96).
127. Guyer (2006, p. 97).

128. Kant (1929, p. 93).
129. Deleuze (1994, p. 86).
130. Kant (1929, p. 74).
131. Kant (1929, p. 68).
132. Kant (1929, p. 74).
133. Kant (1929, p. 75).
134. Deleuze (1994, p. 86).
135. Bergson (1920, p. 198).
136. Lawlor (2019, forthcoming).
137. Lawlor (2019, forthcoming).
138. Lawlor (2019, forthcoming).
139. Lawlor (2019, forthcoming).
140. Deleuze (1994, p. 90).
141. Baross (2006b, p. 32).
142. Widder (2006, p. 409).
143. Olkowski (1999, p. 135).
144. Al-Saji (2004, p. 209).
145. P. Lawlor (1985, p. 830).
146. Olkowski (1999, p. 140).
147. Lorraine (2011, p. 130).
148. Lorraine (2011, p. 131).
149. Olkowski (1999, p. 191).
150. Olkowski (1999, p. 145).
151. Widder (2006, p. 409).
152. "Misrepresentations" is how Critchley defines representations of a Blanchotian death (1996, p. 108).
153. Deleuze (1994, p. 89).
154. McHale (1987, p. 14).
155. Baross (2006b, p. 32).
156. Deleuze (1989, p. 82).
157. Derrida (1982, p. 262).
158. Gasché (1988, p. 293).
159. Gasché (1988, p. 308).
160. Derrida (2007, p. 74).
161. Derrida (2007, pp. 75–76).
162. Derrida (2007, p. 69).
163. Deleuze (1997b, p. 95).
164. Deleuze (1997b, p. 95).
165. Heidegger (2001, p. 177).
166. Jarry (1996, p. 21).
167. Deleuze (1997b, p. 96).
168. Deleuze (1997b, p. 91).

169. Deleuze (1997b, p. 92).
170. Jarry (1996, p. 21).
171. Cited in Hugill (2012, p. 51).
172. Cited in Hugill (2012, p. 51).
173. Deleuze (1987, p. 69).
174. Olkowski (1999, p. 25), italics mine.

CHAPTER 5

1. Rorty (1979, p. 12).
2. Rorty (1979, p. 42–43).
3. Grabes (1982, p. 78).
4. Frappier (1959, p. 136), translation mine.
5. Gasché (1988, p. 43).
6. Gasché (1988, p. 43).
7. Heidegger (2001, p. 177).
8. Dällenbach (1989, p. 156).
9. Dällenbach (1989, p. 157).
10. Kearney (1991, p. 402n).
11. Kearney (1991, p. 17).
12. Kearney (1991, p. 155).
13. Weatherston (2002, p. 1), cites Cassirer.
14. Rorty (1979, p. 4).
15. Rorty (1979, p. 12).
16. Rorty (1979, p. 4).
17. Kearney (1991, p. 253).
18. Kearney (1991, p. 252).
19. Kearney (1991, p. 252).
20. Kearney (1991, p. 285).
21. Derrida (1981a, pp. 194–95).
22. Kearney (1991, p. 286).
23. Derrida (1981a, p. 206).
24. Derrida (1981a, p. 206).
25. Derrida (1981a, p. 206), italics mine.
26. Deleuze (1994, p. 101).
27. Al-Saji (2004, p. 212).
28. Deleuze (1989, p. 70).
29. Deleuze (1989, p. 78).
30. Deleuze (1989, p. 78).
31. Deleuze (1989, p. 79).
32. Bergson (1920, p. 165).

33. Bergson (1920, p. 169).
34. Cited in Dällenbach (1989, p. 16).
35. Al-Saji (2004, p. 215).
36. Al-Saji (2004, p. 213).
37. Bergson (1920, p. 165).
38. Al-Saji (2004, p. 215).
39. Deleuze (1989, p. 69).
40. Deleuze (1989, p. 70).
41. Miller (1993, p. 87).
42. Shetley and Ferguson (2001, p. 68).
43. Cook (1986, p. 96).
44. Deleuze (1989, p. 70).
45. Deleuze (1989, p. 70).
46. Deleuze (1989, p. 70).
47. Rodowick (1997, p. 91).
48. Dieckmann (1962, p. 155).
49. Dieckmann (1962, p. 156), cites Goethe.
50. Dieckmann (1962, p. 157).
51. Dieckmann (1962, p. 156).
52. Deleuze (1994, p. 82).
53. Deleuze (1989, p. 70), italics mine.
54. Ricardou (1973, p. 73). English citation from Deleuze (1989, p. 82).
55. Deleuze (1989, p. 69).
56. Cited in Olkowski (1999, p. 255n).
57. Damisch (1995, pp. 65–66).
58. Olkowski (1999, p. 87).
59. Olkowski (1999, p. 16).
60. Olkowski (1999, p. 29).
61. Olkowski (1999, p. 87).
62. Olkowski (1999, p. 44).
63. Olkowski (1999, p. 118).
64. Deleuze (1989, p. 68).
65. Ricardou (1973, p. 111), translation mine.
66. Ricardou (1973, p. 112), translation mine.
67. Ricardou (1973, p. 29), translation mine.
68. Ricardou (1973, p. 29), translation mine.
69. Bateson (1972, pp. 177–93).
70. Goffman (1974, esp. pp. 124–55).
71. Goffman (1974, p. 67).
72. Harshaw (1984, p. 247).
73. Harshaw (1984, p. 249).
74. McHale (1987, p. 28).

75. Gasché (1988, p. 16-17).
76. Gasché (1988, p. 63).
77. Gasché (1988, p. 93).
78. Gasché (1988, p. 239).
79. Gasché (1988, p. 93).
80. Derrida (1997, p. 36).
81. Gasché (1988, p. 237).
82. Derrida (1981a, p. 33).
83. Gasché (1988, p. 237).
84. Gasché (1988, p. 238).
85. Gasché (1988, p. 238).
86. Kuhn (1996, p. 42).
87. Ricœur (1967, p. 15).
88. Gasché (1988, p. 238).
89. Gasché (1988, p. 171), cites Derrida.
90. Urraca (1992, p. 159).
91. Urraca (1992, p. 155).
92. Urraca (1992, p. 155).
93. Cited in Urraca (1992, p. 159).
94. Urraca (1992, p. 161).
95. Urraca (1992, p. 161).
96. Fink (1974, p. 160).
97. Fink (1974, p. 155), italics mine.
98. Fink (1974, p. 159).
99. Fink (1974, p. 159).
100. Fink (1974, p. 159).
101. Spariosu (1989, p. 129).

CHAPTER 6

1. Spariosu (1989, p. 29).
2. Spariosu (1989, p. 30).
3. Olkowski (1994, p. 124).
4. Olkowski (1994, p. 121).
5. Nietzsche (1961, p. 245).
6. Spariosu (1989, p. 86).
7. Spariosu (1989, p. 101), cites Heidegger (1987).
8. Spariosu (1989, p. 102).
9. Spariosu (1989, pp. 119-20).
10. Spariosu (1989, p. 120).
11. Spariosu (1989, p. 122).

12. Spariosu (1989, p. 127).
13. Fink (2003, p. 171).
14. Spariosu (1989, p. 128).
15. Spariosu (1989, p. 126).
16. Gadamer (2004, p. 109).
17. Gadamer (2004, p. 106).
18. Gadamer (2004, p. 111).
19. Gadamer (2004, p. 484).
20. Gadamer (2004, p. 484).
21. Gadamer (2004, p. 156).
22. Gadamer (2004, p. 470).
23. Gadamer (2004, p. 156).
24. Gadamer (2004, p. 111), italics mine.
25. Spariosu (1989, p. 126).
26. Fink (1974, p. 155).
27. Fink (1974, p. 156).
28. Fink (1974, p. 155).
29. Spariosu (1989, p. 131).
30. Spariosu (1989, p. 129).
31. Fink (1974, p. 159).
32. Fink (1974, p. 156).
33. Fink (1974, p. 160).
34. Fink (1974, p. 160).
35. Spariosu (1989, p. 129).
36. Fink (1974, p. 160).
37. Fink (1974, p. 156).
38. Caillois (1961, p. 44).
39. Gadamer (2004, p. 107).
40. Robbins (1999, p. 145).
41. Levinas (1998, p. 116).
42. Fink (2016, p. 229).
43. Fink (2016, p. 229).
44. Levinas (1998, p. 106).
45. Dällenbach (1989, p. 8).
46. See Kowzan (1976).
47. Deleuze (1994, p. 116), cites Borges.
48. Deleuze (1994, p. 283).
49. Lorraine (2011, p. 137).
50. Deleuze (1990, p. 8).
51. Lorraine (2011, p. 137).
52. Lorraine (2011, p. 137).
53. O'Connor (2014, p. 1100).
54. Visker (2003, p. 276).

55. Visker (2003, p. 276).
56. Hegel (2010, p. 374).
57. Visker (2003, p. 287).
58. Visker (1997, p. 161).
59. Sutton-Smith (1997, p. 133).
60. Cited in Sutton-Smith (1997, p. 136).
61. Sutton-Smith (1997, p. 137).
62. Sutton-Smith (1997, p. 144).
63. Turner (1969, p. viii).
64. Turner (1969. p. 95).
65. Turner (1982, p. 27).
66. Turner (1982, p. 49).
67. Pavel (1986, p. 143).
68. Pavel (1986, p. 42).
69. McHale (1987), drawing on Pavel (1986) and Berger and Luckmann (1966).
70. Cited in McHale (1987, p. 205).
71. Gass (1970, pp. 277–78).
72. Oz (2017, retrieved).
73. Cited in Sutton-Smith (1997, p. 136).
74. Sutton-Smith (1997, p. 207).
75. Turner (1982, p. 49).
76. Lorraine (2011, p. 1).
77. Lorraine (2001, p. 1).
78. Levinas (1998, p. 93).
79. Levinas (1998, p. 18).
80. Smith (2003, p. 62).
81. Smith (2003, p. 62).
82. Visker (2003, p. 273).
83. Bernet (2000, p. 47).
84. Deleuze (1994, p. 283).
85. Deleuze (1994, p. 283), italics mine.
86. Deleuze (1994, p. 284).
87. Deleuze (1994, p. 282).
88. Deleuze (1994, p. 283).
89. Deleuze (1994, p. 283).

CHAPTER 7

1. Gadamer (2004, p. 103).
2. Deleuze (1987, p. 186–87).
3. Deleuze (1987, p. 186).

4. Deleuze (1987, p. 187).
5. Deleuze (1987, p. 188).
6. Deleuze (1987, p. 186).
7. Blanchot (1982, p. 175).
8. Deleuze & Guattari (henceforth "Deleuze") (1986, p. 6).
9. Doležel (1988, p. 20).
10. Deleuze (1987, p. 243).
11. Deleuze (1987, p. 274), italics mine.
12. Blanchot (1999, p. 448).
13. Blanchot (1999, p. 449).
14. Deleuze (1986, p. 13).
15. Deleuze (1986, p. 13).
16. Deleuze (1986, p. 25).
17. Deleuze (1986, p. 26).
18. Deleuze (1986, p. 26).
19. Deleuze (1986, p. 13).
20. Deleuze (1986, p. 28).
21. Deleuze (1986, p. 18).
22. Dällenbach (1989, p. 75).
23. Deleuze (1986, p. 41).
24. Deleuze (1986, p. 28).
25. Deleuze (1986, p. 45).
26. Deleuze (1986, p. 28).
27. Widder (2003, p. 471).
28. Deleuze (1990, p. 67).
29. Deleuze (1986, p. 28).
30. Deleuze (1987, p. 4).
31. Deleuze (1994, p. 151).
32. Morrissette (1985, p. 10).
33. Marks (2000, p. 82).
34. Ricardou (1981, p. 337).
35. Blanchot (2003, p. 226).
36. Gasché (1988, p. 137).
37. Deleuze (1987, p. 7).
38. Deleuze (1987, p. 11).
39. Deleuze (1987, p. 127).
40. Deleuze (1987, p. 21).
41. Deleuze (1987, p. 21).
42. Deleuze (1987, p. 7).
43. Deleuze (1987, p. 9).
44. Deleuze (1987, p. 23).
45. Deleuze (1987, p. 126), italics mine.

46. Deleuze (1987, p. 126).
47. Deleuze (1987, p. 337).
48. Gadamer (2004, p. 156).
49. Gadamer (2004, p. 484).
50. Gadamer (2004, p. 484), italics mine.
51. Gadamer (2004, p. 470).
52. Dällenbach (1980, p. 436).
53. Eco (1989, p. 10).
54. Eco (1989, p. 218).
55. Hutcheon (1980, p. 151).
56. Eco (1989, p. 93).
57. Eco (1989, p. 94).
58. Eco (1989, p. 11).
59. Eco (1989, p. 12), italics mine.
60. Hutcheon (1980, p. 139).
61. Dällenbach (1989, p. 80).
62. Deleuze (1987, p. 12).
63. Foucault (2002, p. 39).
64. Foucault (2002, p. 38).
65. Foucault (2002, p. 20), italics mine.
66. Eco (1989, p. 169).
67. Blanchot (2003, p. 234).
68. Deleuze (1990, p. 3).
69. Deleuze (1987, p. 12).
70. Dällenbach (1989, p. 34).
71. Deleuze (1987, p. 12).
72. Deleuze (1987, p. 337).
73. Baross (2006b, p. 32).
74. Deleuze (1994, p. 91).
75. Deleuze (1994, p. 91).
76. Deleuze (1989, pp. 80-81).
77. Deleuze (1987, p. 127).
78. See Maimonodes's codexing of the halakhah in *Mishneh Torah*, book *Ahavah, Hilkhot Tefillin u-Mezuzah ve-Sefer Torah*, ch. 7 (Touger 1988 trans.)
79. See *m.Yad.* 3:5. The peculiar case of a sacred object that causes impurity by virtue of its sacredness also obtains for the ashes of the red heifer (Num 19:1–10). Though the ashes are prepared for a purification ritual, they render impure—for one day—the priests who participate in their preparation and use.
80. However, "in three places the halakha bypasses the Torah," and one of them is the bypassing of the Torah's demand to write the *get* on a parchment scroll (*y. Qidd.* 1:2). To this day some permit the writing of this *sefer* also upon paper.
81. Rema's (R. Moses Isserles) ruling in Karo 1999 [1488–1575], 125:2.

82. See Holdrege (1989, p. 184).

83. *b. Meg.* 17a.

84. Bal detects various mises en abyme also in the book of Ruth. According to Bal, proper names in this book project the conduct of those who bear them: Orpah would turn back showing her rear, '*oref*; Boaz would be the '*az*, the daring. Bal considers the elders' blessing to Boaz—that he should build with Ruth, "like Rachel and like Leah," "the house of Israel"—to reflect the Bible as a whole, for the Bible is also "entirely consecrated" to this mission (1987, pp. 94–143). However, contrary to the mise en abyme in the (rabbinic) scroll of Esther, Bal's mises en abyme are mild, uncovered only by means of a thorough critical retrospection, the validity of which Dällenbach "calls into question" (1989, p. 49). Mise en abyme, as we saw in chapter 1, "only *becomes* such through the duplicative relationship it admits to with one or other aspect of the narrative," it is a *hic et nunc* relationship, something that happens, or "shines forth," to use Heidegger's term, not something to be inferred from the text.

85. Grossfeld 1991 (trans.) p. 88.

86. Dällenbach (1989, p. 69).

87. Sonnet (1997, p. 79).

88. Dällenbach (1989, p. 101).

89. Yosef Dov Soloveitchik (1983, pp. 161–62) bases this interpretation on *b. Rosh Hash.* 17a: "What is meant by 'wrongdoers of Israel who sin with their body'? — Rav said: This refers to the cranium that does not put on the phylactery."

90. Derrida (1981a, p. 71).

91. Faur (1986, p. xxviii).

92. Foucault (1998, p. 94).

93. Foucault (1998, p. 99).

94. Foucault (1998, p. 94–95).

95. Foucault (1998, p. 95).

96. Foucault (1998, p. 94-95). Cf. Baross: "After more than a century of relentless production by mechanical reproduction . . . an image—a cliché, precisely—is fixed of everything: every gesture, embrace, pose . . . Every phrase of sympathy, mercy, forgiving . . . every future disaster, catastrophe, barbarity . . . This future . . . is the eternity of the cliché: ready-made perceptions, memories, fantasies, desires proliferate and reproduce in the medium of what is called the 'media'" (2006a, p. 113).

97. Foucault (1998, p. 101).

98. Foucault (1998, p. 99).

99. Deleuze (1989, pp. 80–81).

100. Deleuze (1987, p. 142).

101. *Gen. Rab.* 3:7.

102. Deleuze (1987, p. 12), italics mine.

103. Dällenbach (1980, p. 437), cites Hamon.

104. Deleuze (1987, p. 313).
105. Deleuze (1987, p. 380).
106. Deleuze (1987, p. 318).
107. Sonnet (1997, p. 145).
108. Deleuze (1987, p. 314).
109. Deleuze (1987, p. 326).
110. Deleuze (1987, p. 321).
111. Deleuze (1987, p. 337).
112. Deleuze (1987, p. 345).
113. Deleuze (1987, p. 345).
114. Deleuze (1987, p. 346).
115. Deleuze (1987, p. 334).
116. Deleuze (1997b, p. 5).
117. *b. Meg.* 17a.
118. Bogue (2006, p. 219).
119. Deleuze (1987, p. 21).
120. Deleuze (1987, p. 339).
121. Blanchot (1982, p. 269).
122. Blanchot (1982, p. 171).
123. Blanchot (1982, p. 54).

CONCLUSION

1. Carroll (2004, pp. 25–26).
2. Carroll (2004, p. 29).

BIBLIOGRAPHY

Citations from Bal (1978) and Ricardou (1967, 1972, 1973) are my translations unless stated otherwise.

Citations from the Bible follow the Revised English Standard Version (RSV), with minor modifications. Citations from the Babylonian Talmud follow I. Epstein's translation (Soncino Version) with minor modifications. Citations from the Jerusalem Talmud follow J. Neusner's translation (1987). Citations from the Mishnah follow Y. Milstein's translation. Citations from *Genesis Rabbah* and *Song of Songs Rabbah* follow Neusner's translations (1997a and 1997b, respectively). Citations of Rashi (Rabbi Shlomo Itzhaki) follow the Vilna Edition of the Babylonian Talmud.

I use the following abbreviations: *m* for Mishnah, *b* for Babylonian Talmud, *y* for Jerusalem Talmud.

Alter, Robert. 1975. *Partial Magic*. Berkeley: University of California Press.
Al-Saji, Alia. 2004. "The Memory of Another Past: Bergson, Deleuze and a New Theory of Time." *Continental Philosophy Review*, 3: 203–39.
Austin, J. L. 1975 [1962]. *How to do Things with Words*. Oxford: Oxford University Press.
Bal, Mieke. 1978. "*Mise en abyme* et iconicité." *Littérature*, 29: 116–28.
Bal, Mieke. 1987. *Lethal Love*. Bloomington: Indiana University Press.
Baross, Zsuzsa. 2006a. "A Fourth Repetition." In *Deleuze and Philosophy*, C. Boundas (ed.), 98–117. Edinburgh: Edinburgh University Press.
Baross, Zsuzsa. 2006b. "The Future of Deleuze: An Unfinished Project," *Symposium*, 10: 25–33.
Bateson, Gregory. 1972. *Steps to an Ecology of Mind*. Northvale, NJ: Jason Aronson.
Bateson, Gregory. 1979. *Mind and Nature*. New York: E. P. Dutton.
Bearn, Gordon. 2000. "Differentiating Derrida and Deleuze." *Continental Philosophy Review*, 33: 441–65.
Benjamin, Walter. 1998 [1928]. *The Origin of German Tragic Drama*, trans. J. Osborne. London: Verso.
Berger, Peter, and Thomas Luckmann. 1966. *The Social Construction of Reality*. London: Penguin.

Bergson, Henri. 1919 [1896]. *Matter and Memory*, trans. N. Paul. London: George Allen & Unwin.
Bergson, Henri. 1920. *Mind-Energy*, trans. H. Wildon Carr. New York: Henry Holt.
Bernet, Rudolf. 2000. "The Encounter with the Stranger: Two Interpretations of the Vulnerability of the Skin." In *The Face of the Other and the Trace of God*, J. Bloechl (ed.), 43–61. New York: Fordham University Press.
Blanchot, Maurice. 1982 [1955]. *The Space of Literature*, trans. A. Smock. Lincoln: University of Nebraska Press.
Blanchot, Maurice. 1986 [1980]. *The Writing of the Disaster*, trans. A. Smock. Lincoln: University of Nebraska Press.
Blanchot, Maurice. 1988 [1941]. *Thomas the Obscure*, trans. R. Lamberton. Barrytown, NY: Station Hill Press.
Blanchot, Maurice. 1995 [1949]. "Literature and the Right to Death," trans. L. Davis. In *The Work of Fire*, W. Harnacher & D. E. Wellbery (eds.), 300–44. Stanford, CA: Stanford University Press.
Blanchot, Maurice. 1999 [1954]. "The Song of the Sirens," trans. L. Davis. In *The Station Hill Blanchot Reader*, G. Quasha (ed.), 443–50. Barrytown, NY: Station Hill.
Blanchot, Maurice. 2003 [1959]. *The Book To Come*, trans. C. Mandell. Stanford, CA: Stanford University Press.
Bogue, Ronald. 2006. "Fabulation, Narration and the People to Come." In *Deleuze and Philosophy*, C. Boundas (ed.), 202–23. Edinburgh: Edinburgh University Press.
Bordwell, David. 2008. *Poetics of Cinema*. New York: Routledge.
Borges, Jorge Luis. 1962 [1952]. "Partial Magic in the Quixote," trans. J. E. Irby. In *Labyrinths*, D. Yates (ed.), 185–87. New York: New Directions.
Borges, Jorge Luis. 1998a [1941]. "The Garden of Forking Paths." In *Collected Fictions*, trans. A. Hurley, 119–28. New York: Penguin.
Borges, Jorge Luis. 1998b [1944]. "The Library of Babel." In *Collected Fictions*, trans. A. Hurley, 112–18. New York: Penguin.
Borges, Jorge Luis. 1998c [1949]. "The Aleph." In *Collected Fictions*, trans. A. Hurley, 274–86. New York: Penguin.
Borges, Jorge Luis. 1999 [1942]. "John Wilkins' Analytical Language," trans. E. Weinberger. In *Selected Non-Fictions*, E. Weinberger (ed.), 229–33. New York: Viking.
Boundas, Constantin. 2006. "What Difference does Deleuze's Difference Make?" In *Deleuze and Philosophy*, C. Boundas (ed.), 3–28. Edinburgh: Edinburgh University Press.
Caillois, Roger. 1961 [1958]. *Man, Play and Games*, trans. M. Barash. New York: Glencoe.
Carnap, Rudolf. 1937. *The Logical Syntax of Language*, trans. A. Smeaton. London: Kegan Paul.

Carrard, Philippe. 1984. "From Reflexivity to Reading: The Criticism of Lucien Dällenbach." *Poetics Today*, 5: 839–56.
Carroll, Joseph. 2004. *Literary Darwinism*. New York: Routledge.
Cook, Albert. 1986. "The Wilderness of Mirrors." *The Kenyon Review*, 8: 90–111.
Cowan, Bainard. 1981. "Walter Benjamin's Theory of Allegory." *New German Critique*, 22: 109–22.
Critchley, Simon. 1996. "Il y a—Holding Levinas's Hand to Blanchot's Fire." In *Maurice Blanchot: The Demand of Writing*, C. Bailey Gill (ed.), 108–22. London and New York: Routledge.
Dällenbach, Lucien. 1980. "Reflexivity and Reading." *New Literary History*, 11: 435–49.
Dällenbach, Lucien. 1989 [1977]. *The Mirror in the Text*, trans. J. Whiteley. Chicago: University of Chicago Press.
Damisch, Hubert. 1995 [1987]. *The Origin of Perspective*, trans. J. Goodman. Cambridge, MA: MIT Press.
Deleuze, Gilles, and Felix Guattari. 1986 [1975]. *Kafka: Toward a Minor Literature*, trans. D. Polan. Minneapolis: University of Minnesota Press.
Deleuze, Gilles, and Felix Guattari. 1987 [1980]. *A Thousand Plateaus*, trans. B. Massumi. Minneapolis: University of Minnesota Press.
Deleuze, Gilles. 1988 [1966]. *Bergsonism*, trans. H. Tomlinson and B. Habberjam. New York: Zone Books.
Deleuze, Gilles. 1989 [1985]. *Cinema 2: The Time-Image*, trans. H. Tomlinson and R. Galeta. Minneapolis: University of Minnesota Press.
Deleuze, Gilles. 1990 [1969]. *The Logic of Sense*, trans. M. Lester. London: Athlone.
Deleuze, Gilles. 1994 [1968]. *Difference and Repetition*, trans. P. Patton. London: Continuum.
Deleuze, Gilles. 1997a (1983). *Cinema 1—The Movement-Image*, trans. H. Tomlinson. Minneapolis: University of Minnesota Press.
Deleuze, Gilles. 1997b [1993]. *Essays—Critical and Clinical*, trans. D. W. Smith and M. A. Greco. Minneapolis: University of Minnesota Press.
Deleuze, Gilles. 1997c [1953] "Review of Jean Hyppolite, *Logic and Existence*," in *Logic and Existence* by Jean Hyppolyte, L. Lawlor and A. Sen (trans.), 191–95. Albany: State University of New York Press.
de Nooy, Juliana. 1991. "The Double Scission: Dällenbach, Doležel, and Derrida on Doubles." *Style*, 25: 19–27.
Derrida, Jacques. 1973 [1967] *Speech and Phenomena*, trans. D. Allison. Evanston, IL: Northwestern University Press.
Derrida, Jacques. 1978 [1967]. *Writing and Difference*, trans. A. Bass. Chicago: University of Chicago Press.
Derrida, Jacques. 1981a [1972]. *Dissemination*, trans. B. Johnson. London: Athlone.
Derrida, Jacques. 1981b [1972]. *Positions*, trans. A. Bass. Chicago: University of Chicago Press.

Derrida, Jacques. 1982 [1972]. *Margins of Philosophy*, trans. A. Bass. Chicago: University of Chicago Press.
Derrida, Jacques. 1987a [1980]. *The Post Card: From Socrates to Freud and Beyond*, trans. A. Bass. Chicago: University of Chicago Press.
Derrida, Jacques. 1987b [1978]. *The Truth in Painting*, trans. G. Bennington and I. McLeod. Chicago: University of Chicago Press.
Derrida, Jacques. 1988 [1972–1977]. *Limited Inc*, trans. S. Weber. Evanston, IL: Northwestern University Press.
Derrida, Jacques. 1997 [1967]. *Of Grammatology*, trans. G. Chakravorty Spivak. Baltimore, MD: Johns Hopkins University Press.
Derrida, Jacques. 2005 [1986–2004]. *Sovereignties in Question*. New York: Fordham University Press.
Derrida, Jacques. 2007 [1978]. "The Retrait of Metaphor." In *Psyche—Inventions of the Other*, vol. 1, P. Kamuf and E. Rottenberg (eds.), 48–80. Stanford, CA: Stanford University Press.
Derrida, Jacques. 2013 [1980]. "The Law of Genre," trans. A. Ronell. In *Signature Derrida*, J. Williams (ed.), 3–32. Chicago: University of Chicago Press.
Dieckmann, Liselotte. 1962. "Repeated Mirror Reflections: The Technique of Goethe's Novels." *Studies in Romanticism*, 1: 154–74.
Dolcini, Nevia. 2007. "The Analytic/Continental Divide." *Soochow Journal of Philosophical Studies*, 16: 283–302.
Doležel, Lubomir. 1998. *Heterocosmica—Fiction and Possible Worlds*. Baltimore, MD: Johns Hopkins University Press.
Eco, Umberto. 1989 [1962–1968]. *The Open Work*, trans. A. Cancogni. Cambridge, MA: Harvard University Press.
Epstein, Isidor (trans.). 1935. *The Babylonian Talmud*, vols. 1–34. London: Soncino Press.
Faur, José. 1986. *Golden Doves with Silver Dots*. Bloomington: Indiana University Press.
Fink, Eugen. 1974 [1960]. "The Ontology of Play." *Philosophy Today*, 18: 147–61.
Fink, Eugen. 2003 [1960]. *Nietzsche's Philosophy*, trans, G. Richter. London: Continuum.
Fink, Eugen. 2016 [1966]. "Play and Philosophy." In *Play as Symbol of the World and Other Writings*, trans. I. Moore and C. Turner, 229–33. Bloomington: Indiana University Press.
Foucault, Michel. 1986 [1967]. "Of Other Spaces," trans. J. Miskowiec. *Diacritics*, 16: 22–27.
Foucault, Michel. 1998 [1963]. "Language to Infinity," trans. D. F. Bouchard. In J. D. Faubion (ed.) *Aesthetics, Method, and Epistemology*, 89–101. New York: The New Press.
Foucault, Michel. 2002 [1966]. *The Order of Things*. London: Routledge.
Frappier, Jean. 1959. "Variations sur le thème du miroir, de Bernard de Ventadour à Maurice Scève." *Cahiers de l'Association internationale des études francaises*. 11: 134–58.

Füredy, Viveca. 1989. "A Structural Model of Phenomena with Embedding in Literature and Other Arts." *Poetics Today*, 10: 745–69.
Gadamer, Hans-Georg. 2004 [1960]. *Truth and Method*, trans. J. Weinsheimer and D. Marshall. London: Continuum.
Gasché, Rodolphe. 1988. *The Tain of the Mirror—Derrida and the Philosophy of Reflection*. Cambridge, MA: Harvard University Press.
Gasché, Rodolphe. 1996. "The Felicities of Paradox: Blanchot on the Null-Space of Literature." In *Maurice Blanchot: the Demand of Writing*, C. Bailey Gill (ed.), 34–69. London and New York: Routledge.
Gass, William. 1970. *Fiction and the Figures of Life*. New York: Alfred Knopf.
Genette, Gérard. 1972. *Figures III*. Paris: Seuil.
Gide, André. 1956 [1889–1915]. *The Journals of André Gide*, vol. I, trans. J. O'Brien. New York: Vintage Books.
Goffman, Erving. 1974. *Frame Analysis*. New York: Harper and Row.
Gombrich, Ernst. 1960. *Art and Illusion*. London: Phaidon.
Grabes, Herbert. 1982. *The Mutable Glass*. Cambridge: Cambridge University Press.
Gross, Elizabeth. 1986. "Derrida and the Limits of Philosophy." *Thesis Eleven*, 14: 26–43.
Grossfeld, Bernard (trans.). 1991. *The Two Targums of Esther*. In *The Aramaic Bible*, vol. 18, K. Cathcart (ed.). Edinburgh: T&T Clark.
Guyer, Paul. 2006. *Kant*. London: Routledge.
Harshaw (Hrushovski), Benjamin. 1984. "Fictionality and Fields of Reference." *Poetics Today*, 5: 227–51.
Hegel, G. W. F. 2010 [1816–1832]. *The Science of Logic*, trans. G. Di Giovanni. Cambridge: Cambridge University Press.
Heidegger, Martin, 1958. *The Question of Being*, trans. W. Kluback. New York: Twayne.
Heidegger, Martin. 1987 [1961]. *Nietzsche*, vols. 3-4, trans. J. Stambough, D. Farrell, and F. Capuzzi. San Francisco: Harper and Row.
Heidegger, Martin. 1996 [1927]. *Being and Time*, trans. J. Stambaugh. Albany: State University of New York.
Heidegger, Martin. 1998a [1929]. "On the Essence of Ground," trans. W. McNeill. In *Pathmarks*, W. McNeill (ed.), 97–135. Cambridge: Cambridge University Press.
Heidegger, Martin. 1998b [1947]. "Letter on Humanism," trans. F. Capuzzi. In *Pathmarks*, W. McNeill (ed.), 239–76. Cambridge: Cambridge University Press.
Heidegger, Martin. 2001 [1950] "The Thing." In *Poetry, Language, Thought*, trans. A. Hofstadter, 163–84. New York: Perennial Classics.
Heidegger, Martin. 2002 [1950]. "The Origin of the Work of Art." In *Off the Beaten Track*, J. Young and K. Haynes (trans. and eds.), 1–56. Cambridge: Cambridge University Press.
Heidegger, Martin. 2004 [1939]. *On the Essence of Language*, trans. W. Torres Gregory and Y. Unna. Albany: State University of New York Press.
Hill, Leslie. 1997. *Blanchot—Extreme Contemporary*. London: Routledge.
Hobson, Marian. 1982. *The Object of Art*. Cambridge: Cambridge University Press.

Hobson, Marian. 1998. *Jacques Derrida: Opening Lines*. London: Routledge.
Holdrege, Barbara. 1989. "The Bride of Israel: The Ontological Status of Scripture in the Rabbinic and Kabbalistic Traditions." In *Rethinking Scripture*, M. Levering (ed.), 180–261. Albany: State University of New York Press.
Holub, Robert. 1995. "Phenomenology." In *The Cambridge History of Literary Criticism*, vol. 8, R. Selden (ed.), 289–318. Cambridge: Cambridge University Press.
Hugill, Andrew. 2012. *Pataphysics—A Useless Guide*. Cambridge MA: Massachusetts Institute of Technology Press.
Huizinga, Johan. 1949. *Homo Ludens*. London: Routledge and Kegan Paul.
Husserl, Edmond. 1983 [1913]. *Ideas Pertaining to a Pure Phenomenology and to a Phenomenological Philosophy*, vol. I, trans. F. Kersten. The Hague: Martinus Nijhoff Publishers.
Hutcheon, Linda. 1980. *Narcissistic Narrative: The Metafictional Paradox*. Waterloo: Wilfrid Laurier University Press.
Ingarden, Roman. 1973 [1936]. *The Cognition of the Literary Work of Art*, trans. R. Crowley and K. Olson. Evanston, IL: Northwestern University Press.
Irvine, Andrew David. 2009 [retrieved 2016]. "Russell's Paradox." In *The Stanford Encyclopedia of Philosophy*, N. Zalta (ed.). <http://plato.stanford.edu/archives/sum2009/entries/russell-paradox/>
Iser, Wolfgang. 1974 [1972]. *The Implied Reader*. Baltimore, MD: Johns Hopkins University Press.
Iser, Wolfgang. 1993. *The Fictive and the Imaginary*. Baltimore, MD: Charting Literary Anthropology.
Jakobson, Roman. 1990. *On Language*, P. Waugh and M. Monville-Burston (eds.). Cambridge, MA: Harvard University Press.
Jameson, Fredric. 1988. "Cognitive Mapping." In *Marxism and the Interpretation of Culture*, C. Nelson (ed.), 347–60. Urbana: University of Illinois Press.
Jarry, Alfred. 1996 [1911]. *Exploits & Opinions of Dr. Faustroll, a Pataphysician*, trans. S. Watson. Boston: Exact Change.
Johnson, Barbara. 1981. "Translator's Introduction." In *Dissemination* by Jacques Derrida, vii–xxxiii. London: Athlone.
Kant, Immanuel. 1929 [1781]. *Critique of Pure Reason*, trans. N. Kemp Smith. New York: St. Martins Press.
Karo, Joseph ben Ephraim. 1999 [1488-1575]. *Shulḥan Arukh*, Vol. 10 (*Even Ha'ezer*). Jerusalem: Zondel Berman.
Kearney, Richard. 1991. *The Wake of Imagination*. Minneapolis: University of Minnesota Press.
Kowzan, Tadeusz. 1976. "Art en Abyme." *Diogenes*, 24: 67–92.
Kripke, Saul. 1974 [1963]. "Semantical Considerations on Modal Logic." In F. Zabeeh, E. D. Klemke, and A. Jacobson, eds. *Readings in Semantics*, 803–14. Urbana: University of Illinois Press.
Krook, Dorothea. 1967. *The Ordeal of Consciousness in Henry James*. Cambridge: Cambridge University Press.

Kuhn, Thomas. 1996 [1962]. *The Structure of Scientific Revolutions*. Chicago: University of Chicago Press.
Kuiken, Kir. 2005. "Deleuze/Derrida: Towards an Almost Imperceptible Difference." *Research in Phenomenology*, 35: 290–308.
Laporte, Roger. 1996. "Maurice Blanchot Today." In *Maurice Blanchot: The Demand of Writing*, C. Bailey Gill (ed.), 25–33. London: Routledge.
Lawlor, Leonard. 2003. *The Challenge of Bergsonism*. London: Continuum.
Lawlor, Leonard. 2019 (forthcoming). "Bergson on the True Intellect: The Tripartite Concept of Virtuality." In *Interpreting Bergson*, A. Lefebvre (ed.). Cambridge: Cambridge University Press.
Lawlor, Patricia. 1985. "Lautréamont, Modernism, and the Function of Mise en Abyme." *The French Review*, 58: 827–34.
Leibniz, G. W. 1979 [1687]. "Correspondence with Arnauld." In *Discourse on Metaphysics. Correspondence with Arnauld. Monadology*, trans. G. Montgomery, 65–248. La Salle: Open Court Publishing Company.
Leibniz, G. W. 1989 [1686]. "Discourse on Metaphysics." In *Philosophical Essays*, trans. R. Ariew, 35–68. Indianapolis, IN: Hackett.
Le Poidevin, Robin. 1995. "Worlds Within Worlds?" *British Journal of Aesthetics*, 35: 227–38.
Levinas, Emmanuel. 1978. *Existence and Existents*, trans. A. Lingis. Dordrecht: Kluwer.
Levinas, Emmanuel. 1998 (1974). *Otherwise than Being or Beyond Essence*, trans. A. Lingis. Pittsburgh, PA: Duquesne University Press.
Lewis, David. 1968. "Counterpart Theory and Quantified Modal Logic." *Journal of Philosophy*, 65: 113–26.
Lorraine, Tamsin. 2011. *Deleuze and Guattari's Immanent Ethics*. Albany: State University of New York Press.
Magny, Claude Edmonde. 1950. *Histoire du roman français depuis 1918*. Paris: Seuil.
Marion, Jean-Luc. *Being Given*, trans. J. L. Kosky. Stanford, CA: Stanford University Press.
Marks, John. 2000. "Underworld: The People are Missing." In *Deleuze and Literature*, I. Buchanan and J. Marks (eds.), 80–99. Edinburgh: Edinburgh University Press.
May, Todd. 1994. "Difference and Unity in Gilles Deleuze." In *Gilles Deleuze and the Theater of Philosophy*, C. Boundas and D. Olkowski (eds.), 33–50. New York: Routledge.
McHale, Brian. 1987. *Postmodernist Fiction*. London: Methuen.
McHale, Brian. 2006. "Cognition En Abyme: Models, Manuals, Maps." *Partial Answers*, 4: 175–89.
Miller, Joseph Hillis. 1995. "The Disputed Ground." In *Deconstruction Is/In America*, A. Haverkamp (ed.), 79–86. New York: New York University Press.
Miller, Joseph Hillis. 2002. "Derrida and Literature." In *Jacques Derrida and the Humanities*, T. Cohen (ed.), 58–81. Cambridge: Cambridge University Press.
Miller, Stephen Paul. 1993. "Self-Portrait in a Convex Mirror." *Boundary*, 20: 84–115.

Milstein, Yoseph (trans.). 2010. *The Mishnah*. New York: Machon Yisrael Trust.
Morrissette, Bruce. 1972. "Topology and the French *Nouveau roman*." *Boundary 2*: 45–57.
Morrissette, Bruce. 1985. *Novel and Film*. Chicago: University of Chicago Press.
Motzkin, Gabriel. 2000. "Iser's Anthropological Reception of the Philosophical Tradition." *New Literary History*, 31: 163–74.
Neusner, Jacob (trans.). 1987. *The Talmud of the Land of Israel* [Jerusalem Talmud], vols. 1–25. Chicago: University of Chicago Press.
Neusner, Jacob (trans.). 1997a. Genesis Rabbah [*Bereshit Rabbah*]. In *The Components of The Rabbinic Documents from the Whole to the Parts*, vol. IX. Atlanta: Scholars Press.
Neusner, Jacob (trans.). 1997b. Song of Songs Rabbah [*Shir Hashirim Rabbah*]. In *The Components of The Rabbinic Documents From The Whole to the Parts*, vol. V. Atlanta, GA: Scholars Press.
Nietzsche, Friedrich. 1961 [1885]. *Thus Spoke Zarathustra*, trans. R. J. Hollingdale. New York: Penguin Books.
Nietzsche, Friedrich. 1966 [1886]. *Beyond Good and Evil*, trans. W. Kaufmann. New York: Vintage Books.
O'Connor, Brian. 2014. "Play, Idleness and the Problem of Necessity in Schiller and Marcuse." *British Journal for the History of Philosophy*, 22: 1095–117.
Olkowski, Dorothea. 1994. "Nietzsche's Dice Throw: Tragedy, Nihilism, and the Body without Organs." In *Gilles Deleuze and the Theater of Philosophy*, C. Boundas and D. Olkowski (eds.), 119–40. New York: Routledge.
Olkowski, Dorothea. 1999. *Gilles Deleuze and the Ruin of Representation*. Berkeley: University of California Press.
Ollier, Claude. 1988 [1958]. *The Mise-en-scène*, trans. D. Di Bernardi. Elmwood Park, IL: Dalkey Archive Press.
Oz, Amos. 2017 (retrieved). "The teaspoon is very small and the fire is very large." In *Poetry Center Online*. <http://92yondemand.org/amos-oz-teaspoon-small-fire-large-many-us-everyone-us-teaspoo>
Pavel, Thomas. 1986. *Fictional Worlds*. Cambridge, MA: Harvard University Press.
Ricardou, Jean. 1967. *Problèmes du nouveau roman*. Paris: Seuil.
Ricardou, Jean. 1972. *Nouveau roman: hier, aujourd'hui*, vol. 2. Paris: Union générale d'éditions.
Ricardou, Jean. 1973. *Le nouveau roman*. Paris: Seuil.
Ricardou, Jean. 1977. "The Population of Mirrors: Problems of Similarity Based on a Text by Alain Robbe-Grillet." *October*, 3: 35–67.
Ricardou, Jean. 1981 [1967]. "The Story within the Story," trans. J. Kestner. *James Joyce Quarterly*, 18: 323–38.
Ricœur, Paul. 1967 [1960]. *The Symbolism of Evil*, trans. E. Buchanan. New York: Harper and Row.

Ricœur, Paul. 1970 [1965]. *Freud and Philosophy*, trans. D. Savage. New Haven, CT: Yale University Press.
Rimmon-Kenan, Shlomith. 1982. "Ambiguity and Narrative Levels: Christine Brooke-Rose's '*Thru*.'" *Poetics Today*, 3: 21–32.
Rinon, Yoav. 2006. "Mise en abyme and Tragic Signification in the Odyssey." *Mnemosyne*, 59: 208–25.
Robbins, Jill. 1999. *Altered Reading: Levinas and Literature*. Chicago: University of Chicago Press.
Rodowick, David. 1997. *Deleuze's Time Machine*. Durham, NC: Duke University Press.
Ron, Moshe. 1987. "The Restricted Abyss, Nine Problems in the Theory of *Mise en abyme*." *Poetics Today*, 8: 417–38.
Rorty, Richard. 1979. *Philosophy and the Mirror of Nature*. Princeton: Princeton University Press.
Russell, Bertrand. 1922. "Introduction." In *Tractatus Logico-Philosophicus* by Ludwig Wittgenstein, 7–23. London: Routledge and Kegan Paul.
Russell, Bertrand. 1956 [1908] "Mathematical Logic as Based on the Theory of Types." In *Logic and Knowledge: Essays 1901–1950*, R. C. Marsh (ed.), 59–102. London: Allen and Unwin.
Schwartz, Yigal, and Jeffrey Green. 2000. "The Person, the Path, and the Melody." *Prooftexts*, 20: 318–39.
Searle, John. 1977. "Reiterating the Differences: A Reply to Derrida." *Glyph*, 1: 198–208.
Searle, John. 1979. *Expression and Meaning*. Cambridge: Cambridge University Press.
Shetley Vernon, and Alissa Ferguson. 2001. "Reflections in a Silver Eye: Lens and Mirror in 'Blade Runner.'" *Science Fiction Studies*, 28: 66–76.
Smith, Daniel W. 2003. "Deleuze and Derrida, Immanence and Transcendence." In *Between Deleuze and Derrida*, P. Patton and J. Protevi (eds.), 46–66. London: Continuum.
Soloveitchik, Yoseph Dov. 1983. *Shiurim Lezecher Abba Mari*. Jerusalem: Akiva Yosef.
Sonnet, Jean-Pierre. 1997. *The Book within the Book—Writing in Deuteronomy*. Leiden: Brill.
Spariosu, Mihai. 1989. *Dionisus Reborn*. Ithaca, NY: Cornell University Press.
Sutton-Smith, Brian. 1997. *The Ambiguity of Play*. Cambridge, MA: Harvard University Press.
Tally, Robert. 1996. "Jameson's Project of Cognitive Mapping." In *Social Cartography*, R. Paulston (ed.), 399–416. New York: Garland.
Tarski, Alfred. 1956. "The Concept of Truth in Formalized Languages." In *Logic, Semantics, Metamathematics*, trans. J. H. Woodger, 152–78. Oxford: Clarendon Press.
Toloudis, Constantin. 1983. "Metaphor and Mise en Abyme in the Nouveau Roman." *The International Fiction Review*, 10: 27–32.

Touger, Eliyahu (trans.). 1988. *Mishneh Torah by Maimonides*. Jerusalem: Moznaim.
Turner, Victor. 1969. *The Ritual Process*. Ithaca, NY: Cornell University Press.
Turner, Victor. 1982. *From Ritual to Theatre*. New York: PAJ Publications.
Uexküll, Jakob. 1982 [1940] "The Theory of Meaning." *Semiotica*, 42: 25–82.
Urraca, Beatriz. 1992. "Through the Looking-Glass: Borges's Mirrors and Contemporary Theory." *Revista Canadiense de Estudios Hispánicos*, 17: 153–76.
Villani, Arnaud. 1999. *La guêpe et l'orchidée*. Paris: Belin.
Visker, Rudi. 1997. "The Core of My Opposition to Levinas." *Ethical Perspectives*, 4: 154–69.
Visker, Rudi. 2003. "Is ethics fundamental? Questioning Levinas on irresponsibility." *Continental Philosophy Review*, 36: 263–302.
Walton, Kendall. 1990. *Mimesis as Make-Believe*. Cambridge, MA: Harvard University Press.
Waugh, Patricia. 1984. *Metafiction*. London, New York: Routledge.
Weatherston, Martin. 2002. *Heidegger's Interpretation of Kant*. Basingstoke, UK: Palgrave Macmillan.
Widder, Nathan. 2001. "The Rights of Simulacra: Deleuze and the Univocity of Being." *Continental Philosophy Review*, 34: 437–53.
Widder, Nathan. 2003. "Thought after Dialectics: Deleuze's Ontology of Sense." *The Southern Journal of Philosophy*, 41: 451–76.
Widder, Nathan. 2006. "'Time is Out of Joint' and So are We: Deleuzian Immanence and the Fractured Self." *Philosophy Today*, 50: 405–17.
Williams, James. 2003. *Gilles Deleuze's Difference and Repetition*. Edinburgh: Edinburgh University Press.
Williams, James. 2011. *Gilles Deleuze's Philosophy of Time*. Edinburgh: Edinburgh University Press.
Wright, Edmond L. 1976. "Arbitrariness and Motivation: A New Theory." *Foundations of Language*, 14: 506–08.

INDEX

affirmation, philosophy of
  Blanchot, 84, 99, 103, 213
  Deleuze, 9, 34, 68, 105, 114–122, 184–185, 206, 213–214
  Derrida, 80–82, 214–215
  Derrida criticized as philosophy of negation, 71–72, 213–214
Albee, Edward
  Tiny Alice, 196
Allen, Woody
  The Purple Rose of Cairo, 97
Al-Saji, Alia
  mobile mirror in Bergson, 148–149
ambiguity, *see* Blanchot, Dällenbach, Rimmon-Kenan
analytic philosophy, *see also* Le Poidevin, Austin, Russell
  continental-analytic divide, 4–6, 141
  of fiction, as one world frame theories, 42–43, 52
  of fiction, as segregationist theories, 43, 54, 63, 213
animal
  becoming-animal and rhizomatic book, 81, 207
  becoming-animal (Deleuze) and minor literature, *see* minor literature
  biosemiotics and rhizomatic book, 81, 207–210

umwelten and mise en abyme (Uexküll), 81–82, 208
Aristotle
  categorialism and typology of mise en abyme, *see* mise en abyme
  difference in form vs. matter, 106–108, 111, 192
  judgement and equivocity of Being, 107
  preeminence of "specific" difference, 106–107
  vs. Dionysian metamorphoses, 107
Austin, J. L.
  appropriateness conditions, 41, 192
  "infelicitousness" of fictional speech act, 43, 74–75

Bal, Mieke
  Biblical mises en abyme, *see* Bible
  criticism of Dällenbach's intentionalism, 18
  mise en abyme and subject of the work, 12–13
  standardization of mise en abyme, 221n
Barth, John
  Lost in the Funhouse, 52
Beckett, Thomas
  Watt, 26
Benjamin, Walter, *see* symbol

Bergson, Henri, 124–130, 147–151.
   See also virtuality, time
 actor illustration, 123, 148
 chess, multiple game illustration,
   125–126, 133
 cone of memory as self-embedding,
   128–130
 duration and retroaction, 127,
   129–130, 133, 135, 154, 213
 fabulation, *see* Bogue
 memory threads, multiplicity of, 23,
   37, 61, 125, 129–130, 151, 154,
   209
 mirror metaphor, *see* mirror,
   dynamic
 past, paradoxes of, *see* time
 perception-memory, 125, 128–129,
   133–134, 147–148
 pyramid and physiognomy, 133–134
Bible, *see also* scripture, Jewish
 Deleuze's conception of, 191
 mild mises en abyme in (Bal), 242n
Blanchot, Maurice, 83–104. See also
   il y a, worklessness
 ambiguity, philosophy of, 4, 8, 27,
   28, 29, 83–85, 88, 92, 99, 100,
   103, 119, 173, 212
 ambiguity and chiasmatic structures,
   see mirror, double
 ambiguity as affirmation, *see*
   affirmation, philosophy of
 ambiguity vs. fatality of day, 4, 8,
   99–104, 213
 ambiguity vs. mechanism of aletheia,
   86, 88–90
 death and language, 84, 103
 death and the exterior, 83–85, 90,
   91, 92, 99, 103, 173, 209, 210
 Empedocles, 209
 fatality of day as accumulation of
   recrossings, 100–104, 213
 fatality of day vs. mechanism of
   aletheia, 99–100
 Gide's principle of retroaction, *see*
   retroaction
 night-in-itself vs. night of the day,
   85–91, 124, 212
 Thomas the Obscure and reader-text
   re-crossings, 89–91
bipolarism, *see* fictional illusion, theories
   of
Bogue, Ronald
 the "yet to come" in Deleuze, 208–
   209
Borges, Jorge Luis, 160–163
 "The Aleph," *see* mise en périphérie
 "The Analytical Language of John
   Wilkins," *see* Chinese encyclopedia
   under iterability
 "Averroës' Search," 39
 "The Garden of Forking Paths" and
   pragmatic signification, 206
 "The Library of Babel" and modern
   language, *see* Foucault
 The Library of Babel and possibilia
   (Pavel), *see* possible worlds
 "The Lottery in Babylon," *see* divine
   game
 mirroring and doubles in, 160–161
 "Partial Magic in the Quixote"
   (Night 602), 2, 62
Brooke-Rose, Christine
 Thru, 46–48, 62

Cervantes, Miguel de
 Don Quixote, 26, 48
Caillois, Roger
 play, corruption of, 172, 181, 215
 play, deconstruction of, 173
 play, end of, and ambiguity
   (Blanchot), 172–173, 174
 play, four categories of, 172

INDEX

Carroll, Joseph, *see* post-structuralism, criticism of
cinema
  and the affect, *see* qualia
  image, as actual-virtual unity, 147, 118
  image of, as pataphorical, *see* pataphoricity
  "liberation" effects, *see* Ricardou
coexistence principle, 16–23, 119–122, 147–156, 213–217. *See also* affirmation, retroaction
accumulation of fictionalizing acts, *see* Iser
accumulation of recrossings and fatality of day, *see* Blanchot, Laporte
accumulation of transcoding acts, *see* rhizomatic book
actual-virtual in cinematic image, *see* cinema
actual-virtual in perception-memory, *see* Bergson
compossibility of monads, *see* Leibniz
difference as coexistence of disparates (Deleuze), *see* difference-in-itself
double bind and, in mise en abyme, 5, 16–23, 27, 28, 29, 36, 47, 53, 71, 72, 82, 119–122, 147–156, 158, 160, 162, 125, 213–217
  in mirroring, *see* the following under mirror, dynamic: sensory vs speculative bimodality; actual-virtual, indiscernibility of; semiotic-pragmatic, indiscernibility of; actual-virtual, coexistence of
repetition, vertical-horizontal, *see* repetition-for-itself
self-other, *see* otherness
semiotic-pragmatic, *see* mirror, dynamic; rhizomatic book

words-things, *see* Renaissance, under Foucault
Cook, Albert
convex mirroring, 150
crystalline
  as centrifugal mise en abyme, 6, 137, 197
  diffused reflection in, 149, 151
  as symbol of time, 149

Dällenbach, Lucien, 11–38
  dynamic relation between species, 27–29, 71–72
  dynamic relation between types and species, 27
  methodological ambiguity and Blanchot, 27–29, 35–36, 71, 119, 212, 221n
  mirroring, static vs. dynamic, 11–16
  mise en abyme as becoming, 7, 19, 29
  mise en abyme as between symbol and allegory, *see* symbol
  mise en abyme, centripetal vs. centrifugal, 196
  mise en abyme, definition of, 14, 221n
  mise en abyme, immanence of, *see* mise en abyme
  mise en abyme, relational, 12–13, 14
  mise en abyme, species of, 25–29, 71, 72. *See also* the following under mise en abyme: of enunciation; of text; of utterance; transcendental
  mise en abyme, types of (simple, aporetic, infinite), 1–2, 15, 25, 27, 28, 34, 35, 111, 196
  new vs. new new novel, 7, 30–36. *See also* new novel, new new novel

Dällenbach, Lucien *(continued)*
   reader, implied vs. empirical, 36–38, 4, 193
   reflection, degrees of analogy in, 27
   reflective utterance, multisignificance of, 16, 17, 18, 19, 44, 51, 212
   temporal disruption, 19–23. *See also* prospective; retrospective; retroprospective, under mise en abyme
   typology and Derrida, 27, 34, 36
   typology and Jakobson, 27, 28, 29
Damisch, Hubert
   misconception of double mirror, 152–153
death
   and end of play, *see* Caillois
   and language, *see* Blanchot, Foucault
   as "my own" of dasein, *see* Heidegger
   as otherness and ambiguity, *see* Blanchot
Deleuze, Gilles, 105–140, 147–152, 174–185, 187–210. *See also* cinema, crystalline, difference-in itself, pataphoricity, divine game, line of flight, minor literature, repetition-for-itself, rhizomatic book, virtuality
   becoming-animal, *see* animal
   being, univocity of (Scotus), 9, 44, 110–111, 117, 121, 125, 166, 184, 214. *See also* presupposed multiplicity as pitfall, under possible worlds, multiculturalism, Hegel
   on Aristotle, 106–108, 110, 111, 113, 192
   on Bergson, 23, 61, 124–130, 134, 135, 136, 137, 147–152
   and Blanchot, 85, 119, 122, 124, 127, 130, 152, 188, 209–210, 211, 213
   chess vs. Go, 35, 112
   diagram, *see* map
   ethics of becoming *see* ethics
   expression preceding expressed, 78, 114, 118
   on Hegel, 106–109, 110, 111, 114
   on Heidegger, 9, 85, 105, 109, 110, 114–115, 138, 176, 192
   on Hume, 122
   intensity, indivisibility of, 112, 147, 103–104
   on Kafka, 188–189
   on Kant, 130–132, 134, 136, 137, 197
   on Leibniz, 8, 111–113, 216
   logic, nomadic vs. sedentary, 110, 111, 112
   as metaphysician, 105
   and mirroring, *see* mirror, dynamic
   on Nietzsche *see* eternal return, affirmation, divine game
   on Plato, *see* Plato
   qualia, *see* qualia
   sense and ontology of sense, 78, 110, 114, 118, 189
   on Spinoza, 114
   thinker of both disjunction and univocity, 9, 34, 120, 121, 122
   time, syntheses and paradoxes of, *see* time
   vs. Derrida on completeness of signification, 68, 71, 116–119, 214
de Nooy, Juliana
   criticism of Dällenbach's typology, 36, 71
Derrida, Jacques, 57–82. *See also* supplement, *différance*, iterability
   anti-mimetology, *see* mimetism
   and Austin, 74–75
   deconstruction, 62, 72, 73, 146, 158, 178, 220n
   Deleuzian criticism of, *see* Deleuze

INDEX

dichotomies as totalitarianism, 43, 60, 105
Heidegger's *abgrund*, 88
Heidegger's Being as "transcendental signified," 18, 59–60, 138
Husserl's expression/indication divide, 61–62
Husserl's levels of memory, *see* Husserl
metaphoricity, *see* metaphoricity
mise en abyme, opposing the logocentric, 5, 8, 18, 34, 64–66, 69–72, 121, 214
and Nietzsche, *see* eternal return, affirmation
precedence of signified in metaphysics, 59–60, 71, 73, 138
quasi concepts (supplement, *différance*, iterability, trace) as vertical infrastructural gap, 7, 64, 68
trace, quasi concept of, 60, 61, 64, 66, 84, 101, 212
signification, the parergon of, *see* language and signification
simulacral mirroring in Mallarmé, *see* mimetism
tain of mirror, *see* Gasché
textualistic reading of, 73–104, 214–215
transcendental reading and critique of, 68–72, 108, 116, 117, 118, 119, 121, 183, 206, 214, 215
two readings of, 8, 73–74
Descartes
and "internalization" of philosophy, 57
Kantian critique of (Deleuze), 130
mind as mirror (Rorty), 141
différance (Derrida)
mise en abyme as emblem of, 64, 69
and pure past, 61
quasi concept of, 7, 61, 63, 64
as vertical difference, *see* Derrida

difference-in-itself (Deleuze)
as coexistence of disparates, 8, 9, 34, 71, 109, 112, 115, 120, 121, 122, 126, 127, 128, 132, 147, 148, 154, 162, 216
generative rather than presupposed, 5, 44, 110. *See also* retroaction principle
governed by no preexisting organizing principle, 29, 109, 110, 111, 116, 132, 166, 194, 195, 211
as originating from "indifference," 34, 44, 110
and repetition, *see* repetition-for-itself
unmediated by identity, 35, 43, 106, 107, 108, 110, 112, 134, 153, 178, 214
as vertical, 111, 114, 122, 131, 133
vs. contrariety, 3, 34, 105, 106, 107, 108, 111, 117, 130, 148, 191, 212
difference, *see also* Aristotle, *différance*, difference-in-itself, otherness
ambiguity (Blanchot), *see* Blanchot
ambiguity (poetics) *see* Rimmon-Kenan
derived from mise en abyme, *see* "double bind" under coexistence
identity, coded vs. situational, 7, 12, 30, 35, 43, 47, 60, 91, 112, 160, 177, 178, 204, 214
inessential (Leibniz), 41, 111–112, 113, 115, 192
infinitely small (Leibniz), 112
ontico-ontological (Heidegger), 3, 4, 19, 58, 59, 86, 142
pure ontic (post-Heideggerian), 5, 59–60, 64, 83, 85–91, 100, 144, 169, 172, 173, 174, 175, 192
vs. binary divisions, 3, 14, 16, 40, 43, 44, 45, 47 61, 63, 72, 96, 101, 105, 142, 160, 204, 166 171 177, 130, 143, 158, 166, 204, 212, 214, 215

260 INDEX

distantiation (Brecht), *see* rhizomatic book
divine game, 174–185. *See also* Deleuze, play
  and ethics of becoming, *see* ethics
  and "Lottery in Babylon," 175
  as play within play, 175
  pragmatics as part of game, 9, 117, 175, 212
  roll as reconstituting rules in its favour, 117, 125, 140, 166, 184–185, 193, 215
Doležel, Lubomír
  "one world frame" theories, 42–43
  possibilia and paradox of metafiction, 44, 45, 47, 213
Duns Scotus
  being, univocity of. *See* Deleuze
Duras, Marguerite
  India Song, 151

Eco, Umberto
  mirrors and doppelgangers, 161
  open work, 193–194
  reader, implied and empirical, 194
  seriality, 37
Escher, M. C.
  Drawing Hands, 46
eternal return (Nietzsche)
  Deleuze's conception of, 114–116
  Deleuze's third synthesis of time, 134, 140, 197
  Derrida's conception of, 114–116
  Heidegger's conception of, 114
ethics 173–185
  of becoming, and act of responsibility directed towards situational otherness, 176, 177, 178
  of becoming, and act of responsibility fated to succeed, 154–155
  of becoming, as devoid of ideology, 177
  and freedom of play, *see* Schiller
  ludic, and idolized otherness *see* play
  as preceding ontology (Levinas), 174

Faur, José
  parchment scrolls as self-referential, 204–205
fictional illusion, theories of
  bimodality, sensory vs speculative, *see* mirror, dynamic
  bipolarist vs. bimodalist, 40, 155–156
  make-believe theory (Walton) and embedded fiction, 49–52. *See also* appearing-to-be, under Fink
Fink, Eugen, 169–172
  appearing-to-be and water reflection, *see* mirror, dynamic
  appearing-to-be as mise en abyme, 171
  appearing-to-be as symbol of world's totality, 4, 9, 162, 170–171, 173
  play as generative of Being, 171, 212
Foucault, Michel
  heterogenous space, 103
  language of antiquity ("rhetoric"), 205
  language of modernity and "Library of Babel," 205–206
  language of Renaissance, 195, 208
  mirroring, death, and reduplication of language, 93, 97, 152, 245
  murmuring and density, 103, 205, 213
Füredy, Viveca
  intact and multiplying boundary, 53–54
  intact but reified boundary, 52–53, 91

interaction across a previously intact boundary, 54–55
lacunal mise en abyme, 52–53, 69
segregationism, resort to, 55, 63, 213

Gadamer, Hans-Georg, 168–169
being of literature, 4, 9, 168–169
being played vs. playing subject, 168, 174, 175
as bipolarist theoretician, 172
play, ontological valence of, 4, 9, 168
play as to and fro movement, 88, 168, 187
player/reader implied rather than empirical, 41, 88, 192, 193, 194
and symbol, *see* symbol
to and fro movement as monocentrism, 60, 100, 169, 175, 192–193
Gasché, Rodolphe, 156–160
Derrida's infrastructural gaps, 60, 64
double mirroring in Hegel, 156–158
fatality of day and question of being, 100
tain and Borges's mirrors (Urraca), 160–161
tain as allegory rather than symbol, 9, 159–160, 215
tain of mirror vs. specular play, 5, 109, 156–159
Gass, William, *see* play
generative novel, *see also* Roussel, Ollier, Ricardou, Morrissette
reference modeled on linguistic generators, 24, 25, 73, 94, 98, 136, 189, 190
specifity of text, 24, 190
Genette, Gérard
and narrative levels, 16
Geneva school
intentionality of text, 227n

Gide, André
charter of mise en abyme, 1, 11–14
convex mirroring, 11, 14
The Counterfeiters, 15
double mirroring, *see* mirror, dynamic
immanence of mise en abyme, *see* mise en abyme
La Tentative amoureuse, 12–13
mechanism of retroaction, *see* retroaction
shield emblem and its reception, 1, 7, 15, 30, 33, 52–53, 65, 71, 72, 120, 121, 129, 137, 211, 212. See also "preindividuation" under new novel; lacunal mise en abyme under Füredy
Goethe, J. V. *See* mirror, double

Hartley, L. P.
"From W.S," 54
Hegel, G. W. F.
absolute reflection, 5, 108, 109, 157, 158. *See also* "specular play" under Gasché
difference as contradiction, 61, 106, 108, 143, 158
language and annihilation, 84
triadic dialectics as presupposed, hierarchized multiplicity, 108, 109, 110, 213
Heidegger, Martin, 57–59, 85–89, 142–144
abgrund as quasi mise en abyme, 86–89
adequatio vs. aletheia, 17, 58, 88, 89, 100, 101, 142, 192, 205, 210
death and dasein, 83, 84. 85, 173
earth vs. world, 85, 86, 88, 89, 173, 204, 209, 210
eternal return, take on, *see* eternal return

Heidegger, Martin *(continued)*
  heralding post-Heideggerian thought, 9, 215
  hermeneutic circle, 6, 18
  language, *see* language and signification
  metaphysical tradition, 57, 58, 59, 105, 138, 141, 145, 167
  and mirroring, *see* mirror, dynamic
  ontico-ontological difference, *see* difference
  ontico-ontological privileged entities, 4
  play of being, 162, 167, 168, 169, 173, 192
  question of being, 58, 59, 99, 176
  technology, 205
  temporality of Dasein, 58, 59
  the Thing, 138, 142–144
Hobson, Marian
  bipolarism vs. bimodalism, *see* fictional illusion, theories of
  Derrida's citationality, 65
Homer
  Odyssey, 2, 94
Huizinga, Johan
  play as segregated space-time, 170, 172, 175
  play, broad definition of, 9, 172, 178, 187
  play, corruption of, 181
Husserl, Edmond
  expression/indication divide, *see* Derrida
  levels of memory and *Dresden Gallery*, 62–63
  phenomenological reduction and gaps of indeterminacy (Ingarden), 37; and acts of fictionalization (Iser), 96; vs. substance ego, 57; and "withdrawal" (Heidegger), 86

Hutcheon, Linda, *see also* metafictional paradox
  as bimodalist, 155
  failing to concern empirical reader, 41, 42, 194
  heterocosm, "ontological status" of, 39, 40
  narcissistic narratives and mimesis of process, *see* mimetism
  narcissistic narratives, mise en abyme as central mode of, 38, 39, 40
  resuccumbing to structuralism, 5, 40

il y a
  and fatality of day, 8, 102
  as mise en abyme, 101
  pre-personal existence, 100, 101, 122, 209, 211
  and rhizome, 102
Ingarden, Roman
  concretization of texts, 36, 37, 86, 193
Iser, Wolfgang, 95–98
  accumulation of fictionalizing acts, 98, 99
  fictionalization and mirroring, *see* mirror, dynamic
  fictionalization as mechanism of worklessness, 8, 95–98
  the fictive and the transcendent, 95, 96, 98
  the fictive as third value, 96, 130
  gaps of indeterminacy, 36, 37, 38
  textual vs. referential reading, 98
iterability (Derrida), 66–70, 73–82
  and Chinese encyclopedia (Borges), 67, 68
  and citationality, 18, 45, 66, 72, 74–76
  and incompleteness of signification, 68
  and lacunal mise en abyme, 69–72

mise en abyme, over and under
"emancipation," 72
and pitfall of representation, 68–72,
108, 116, 117, 118, 121, 183,
206, 214, 215
as quasi concept, 7, 60
re-citation as analogical signification,
77, 79, 80, 81, 214
re-citation as prospective mise en
abyme, 75, 76, 78, 80
as repeatability, 66, 67, 68
Searle's misconception of, 68

Jakobson, Roman
"dominant," concept of, 29
dynamic synchronicity, 27, 221
paradigmatic/syntagmatic axis, 130, 221
verbal communication, categories of,
28
Jameson, Fredric, *see* map
Jarry, Alfred, *see* pataphoricity
Joyce, James
Finnegan Wake, 193
Ulysses, 193

Kafka, Franz *see* minor literature
Kant, Immanuel, 130–132
the determinable as third value, 130
and Heidegger, 145
and lamp paradigm, *see* Kearney
and mirror paradigm, *see* Rorty
schema and infinite regress (Guyer),
131
schema and third synthesis (Deleuze),
134, 136, 137
schema as mise en abyme, 131–132,
134, 136, 197, 213
Kearney, Richard
failure to study empirical double
mirror, 145
mimetic paradigm of mirror, 144

parodic paradigm of labyrinth of
mirrors, 145
productive paradigm of lamp, 144,
145
three paradigms of imagination, 9,
144–147
Klein form
as denying identifiable center of
consciousness, 43, 46, 47, 137
and new new novel, 7, 9, 33, 137, 212
and pataphoricity, 137, 140
and rhizome (Deleuze), 34
and third synthesis (Deleuze), *see*
time
Kowzan, Tadeusz
mimetism of mise en abyme, 47
Kuhn, Thomas
"paradigm" compared to Ricœur's
"symbol," 9, 144, 109, 215,
159–160
Kuiken, Kir
Deleuze vs. Derrida on the
simulacrum, 114–115

language and signification, *see also*
Austin, Jakobson, Foucault,
iterability, metaphoricity,
pataphoricity, mimetism, Saussure
analogical vs. digital signification, *see*
iterability
annihilation and language, *see* Hegel
arbitrariness of signification, *see*
Saussure
biosemiotic, *see* rhizomatic book
completeness of signification, *see*
Deleuze
death and language, *see* Blanchot
expression/indication divide
(Husserl), *see* Derrida
as "house of Being" (Heidegger),
138, 167

language and signification *(continued)*
  incompleteness of signification (Derrida), *see* iterability
  meta-language/object-language division, 19, 44, 46, 51, 52, 54, 63, 213
  parergon of, in metaphysics, 27, 41, 159, 192, 204
  Quine's indeterminacy of reference (Pavel), 44
  rhizomatic vs. arborescent conceptions of, 77
  semiotic-pragmatic coexistence, *see* mirror, dynamic; rhizomatic book; divine game
  transcoding, *see* rhizomatic book
Laporte, Roger
  fatality of day and coexistence of "slopes," 100–101
Lawlor, Leonard
  double cone in Bergson, 129–130
  physiognomy in Bergson, 133–134
Lawlor, Patricia
  de Man's "modernist project," 135
Leibniz, G. W.
  compossibility of monads, 112, 121, 213
  continuity, law of, 112
  identity of the indiscernibles, law of, 112
  inessential difference, *see* difference
  infinitely small difference, *see* difference
  monads as "pre-individual" entities, 112
Le Poidevin, Robin
  embedded fiction and make-believe theory, 48–52
  embedded fiction, epistemological paradox, 51
  embedded fiction, ontological paradox, 51–52
  embedded fiction, pathological, 50–52, 54
  resort to segregationism, 52, 54, 55, 63, 213
  simultaneity of narrative levels, 51, 52, 102, 154
Levinas, Emmanuel, see also *il y a*
  ethics as primordial, 174, 176, 183, 184
  infinite responsibility and pitfall of negation, 9, 10, 183, 184, 215
  player's "egoist fate," 173, 174, 175, 182
Lewis, David
  counterpart relation (possible worlds), 43
liminality (Turner)
  as between and betwixt, 178, 179
  and communitas, 179, 182
  ludic communitas, *see* play
line of flight (Deleuze)
  and Blanchot's gaze to the exterior, 92, 143
  destination did not pre-exist line, 92, 143, 177, 185, 207
  in minor Literature, 190
logical types, theory of, *see* Russell
Lorraine, Tamsin
  ethics of becoming, *see* under ethics

Mallarmé, Stéphane
  Le Livre and transcoding, 100, 190
  Mimique and simulacral mimicry (Derrida), 146
map
  cognitive (Jameson), 48
  diagram (Deleuze) as map containing mapping, 48, 131, 194, 196, 206, 211
  mise en abyme as cognitive (McHale), 48

rhizomatic book as, *see* rhizomatic book
Marion, Jean-Luc
  discontinuity of gift, 93
May, Todd
  Deleuze's multiplicity-univocity irony, 121
McHale, Brian
  cognitive map, *see* map
  composite mise en abyme, 32
  mirroring, *see* mirror, static
  postmodernist fiction, 179
Melville, Herman
  Moby-Dick, 188
metafiction, paradox of (Hutcheon, Waugh)
  as invoked by Doležel, *see* Doležel
  reader's submission to fictional illusion is at same time its laying bare (Waugh), 40
  resources invested by reader to decode fiction form part of latter (Hutcheon), 38
  significance to non-reflexive fiction, 5, 40
metaphoricity, *see also* pataphoricity
  in Derrida, 30, 137–138, 211
  in *nouveau nouveau roman,* 30
Miller, Joseph Hillis
  Derrida, textualistic vs. transcendental reading of, 73
Miller, Stephen Paul
  convex mirroring, 149
mimetism, *see also* map
  anti-mimetology, 40, 42, 43, 144, 177, 191, 209
  anti-mimetology and metaphysical pit, 30–36, 72
  of mise en abyme, *see* Kowzan, Rimmon-Kenan
  and *nouveau roman,* 7, 30–36
  and paradigm of mirror, 144, 156
  of product vs. process, 5, 38–39, 194
  of simulacra (Derrida/Mallarmé), 47, 146, 147
minor literature, 187–190
  as becoming-animal, 188
  English nonsense as, 189
  expression precedes expressed, 189
  generative novel as, 189–190
  Kafka as, 188–189
  as non-ideological, 190
  signifying in a language it generates, 189
mirror, static, 11–16, 141–163. *See also* mirror, dynamic; Rorty; Kearney
  as consisting of bipolarity, 14, 152, 160
  conveying adequatio and totalitarianism, 12, 14, 30, 48, 65, 142, 143, 145, 148, 153
  in Dällenbach, *see* Dällenbach
  and "double decker" reality (McHale), 156
  as implying doppelgangers, *see* Borges, Eco
  meaning of left-right illusion, 161–162
  as metaphor in scholastic thought, 142
  the tain of, *see* Gasché
mirror, dynamic (double), 11–16, 141–163
  and acts of fictionalization (Iser), 97
  actual-virtual, coexistence of, 13–14, 115, 147, 148, 149, 152, 153, 154, 155, 159–160, 171, 215
  actual-virtual, indiscernibility of, 25, 47, 63, 98, 108, 115, 146, 147, 151, 152, 159, 160, 171
  convex and concave as, 14, 149–151
  crystalline as, 149

mirror, dynamic (double) *(continued)*
    in Dällenbach, *see* Dällenbach
    and "enkindling" of memory
        (Goethe), 151
    failure to study empirical device, *see*
        Kearney, Damisch, Al-Saji
    in Gide, 13, 148
    and language, *see* Foucault
    the mirroring process as the object
        of reflection, 28–29, 94, 143, 152
    as paradigm shift in imagination, *see*
        Kearney
    as paradigm shift in philosophy, 5,
        9, 14, 16, 141–163, 215
    perception-memory as (Bergson and
        Deleuze), 125, 129, 147–156
    in Ricardou, *see* Ricardou
    semiotic-pragmatic, indiscernibility
        of, 109, 154, 158, 159, 160
    sensory vs. speculative bimodality,
        154–155, 159–160, 162, 215
    simulacral mirroring (Derrida), *see*
        Mallarmé
    subject of as situational, 12, 13, 20,
        69, 70, 79, 93, 108, 152, 153,
        157
    as symbol of mise en abyme, 5, 6,
        11–16
    the Thing (Heidegger), 138,
        142–144
    water reflection and (Fink), 162–163
    and worklessness, 95
mise en abyme, *see also* Dällenbach,
    Ricardou, Gide, Klein form, Ron,
    Füredy, Rimmon-Kenan, Kowzan,
    Foucault, Bal, Le Poidevin,
    time, repetition, McHale, mise
    en périphérie, *il y a*, Moebius
    strip, crystalline, iterability,
    metaphoricity, pataphoricity,
    supplement, *différance*, difference-
in-itself, repetition-for-itself, divine
    game, rhizomatic book, dynamic
    mirror, retroaction, coexistence,
    worklessness
    appearing-to-be as, *see* Fink
    Bergson's cone as, *see* Bergson
    Bergson's duration as, *see* past,
        paradoxes of, under time
    Bergson's pyramid as, *see* Bergson
    categorialism (Aristotle) and the
        typology of, 29, 106
    centrifugal, 10, 77, 127, 196–210,
        211. See also mise en périphérie,
        Klein form
    citationality as, *see* Derrida
    cognitive map as, *see* map
    compossibility and monadology as,
        see Leibniz
    de Man's modernist project, *see*
        Lawlor, Patricia
    diagram as, *see* map
    of enunciation, 26, 90, 91, 94,
        203
    and fatality of day, *see* Blanchot
    as heterogeneity of plenitudes,
        70–71, 98, 103, 111, 116–
        122, 125, 129, 213. See also
        coexistence principle, retroaction
        principle
    immanence of as diegetic or
        metadiegetic, 16
    immanence-transcendence dialectics,
        1, 16–19, 96, 98, 131
    "jigsaw" vs. "unit-like" in *nouveau
        nouveau roman*, *see* new new novel
    Kant's schema as, *see* Kant
    law of law of genre as (Derrida),
        78–80
    logocentric, *see* Derrida
    as a mode of textual narcissism, *see*
        Hutcheon

monocentric conception of, *see* triadic dialectics (Hegel), levels of memory (Husserl), logical levels (Russell), *abgrund* (Heidegger), Iterability (Derrida), resort to segregationism (Le Poidevin, Füredy), infinite responsibility (Levinas), possibilia and logical levels (possible worlds)
naturalistic, *see* rhizomatic book; scripture, Jewish
as the other in the text's reception, 38
as paradigm shift, 4–5, 141–163, 165–185
as pre-individuated entity, *see* new novel, Leibniz
prospective, 20–21, 75–82, 122–124, 214
"proximity" as (Levinas), 101–102, 183–184
quasi concepts as (Derrida), *see* Derrida
retro-prospective, 22–23, 124–130, 135
retrospective, 21–22
sefer as, *see* Jewish scripture
subject of reconstituted by the added circuit, 35, 37, 70, 71, 102, 109, 112, 116, 118, 121, 125, 184, 197, 206, 209, 213, 216. *See also* coexistence principle; retroaction principle; subject as situational, under mirror, dynamic
of text, 24, 25–26
transcendental, 26, 27, 28, 29, 71, 72, 160, 161
Triptyque and threefold of the Thing (Heidegger), 144
umwelten and (Uexküll), *see* animal
of utterance ("fictional"), 25, 26, 27, 29, 114

the virtual as (Deleuze), 126
mise en périphérie
"The Aleph" (Borges), 95
definition of (Ricardou), 21
La Mise en scène, *see* Ollier
play as, *see* Fink
and retrospective mise en abyme, 21
and rhizomatic book, *see* rhizomatic book
and worklessness, 94–95
Moebius strip
and primordiality of expression over expressed (Deleuze), 118
and outside of the self (Levinas), 184
Morrissette, Bruce
and generative novel, 25, 98
multiculturalism
and ludic ethics, *see* play
pitfall of presupposed multiplicity, 177
and substance-other, 177–178, 182, 188, 212, 216

narcissistic narratives, *see* Hutcheon
new novel, *see also* new new novel, generative novels
and epistemological dominant, 179
prevailing of mise en abyme in, 2–3, 30
"tidy embedding" as preindividuation, 35
new new novel (*nouveau nouveau roman*), 30–36, 134–140. *See also* Klein form
and Deleuze's synthesis of future, 36, 134–140
"jigsaw" vs. "unit-like" mise en abyme, 7, 65, 189
and ontological dominant, 179
partition from new novel, 7, 30
pitfall of ideology (Dällenbach), 34–36

Nietzsche, Friedrich. *See also*: eternal return; affirmation, philosophy of; divine game
  "internalization" of world, 57
  play and will to power, 165–168, 172
Novalis
  Heinrich von Ofterdingen, 22, 23, 127, 129

O'Brien, Flann
  At Swim-Two-Birds, 50
Olkowski, Dorothea
  body and the pragmatics of mirroring, 153–154
  minor signification and synthesis of future, 135–136, 140
Ollier, Claude
  La Mise en scène, 3, 16, 21–22
ontology
  density-less modern language, *see* Foucault
  Heideggerian: ontico-ontological difference, *see* difference
  heterocosm, ontological status of, *see* Hutcheon
  of Language of Renaissance, *see* Foucault
  of play, *see* Fink, Gadamer
  post-Heideggerian: pure ontic, *see* difference
  rhetoric, ontological density of, *see* Foucault
  of sense vs. essence, *see* Deleuze
  Torah, ontological status of, *see* scripture
  univocity of Being, *see* Deleuze
oral book, *see* rhizomatic book
otherness, 174–185. *See also* Levinas, difference, difference-in-itself, *différance*, multiculturalism, Hegel, ethics, Gasché
  death of other, *see* Blanchot
  as middle between self and other, 10, 34, 122, 93, 178, 215, 216
  of self vs. otherness in its own right, 3, 60, 108
  situational vs. coded, 108, 157, 177, 178, 182, 191, 215
Oz, Amos
  self-marginalization as function of power, 180–181

Pabst, Georg Wilhelm
  Pandora's Box, 118
pataphoricity, *see also* metaphoricity, Klein form, mise en périphérie
  cinematic image as (Deleuze), 137, 197
  infrastructural reality (rhizomatic book) as, 211. *See also* rhizomatic book
  pataphors and pataphysics (Jarry), 138–140
  play as (Fink), 171
  sign as "showing" (Deleuze), 138–139
  synthesis of future (Deleuze), *see* time
Pavel, Thomas
  logical levels and possiblia, *see* possible worlds
  ontological landscape, *see* play
  segregationist theories, *see* analytic philosophy
Plato
  desire, 68
  myth and the testing of claimants, 113–114
  overturning Platonism, 34, 58, 113, 146, 163, 170, 171, 187
  and skepticism of ludic, 180
play, 165–185. *See also* divine game, Huizinga, Gadamer, Fink,

Spariosu, Heraclitus, Caillois, Schiller
actor example, *see* Bergson
of being, *see* Heidegger
between world and earth (Heidegger), 167
chess vs. go, *see* Deleuze
and "egoist fate," *see* Levinas
and groundlessness (Heidegger), 167
of Language as "house of being" (Heidegger), 167
ludic communitas and ontological landscape, 179
ludic communitas as a function of power (Gass, Sutton-Smith), 179–183
ludic ethics and idol-other, 177–178, 182, 188, 212, 215, 216
multiculturalism and postcolonialism as ludic ethics, 178, 182
multiple chess game, *see* Bergson
skepticism of ludic (Plato), *see* Plato
and will to power, *see* Nietzsche
within play, *see* divine game
Poe, Edgar Allen
"The Fall of the House of Usher," 11, 24, 76
possible worlds, 42–55
as braking with Russell's semantics, 43, 213
counterpart relation, *see* Lewis
logical levels in (Pavel), 44–45
pitfall of presupposed multiplicity, 43–44, 110
postcolonialism, *see* play
post-structuralism, criticism of
between affirmativity and "perverse negativity," 215–216
between introversion and extroversion, 216–217
Proust, Marcel
Remembrance of Things Past, 26

qualia
as assimilating "state of affairs," 118

reader-response criticism, 36–42. *See also* Iser, Hutcheon, Waugh, Eco, rhizomatic book, Ingarden
as failing to concern empirical reader, *see* Dällenbach, Hutcheon, Gadamer, Eco, rhizomatic book
and structuralist closure, 7, 36
repetition-for-itself (Deleuze), 105–140. *See also* iterability, worklessness, coexistence, retroaction, difference-in-itself, eternal return, divine game, Bergson
aporetics in, 111
of difference and plenitudes, 8, 35, 105–114, 129, 166, 193
instance reconstituting whole, 116, 121, 137, 197, 213
and Kant's schema, 131
repetition, mechanical, 67. *See also*: triadic dialectics, under Hegel; levels of memory, under Husserl; *abgrund*, under Heidegger; incompleteness of signification, under iterability; infinite responsibility, under Levinas
vertical as coexisting with horizontal, 119–120, 123, 214
vertical vs. horizontal, 8, 67, 111, 114–115
retroaction principle, *see also* coexistence principle
act of selection as reconstituting reading, *see* seriality, under Eco
act of perception as reconstituting memory, *see* memory threads, under Bergson
circuit as reconstituting mise en abyme, *see* mise en abyme
duration, *see* Bergson

retroaction principle *(continued)*
  first paradox of past (Deleuze), 126–127
  Füredy, 53
  Gide, 13, 14, 23, 88, 91, 93, 95, 127, 212
  instance as reconstituting repetition, *see* repetition-for-itself
  in mirror, *see* situational subject, under mirror, dynamic
  move as reconstituting chess game, *see* Bergson
  roll as reconstituting rules, *see* divine game
  token as reconstituting language, *see* completeness of signification, under Deleuze
  worklessness (Blanchot), 28, 91–95, 98
rhizomatic book, 187–210
  and analogical re-citation (Derrida), 77, 81–82
  as centrifugal mise en abyme, 197, 205–210
  as diagram and naturalistic mise en abyme, 194, 196, 204, 206, 207, 208
  diegesis as accumulation of transcoded biosemiotic acts, 207, 208, 209
  different with every recipient, 191
  empirical rather than implied reader (vs. reader-response criticism), 10, 42, 77, 193–194
  and generative novel, 189–190
  infrastructural reality and pre-signified things, 209–210
  infrastructural reality vs. Brecht's distantiation, 195–196
  as mise en périphérie, 196, 206
  and open work, *see* Eco
  oral book as, 113, 191, 198
  Ricardou and Mallarmé as heralds of, 26, 100, 190

  sefer as, 197–205, 207
  semiotic-pragmatic coexistence, 10, 77, 81–82, 95, 140, 192, 194, 203, 204
  and transcoding, 10, 77, 205–210, 217
  unimaginability of centrifugal circuit, 197, 206, 207, 208, 209, 210, 211, 217
  vs. arborescent book, 191
  vs. Gadamer's hermeneutics, 192–193
rhizome, *see also* rhizomatic book
  and diagram (Deleuze), 48, 194–196
  and *il y a*, 102
  and Klein form, 34
  rhizome paradigm vs. tree, 190–191, 193
Ricardou, Jean, *see also* mise en périphérie, generative novels
  and attack-revenge dialectics, 20, 21, 23, 121, 124
  cross of auto-representation, 23–25
  herald of rhizomatic book, *see* rhizomatic book
  inverse proportion between textual and referential levels, 155
  La Prise de Constantinople, 25
  Les Lieux-Dits: anagrams and mise en abyme, 31
  "liberation" technique in cinema, 154
  mise en abyme and mirroring, 12, 14, 69, 152
  strife between textual/generative and ideological/referential vectors, 23–25, 31, 34, 42, 93, 94, 190, 194, 211
Ricœur, Paul
  hermeneutics of faith, 18, 159
  symbol vs allegory, *see* symbol
Rimmon-Kenan, Shlomith
  ambiguity vs. Russell's logical types, 46, 47, 213

mimetism of mise en abyme, 47, 48, 63
poetical ambiguity, 45–48
Robbe-Grillet, Alain
  Projet pour une révolution à New York, 32, 33, 34
  "Three Reflected Visions," 25
Ron, Moshe
  immanence of resemblance, 222n
  irrepleteness of duplication, 76
Rorty, Richard
  mind as mirror in western thought, 9, 14, 141–142, 144, 145
  ontological/analytic divide, 6, 141–142
Roussel, Raymond, *see also* generative novel
  "Parmi les noirs," 24, 190
Russell, Bertrand
  class paradox and theory of logical types, 44, 46, 47, 53
  logical levels as quasi mise en abyme, 19, 45–55, 79, 157, 213
  and segregationism, 42, 43, 52, 54, 55, 213

Saussure, Ferdinand de
  arbitrariness of signification, 60, 65, 66, 119
schema, 130–134
  in Bergson, as second power physiognomy, 133–134, 213
  in Deleuze, 130, 136, 137, 213
  in Kant, as prone to infinite regress, *see* Kant
  in Kant, as replica of apperception, *see* Kant
Schiller, Friedrich
  play and freedom, 165, 168, 177
scripture, Jewish, 198–205
  Book of Esther and kairological time, 202
  Book of Esther as mise en abyme, 201–202
  Book of Esther as sefer, 200–201
  Book of Torah as archetype of sefer, 200
  Book of Torah as blueprint of creation, 200
  Book of Torah as blueprint of multiple creations, 207
  Book of Torah as mise en abyme, 202–203
  Book of Torah, "ontological status" of, 200
  as sefer, category applied to five texts, 198
  sefer as rhizomatic book, 198–205
  sefer requiring ritual format and use, 198
  sefer as parchment scroll, 198
  sefer and non-anthropocentric signification, 207
  tefillin as sefer, 199
  tefillin as mise en abyme, 201
  mezuzah as sefer, 199
  mezuzah as mise en abyme, 201
  get as mise en abyme, 201
  get as sefer, 199
  get performs rather than corroborates divorce, 199–200
  poetic vs. corporeal (naturalistic) mise en abyme, 203–204
  scroll vs codex as cross referential, 204–205
Searle, John
  and criticism of iterability, 68, 214
  referential value of fictional propositions, 43, 68
Shakespeare, William
  Hamlet, 1, 11, 135, 206
Shetley Vernon & Ferguson Alissa
  convex mirroring, 150
shield, emblem of, *see* Gide

Simon, Claude
  Triptyque, 31, 144
Smith, Daniel
  infinite justice (Derrida), 183
Sonnet, Jean-Pierre
  the generative Torah beyond Moses, 207
  mise en abyme in the Torah, 202–203
Sophocles
  Oedipus the King, 20, 75, 123, 135
Spariosu, Mihai
  concept of play in Greek and post-Kantian thought, 165–168
supplement (Derrida)
  chain of supplements and world of "text," 45, 47, 63–64, 65, 138, 146
  as supplement of supplement, 7
  supplement/origin divide, 45, 47, 63–64, 113, 138, 150, 158, 171
Sutton-Smith, Brian, *See* Play
symbol, *see also* metaphoricity; pataphoricity; mirror, static; mirror, dynamic; play; crystalline
  compared to "paradigm," *see* Kuhn
  double mirror vs. tain of mirror as, 159–160
  mise en abyme as, 4–6
  mise en abyme as between symbol and allegory, 17–18, 21
  play as, *see* Fink
  vs. allegory in Benjamin, 220n
  vs. allegory in Ricœur, 4–6, 17, 18
  vs. icon 76, 81, 133, 214

time, *see also* Bergson, eternal return
  différance and pure past see *différance*
  first paradox of past and Gide's retroaction, *see* retroaction, 126–127
  fourth paradox of past and Bergson's cone, 127–129
  prospective mise en abyme and synthesis of present, 122–124
  retroprospective mise en abyme and synthesis of past, 124–130
  second paradox of past and polycentrism of mise en abyme, 127
  synthesis of future and schema, *see* Kant
  synthesis of future: pataphoricity, Klein form, and mise en périphérie, 134–140
  temporality of Dasein, *see* Heidegger
  third paradox of past and centripetality of mise en abyme, 127
  transcoding and the "yet to come," *see* rhizomatic book
Torah, book of, *see* scripture
Turner, Victor, *see* liminality

Uexküll, Jakob, *see* animal
Urraca, Beatriz
  Borges, Gasché and mirroring, 160–161

van Eyck, Jan
  Arnolfini Marriage, 150
virtuality (Deleuze/Bergson)
  cinematic image, actual-virtual unity in, *see* cinema
  memory image, actual-virtual unity in, 147, 148, 149, 154
  mirroring, 147, 148, 149, 150, 151, 152
  as mise en abyme, *see* mise en abyme
  repetition, 113, 115–116, 118, 120, 122, 124, 126

threads of memory, 123, 124, 126, 129, 130, 151, 154
Visker, Rudi
　multiculturalism as totalitarianism, 177–178

Walton, Kendall, *see* fictional illusion
Waugh, Patricia, *see* Fiction, paradox of
Welles, Orson
　Citizen Kane, 151
　The Lady from Shanghai, 151
Widder, Nathan
　duration and representation, 134, 136
　Hegel and Deleuze's project of immanence, 109
worklessness (Blanchot), 91–95. *See also* Foucault

accumulation of recrossings as space of literature, 103. *See also* fatality of day, under Blanchot
fictionalization as mechanism of, *see* Iser
freeing work from ideology, 93–94
and *il y a*, 102
mechanism of retroaction, *see* retroaction
and mirroring, *see* mirror, dynamic
and mise en périphérie, *see* mise en périphérie
and myth of Orpheus and Eurydice, 91–92
object of recrossings not preexisting the act, 152
as recrossings to absolute exterior, 8, 20, 53, 91–95, 212

www.ingramcontent.com/pod-product-compliance
Lightning Source LLC
Chambersburg PA
CBHW020642230426
43665CB00008B/277